MODER

THE STRANGE STORY OF ART AND MUSIC IN THE TWENTIETH CENTURY

Max Ridgway

Front Image: Franz Kline, *Turin* (1960)

Back Image: Bo Gorzelak Pedersen, *Murder Painting* (2016)

Special thanks to Victor Hugo Rodriguez Sandoval and Ron Hoggard for proofreading assistance.

© Max Ridgway, 2018

CONTENTS

4	Chapter One: Setting the Stage
26	Chapter Two: Impressionism – A New Art Emerges
45	Chapter Three: Primitivism – The Old is New
68	Chapter Four: Expressionism – The Art of Angst
98	Chapter Five: Futurism – Speed, Noise, and Machines
113	Chapter Six: Dada – The Anti-Art
142	Chapter Seven: Neoclassicism – Calls to Order
160	Chapter Eight: Art and Music in the Soviet Union
179	Chapter Nine: Art and Music in Postwar Europe
205	Chapter Ten: Art and Music in Postwar America
223	Chapter Eleven: John Cage
238	Chapter Twelve: Postmodernism
270	Postscript: What Comes Next?

CHAPTER ONE: SETTING THE STAGE
INTRODUCTION

This is a book about the art of the twentieth century, art being defined in its broadest sense, encompassing all the various branches of creative human activity - music, painting, literature, and film - and discovering the connections between these various branches of art. As a word, "art" is related to words like "artifice" and "artificial", emphasizing the fact that art is not something that spontaneously appears in nature, but instead is made by humans, deliberately, and with intent. The intent of the artist, of course, is not always known, but may be inferred by examination of the art object itself, which might be better described as an "artifact" (a "fact of art"), a tangible reflection of the artist's otherwise intangible ideas. By careful scrutiny of the artifacts of modern art (its paintings, music, literature, etc.), and especially by comparing the art of one field with another, the ideas that inspired these works begin to become clear.

Music is arguably the most abstract of all the arts. Consisting as it does of nothing but sound, it is perceived by the mind through only one of the five senses. Unlike painting or sculpture, a piece of music offers nothing to see, nothing to touch. Furthermore, music exists only in time and it must, therefore, be apprehended in real time. While a painting may be inspected at close range or at a distance, and contemplated for an unlimited amount of time, music is a fleeting experience. It is the least concrete of all the arts, and therefore, seemingly the most difficult to understand and appreciate. To compound the problem further, modernist composers of the twentieth century frequently employed idiosyncratic modes of musical discourse. Their musical language was, in many cases, one of dissonance, density, difficulty, and complexity, often leaving listeners bewildered, perplexed, or to varying degrees, hostile.

However, the music of the twentieth century becomes comprehensible when considered within the context of the time and culture which gave birth to it. For that reason, this is also a book about Modernism, since it is this movement that gave birth to all the radical and controversial works that appeared in the early twentieth century and continued to be the guiding impulse for the various art movements that appeared throughout the century, continually regenerating and redefining itself as the century progressed. In short, Modernism is the unifying narrative that ties the twentieth century together and makes all of its art comprehensible.

WHAT IS MODERNISM?

What do we mean when we say that something is modern? In one sense, the word "modern" simply means "contemporaneous". Understood in this way, all art is modern in the time in which it is created. The *Mona Lisa* was modern art in 1503, if we understand the word "modern" simply to mean "contemporaneous". Even the cave paintings in the Chauvet Cave in France could be said to have been examples of modern art when our Paleolithic ancestors first made them 35,000 years ago.[1]

However, when considering the Modernism of the early twentieth century, "modern" means something more than simply "contemporaneous". By adding the suffix "ism", the word "modern" takes on a new kind of life. Beyond simply referring to the art of the present day, Modernism represents a distinctive kind of practice, a philosophy of art, standing apart from everything that preceded it.

Merriam-Webster tells us that Modernism represents "a self-conscious break with the past and a search for new forms of expression."

---

[1] By comparing these cave paintings with many of Picasso's line drawings it could be argued that the cave paintings are "modern" even by other definitions.

The idea of "a self-conscious break with the past" in this definition is especially enlightening. This indicates that the modernist artist (whether poet, writer, painter, or composer) was not simply creating a work of art, but consciously attempting to "break with the past". In other words, for the modernist it was not enough to merely make a positive statement, so to speak, in the form of a work of art, but it was also necessary to make a negative statement at the same time, by a "break with the past", a negation of what came before. This discarding of past practices then made necessary the "search for new forms of expression", giving rise to the revolutionary works of art that so shocked and scandalized the public in the early years of the century. But before examining these radical new forms of expression, it is useful to take a broad view of the culture the modernists were rejecting and to also consider the impact of a host of world-transforming new ideas, all of which seemed to appear at or around the turn of the century, lending weight and even logic to the modernist impulse to break with the past.

THE VICTORIAN ERA AND THE TURN OF THE CENTURY

The appearance of Modernism roughly coincides with the turn of the century,[2] and coincidentally, the end of the Victorian Age, named for the monarch who ruled the British Empire from 1837 until her death on January 22, 1901, the event which seemed to symbolically proclaim the end of the era which bore her name. The Victorian Age was a time of industrial expansion and scientific progress.

---

[2] The chronological beginning point for Modernism is the subject of some debate and disagreement among authors and historians. For the sake of convenience, I am using the beginning of the twentieth century as a loose starting point, although many of the ideas and much of the art coming under the umbrella-like label of Modernism actually appeared in the late nineteenth century.

It produced some of the greatest authors of the English language, among them Charles Dickens, Charlotte Brontë, Thomas Hardy, and Alfred Tennyson. It was a period marked by prosperity and optimism, by political stability and social reform. However, the rigid Victorian norms of social conformity coupled with a general attitude of sexual repression cumulatively created, over the five decades of the Victorian Era, an atmosphere ripe for social rebellion and artistic revolution.

But it was not the declining influence of Victorian mores alone which led to the advent of Modernism. Other factors added weight to the general sense that an old order was passing away and that a new, modern world was about to appear, superior to the old world in every way. A rapid succession of technological inventions and scientific innovations, the electric light bulb and the X-ray, the automobile and the airplane, the gramophone and the machine gun, all appearing around the turn of the century, gave the impression that a radical transformation of Western society was underway.

In addition, the early years of the twentieth century saw the publication of several groundbreaking new theories which led artists and intellectuals to question and ultimately to abandon many fundamental assumptions about the nature of the world and man's place in that world.

One such theory appeared well before the dawn of the new century but nevertheless continued to exert great influence at the beginning of the 20th century. In his 1859 book, *On the Origin of Species*, Charles Darwin suggested that biological life arose through descent from a common primordial ancestor and that, through a process of evolution taking place over millions of years, particular populations have evolved and changed through a process of natural selection.

Even though Darwin's book did not explicitly promote the notion of the animal origins of humanity, this soon became the central point of controversy. Ultimately, however, Darwin's work served to undermine the importance of religious faith, a central pillar of Victorian-era morality.[3]

Another influential and important work, Sigmund Freud's *Interpretation of Dreams*, appeared in 1900, at the very beginning of the 20th century. According to Freud, the dream reveals the hidden workings of two distinct processes of the unconscious mind. The first involves the expression of a wish for something that is morally or socially forbidden. The second consists of a kind of mental censorship in which the unconscious mind attempts to repress the morally unacceptable desire, creating a kind of internal tension which is played out in the dream, albeit in a distorted or disguised form. Freud further believed that guilt, arising from the suppression of desire, was the root cause of mental, and in some cases even physical illness and that this guilt is primarily the product of cultural and religious norms of morality.[4]

Though many of Freud's ideas have now fallen into disfavor in the psychological community, at the turn of the century his work was extremely influential, and it served to further undermine Victorian norms of morality.

Freud and Darwin were, in effect challenging conventional ideas about the nature of man. Albert Einstein, with the 1905 publication of his *Theory of Special Relativity*, effectively destabilized time-honored notions about the physical world and the universe itself.

---

[3] In his excellent book *Modern Times*, the historian Paul Johnson argues convincingly that Darwin's notion of the survival of the fittest is "a key element both in the Marxist concept of class warfare and of the racial philosophies that shaped Hitlerism." He further suggests that the social and political consequences of Darwin's ideas have yet to completely work themselves out of the culture.

[4] Freud admitted, however, that cultural and religious restraints on morals and behavior were necessary for a functioning society.

If the general public could not comprehend the science behind Einstein's theories, the idea that the world was in reality not what it had always been assumed to be, was abundantly clear.

> All at once nothing seemed certain in the movements of the spheres. 'The world is out of joint', as Hamlet sadly observed. It was as though the spinning globe had been taken off its axis and cast adrift in a universe which no longer conformed to accustomed standards of measurement.[5]

It was probably inevitable that Einstein's strictly scientific theory of relativity would eventually become confused in the public mind with the completely unrelated ethical idea of relativism. If time and space were relative, then surely good and evil were also relative and therefore the belief in absolutes of any kind was now passé. Einstein was disturbed by this misapplication of his theories. He wrote to a friend that he felt "like a man in a fairy-tale who turned everything he touched to gold, so with me, everything turns into a fuss in the newspapers."[6]

Nevertheless, Einstein's theories, along with those of Darwin and Freud, effectively undermined long-accepted, and broadly held assumptions. It was as though all former certainties were now called into question. Previously settled truths now seemed to be sadly out of step with the modern world.

---

[5] Paul Johnson, *Modern Times*, pg. 4

[6] ibid

A RADICAL BREAK WITH THE PAST

Artists, living as they do within the broader culture, were susceptible to the influence of the widely publicized views of Darwin, Freud, and Einstein, views which were making a tremendous impact in the culture at large. But in the more arcane world of philosophical ideas, calls for a radical break with the past were even more direct and provided additional intellectual justification to the early modernists.

Writing in 1863, Matthew Arnold, in his influential *Lectures and Essays in Criticism*, presciently expressed the attitude that would be wholeheartedly embraced by the modernists of the next century. He wrote that modern man finds himself burdened with

> an immense system of institutions, established facts, accredited dogmas, customs, rules, which have come to [him] from times not modern. In this system [his] life has to be carried forward, yet [he has] a sense that this system is not of [his] own creation, that it by no means corresponds exactly with the wants of [his] actual life, that for [him] it is customary, not rational. The awakening of this sense is the awakening of the modern spirit.[7]

Friedrich Nietzsche in his *Will to Power* (published posthumously in 1901) wrote, "what is needed, above all, is an absolute skepticism toward all inherited concepts."[8] He warned philosophers (and the same would certainly apply to artists) against embracing concepts handed down from bygone days as though they were "a wonderful dowry from some kind of wonderland". Instead, he encouraged philosophers (and by extension, artists) to make and create brand new concepts and to present them convincingly.

---

[7] Matthew Arnold, *Lectures and Essays in Criticism*, pg. 109

Nietzsche is probably most famous for asserting that "God is dead." Though this pronouncement is well known, its meaning is not. The idea appears in his *Parable of the Madman*. The madman cries in the market, "I seek God". The passersby mock him, saying, "Why, has he gotten lost?" The madman replies, "We have killed him – you and I. We are his murderers."[9] Nietzsche was an atheist, and he certainly did not mean to suggest that he believed that there was a God who had now died. What he meant was that our idea of God has died. Nietzsche thought that the practical result of the Age of Enlightenment was ultimately to eliminate God and Christianity from its formerly central role in European civilization. His statement is actually a warning to nontheists that they now have a problem: how does one retain any values at all in the absence of divine order?

Nietzsche was not, of course, arguing in favor of Christianity. Instead, he maintained that in the absence of Christian values, modern man must create his own new values. He called for what he described as a "transvaluation of all values", that is, a re-evaluation of all values, which he depicted as "a declaration of war...against all the old concepts of 'true' and 'not true'."[10]

The impulse towards withdrawal from social and moral consensus led early modernists to see themselves as outsiders, divorced from and marginal to the society in which they lived. Like Nietzsche, they tended to see the world as devoid of meaning or inherent significance.

As they saw it, the task of the artist was not to discover meaning in life, but to create new meaning out of the increasing disorder of modern life.

---

[8] Friedrich Nietzsche, *The Will to Power*, pg. 409

[9] Friedrich Nietzsche, *The Gay Science*, pg. 181-182

[10] Friedrich Nietzsche, *The Anti-Christ*, pg. 26

This led the early modernists to look for meaning in places previously considered to be meaningless; to value what was previously without value.[11]

In his *Flowers of Evil* (1857), Charles Baudelaire found value in decadence. In this collection of poems written during a large-scale renovation of Paris, Baudelaire laments the disappearance of the beggars, the blind, the gamblers and the prostitutes from the streets of Paris, all replaced by clean, symmetrical boulevards inhabited by an anthill of identical middle- class citizens, living meaningless lives.

Anton Chekhov wrote his short story, *Mire*, in 1886, finding value in a dunghill. His intent was to suggest that the seamy side of life is just as relevant as the usual, idealized subjects of literature. He explained, "A writer must be as objective as a chemist …He must realize that dunghills play a very respectable role in the landscape and evil passions belong to life just as much as good ones do."[12]

Luigi Russolo found value in noise. In his 1913 Futurist manifesto, *The Art of Noises*, Russolo argues that the human ear has become so accustomed to the speed, energy, and noise of the urban industrial world, that a new kind of music, one based on electronics and technology, is called for.[13]

In *Lady Chatterley's Lover*, D. H. Lawrence placed value on obscenity. First published in 1928 in Italy, the unexpurgated version did not appear in England until 1960, and then only after a landmark obscenity trial.

---

[11] I have borrowed this list of examples from Daniel Albright, *Putting Modernism Together*, pg. 1 – however, I have filled out his list with explanation and description

[12] Michael Ryan, *A Difficult Grace: On Poets, Poetry, and Writing*, pg. 152

[13] Luigi Russolo, *The Art of Noise*, pg. 6

Part of the controversy revolved around Lawrence's use of several words and expressions which are now common, but which were at the time not considered to be appropriate in print.[14]

Erik Satie placed value in triviality when he wrote his *Furniture Music* in 1917. It is music designed to be heard but not listened to – a sort of turn of the century muzak. Another similarly conceived work by Satie is called *Vexations*. It consists of a short musical phrase which, according to instructions provided by the composer, should be repeated 840 times. It received its first public performance only in 1963 and took 18 hours to perform. Only one individual was able to endure until the end. The performance reportedly induced hallucinations and altered states of consciousness in some members of the audience.[15]

The inclination of the modern artist toward what is abhorrent or contemptable may be partially attributed to the influence of Freud, who contended that we are often motivated by needs and fears which have nothing in common with the high ideals of reason or beauty. Art historian Norbert Lynton explains that

> ...the apparent negative preference of much modern art – substituting disorder for order, ugliness or distortion for beauty and proportion, obscurity...for clarity of meaning – represents a productive engagement with aspects of experience previously considered abnormal and not art-worthy but now recognized philosophically, creatively, and scientifically as central to humanity.[16]

---

[14] Though, as I say, these words are common enough today, they will, nevertheless not appear in print here. Anyone who is curious may easily discover the offending passages by consulting any one of a multitude of Internet sources.

[15] Sam Sweet, *A Dangerous and Evil Piano Piece*, The New Yorker, September 9, 2013

[16] Norbert Lynton, *The Story of Modern Art*, pg. 40

Another possible explanation for the motives of the modern artist may be found in the writings of the Russian literary theorist Viktor Shklovsky. He wrote that the distinctive contribution of art is defamiliarization. By this, he meant that we typically see the world through inherited conventions, what Nietzsche called "metaphors which are worn out and have lost their power"[17]. In other words, we perceive familiar things by a kind of mental shorthand which allows us to take in our surroundings with little or no conscious thought. Shklovsky argues that art can revive these conventions by making ordinary things seem strange. "The technique of art is to make objects unfamiliar; to make them difficult...Art is a way of experiencing the artfulness of an object – the object itself is not important."[18] Therefore, when Chekhov invites us to contemplate a dunghill he is actually forcing us to perceive the world in a new and different way.

On the other hand, it cannot be denied that modern art often seeks to be intentionally provocative. In consciously breaking from the norms of the past and by deliberately rejecting the consensus language of their craft, modern artists at the turn of the century became obsessed with a desire to discover the outer boundaries of artistic possibility.

In contrast to the general practice of the Victorian Era, in which both artist and audience shared a non-confrontational, comfortable middle ground of shared expectations and values, the modern artist preferred to "push outwards to the freakish circumference of art."[19]

This "adventurous" aspect of modern art is explained beautifully by Daniel Albright in his erudite book on Modernism:

---

[17] Friedrich Nietzsche, *On Truth and Lies in the Nonmoral Sense*

[18] Viktor Shklovsky, *Art as Technique*, pg. 2

[19] Daniel Albright, *Putting Modernism Together*, pg. 5

I think that modernist art will always appeal to those of us with an itch to explore. The trek to the South Pole, the quest for the source of the Nile, the search for birds of paradise in the interior of New Guinea, the climb up Mount Everest, the bathysphere descent into the Marianas Trench – Modernism provides something equivalent, in the domain of art. It matters to those who want to peer inside the human mind or to investigate the horizons of the human.[20]

BEFORE THE STORM: EUROPEAN MUSIC AT THE END OF THE 19TH CENTURY

For a period of roughly two hundred years, approximately 1700–1900, all Western European musicians and composers accepted a general set of propositions concerning harmony and musical form. This set of propositions is called *tonality*. The concept of tonality is that musical tones function in a hierarchical way in relation to a central tone called *tonic*. The tonic is the "center of gravity" and all other pitches function in relation to it.

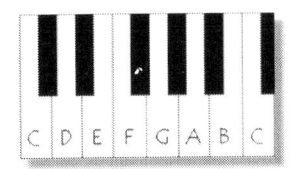

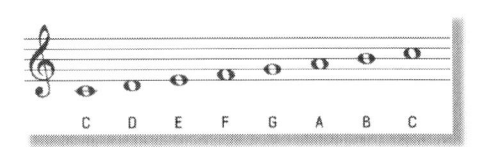

Using a piano keyboard as an illustration, the white keys represent the tonality (or key) of C, with the single pitch, "C", being the tonic note.

---

[20] Ibid., pg. 6

The other notes (D, E, F, G, A, B) are used as departures from tonic and all melodies and harmonies are expected to ultimately resolve back to tonic (either the note or the fundamental harmony built on tonic). These pitches taken together (including the tonic note) form a seven-note scale of pitches available for use within the context of that particular tonality or key.[21]

In this system, tonality is established by the use of these seven notes and equally importantly, the exclusion of the five tones represented by the black keys. In the Middle Ages (before the evolution of this tonal system), church music (i.e., Gregorian chant) made use of these letter-named notes exclusively for melodies. After the tonal system was developed, the seven-note scale was still the primary basis for tonality, but the five excluded notes (represented by the black keys) began to be used sparingly to add interest. These excluded notes were called "chromatic" notes because they added "color" to the music.[22]

Composers liked to use the chromatic notes for the simple reason that they sounded good. Being strictly limited to only the seven-note scale would be like being restricted to only vanilla ice cream – there's nothing wrong with it, but it gets boring after a while. As time passed, and especially as the 19th century unfolded, composers began to employ chromaticism with increasing frequency, avoiding resolution to tonic for longer and longer periods of time.

A kind of breaking point was reached when Richard Wagner created an opera entitled *Tristan and Isolde*.[23]

---

[21] It should be added that tonality is not limited exclusively to the white keys on the piano. Any pitch can be designated as "tonic" and the appropriate scale built upon it.

[22] The word *Chromatic* comes from the Greek *chroma*, meaning "color"

[23] Wagner did not like Italian opera, and did not want his work associated with it, so he refused to use the word "opera", preferring instead the term,

RICHARD WAGNER: *TRISTAN AND ISOLDE*

Richard Wagner was born in Leipzig, Germany in 1813, the ninth child of a minor town official. When his father died only six months later, Wagner's mother married an actor/playwright named Ludwig Geyer, whom Wagner later suspected of being his real father.

It is no surprise then, to learn that Wagner's early interests were in theater, as well as music. Wagner began writing operas in the 1830s and in 1836 married a soprano named Minna Planer. Although he remained married to Minna until her death in 1866, he had affairs with numerous other women.

In 1849 Wagner participated in a street demonstration which turned violent, resulting in many arrests. When he learned that a warrant had been issued for his arrest, he immediately fled to Zurich, leaving Minna behind in Dresden. While in Zurich, Wagner met a wealthy silk merchant named Otto Wesendonck, who agreed to support him financially and bankroll his projects. He even invited Wagner to live in a cottage on the grounds of his estate.

It was during his time in Zurich that Wagner became obsessed with the medieval love story, *Tristan and Isolde*, and decided to set it to music as an opera, even though it required him to temporarily suspend work on his magnum opus, *Der Ring des Nibelungen*. Part (or all) of Wagner's interest in the subject matter may perhaps be explained by the fact that he had become involved in a passionate love affair with Mathilde Wesendonck, the wife of his wealthy patron.

"Gesamtkunstwerk", meaning "total art work", that is, a work of art employing many different art forms, for instance, music, drama, costume, artistic set design, etc. In other words, an opera.

As he was nearing completion of the opera, Wagner's wife, Minna, who had by now joined him in Zurich, intercepted an intimate note written by Wagner to Mathilde. Needless to say, Zurich soon became an environment not conducive to creative work, and Wagner eventually left both Minna and Mathilde for Venice, where he finally completed work on *Tristan and Isolde* in 1858.

The story is a tragedy concerned with two lovers fated to share forbidden and ultimately frustrated love. Tristan is a Cornish prince who kills an Irish warrior, the uncle of the Irish princess, Isolde. Tristan kidnaps Isolde in order to bring her back to Cornwall as a bride for King Mark. During the journey, Isolde asks her handmaiden to prepare a strong poison, with which she plans to kill Tristan, and then herself. Instead, the handmaiden prepares a strong love potion. Isolde then invites Tristan to share a drink with her. Of course, instead of dying from poison, Tristan and Isolde, under the influence of the love potion, fall passionately in love. Because she will be the bride of King Mark, the love between Tristan and Isolde is forbidden, but because of the love potion, it is overpowering and real.

Notwithstanding the circumstances of its composition, *Tristan and Isolde* is a truly remarkable work. In order to express the tragic, unfulfilled longing of Tristan and Isolde, Wagner created music that is never allowed to resolve to any tonic. Along the way, he introduced harmonies which, until this time, were unheard of and theoretically impossible.

The prelude to *Tristan and Isolde* opens with a chromatic melody line culminating on the fourth note in a harmony that has sparked debate ever since.[24] This so-called "Tristan chord" (in brackets) has been called "The Chord that Changed the World", and "The Most Significant Chord in the World".[25]

Why all the fuss? The key signature for the *Prelude* to *Tristan and Isolde* has no sharps or flats which implies either the key of C or A minor. The "Tristan chord" is spelled F–B–D#–G#. The altered, chromatic pitches make this chord a dissonant chord in relation to the implied key. Dissonant chords containing altered, chromatic pitches were not unheard of in the 19th century. But this chord, spelled as it is, represented an entity not encountered before, a harmony that defied musical analysis in Wagner's day.

---

[24] If Wagner had been a jazz guitarist living 100 years later, this harmony (with slight spelling alterations) would be entirely conventional: Fm7(b5), E7(#11).

[25] Other equally hyperbolic descriptions can be found in the same place I found these, through a Google search.

What was even more revolutionary, at least in terms of long-term influence, was not just the Tristan chord, but where the music went next. Ordinarily, in tonal music, a dissonant harmony like the Tristan chord should resolve into consonant harmony. In the tonal system, consonance is the norm and dissonance represents a temporary disruption of the norm. Dissonance represents a momentary state of tension, and consonance represents a release of that tension. However, in *Tristan and Isolde*, the dissonant Tristan chord does not resolve into a consonance – instead, it dissolves into another dissonant harmony, which likewise dissolves into yet another dissonant harmony, continuing throughout the prelude. Ultimately, this unstable, constantly shifting harmony seemed to call into question the entire theory of tonality as it had been understood for the previous 200 years.

Wagner's music was so far ahead of his time that *Tristan and Isolde* proved to be almost impossible to stage.

> The music was so unusual that, at first, musicians struggled to play it...The first performance was supposed to be in Vienna in 1862. But after more than 70 rehearsals, the production was canceled. The singers could not find their notes and the orchestra struggled to keep time. Only by 1865, with its premiere in Munich, had the musicians caught up with Wagner and his "Tristan". The critics were less convinced: the singing was "nothing but screaming and shrieking", fumed one, while the orchestra indulged in the "most outrageous discords".[26]

---

[26] "A spine-tingling and blissful infinity", *The Economist*, December 30, 2014

At the eventual premiere, Hans von Bülow was chosen to conduct the orchestra, despite the fact that Wagner was by then having an affair with von Bülow's wife, Cosima. The parts of Tristan and Isolde were sung at the premiere by a husband and wife team, Ludwig Schnorr von Carolsfeld and Malvina Schnorr von Carolsfeld. Just over one month after the premiere, Ludwig died suddenly, having sung the role only four times, prompting speculation that the extreme exertion required had done him in.

Despite its revolutionary character, the musical language of *Tristan and Isolde* was still well within the boundaries of the tonal system. But by delaying a final resolution to tonic through extreme chromaticism, his music, in effect "suspended" tonality, and his example would reverberate well into the 20th century.

Richard Wagner died in 1883. The seventeen year period between his death and the beginning of the twentieth century was dominated by two German composers, Richard Strauss and Gustav Mahler, whose music built upon the innovations of Wagner, further stretching and weakening the sense of tonality and paving the way for the more extreme music of the 20th-century modernists.

RICHARD STRAUSS

In the first years of the twentieth century, Richard Strauss wrote two operas, *Salome* (1905) and *Elektra* (1909), both extremely controversial, on account of their subject matter and because of their strident musical dissonance. *Salome*, based on Oscar Wilde's 1891 play, was guaranteed to create a scandal with its mix of a biblical story with bloody violence and eroticism.

The Austrian premiere of *Salome* on May 16, 1906, was so widely anticipated that some musical enthusiasts traveled from miles around to witness the spectacle.

Adolf Hitler later told Strauss's son that he had borrowed money to make the trip, but it is uncertain whether he actually attended the performance.[27]

Salome was met with enthusiasm, especially among the younger generation of musicians, who were thrilled by its audacious innovations.

Even more daring was Strauss's 1909 follow-up to *Salome*, a one-act opera based on ancient Greek mythology entitled *Elektra*. The story of what is perhaps the bloodiest opera in the entire repertoire revolves around what is perhaps the most dysfunctional family of all time.

The head of the household is Agamemnon, who has returned from the battle of Troy only to be promptly hacked to death by his ax-wielding wife, Clytemnestra, who, in his absence, has taken up with another man.

Strauss's opera begins here, with Agamemnon's daughter, Elektra reacting to the murder of her father. She has obviously lost her mind, and she is described in the libretto as acting "like a beast in its lair". Her solution is to convince her brother, Orestes, to murder their mother, after which she will dance with joy at her father's grave.

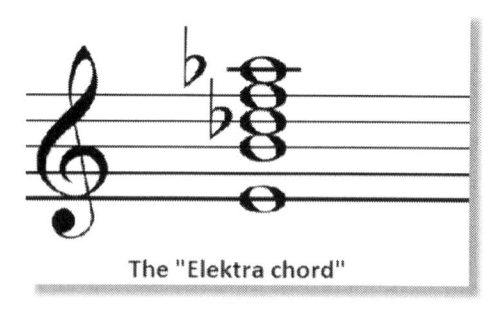

The "Elektra chord"

---

[27] Alex Ross, *The Rest is Noise*, pg. 4

The music of *Elektra* creates extreme dissonance by exploiting ideas such as bitonality (two simultaneous key centers), as illustrated by the so-called "Elektra chord", which consists of a D-flat major chord stacked above a perfect fifth in the key of E. This chord is regarded as Elektra's "harmonic signature" and is used at important points in the opera to indicate Elektra's conflicted personality.

The idea of two simultaneous and conflicting key centers would be taken up again by the next generation of full-fledged modernist composers, most notably Igor Stravinsky, who employed the idea in his ballet score, *Petrushka*, in order to suggest the divided personality of the titular character. *Elektra* marks the furthest extreme of Strauss's experiment with Modernism, a point from which he afterward retreated, returning to more conventional modes of expression for the rest of his life.

GUSTAV MAHLER

The music of Gustav Mahler also built upon and extended the ideas of Wagner, and like Strauss, his music had the effect of further weakening the sense of tonality. However, unlike Strauss, who made his name writing adventurous operas, Mahler's language of musical discourse was primarily that of the symphony. His symphonies tended to be gargantuan, noisy affairs, full of emotional turbulence and angst.

Mahler and Strauss were occasionally rivals, but more often they were friends and enthusiastic promoters of one another's work. When Mahler died from a bacterial infection on May 18, 1911, Strauss was devastated and could not speak for several days.[28]

---

[28] Ibid, pg. 31

Mahler died only one decade into the remarkable new century, but his influence on the next generation of composers, especially Arnold Schoenberg, would be strong. Strauss was destined to have a longer, stranger story.

As the twentieth century opened, the artists, writers, and composers who would create Modernism shared a common conviction: the long-standing consensus language of their various disciplines had exhausted itself. They felt an urgent necessity to create a new mode of expression, more closely attuned to the modern world which was just dawning. For writers like James Joyce and T. S. Eliot, it meant radically undoing traditional narrative styles and embracing experimental techniques such as stream of consciousness, absurdity, and symbolism. For artists like Pablo Picasso and Wassily Kandinsky, it meant leaving behind traditional figurative painting in favor of abstracted or geometric shapes. For composers like Arnold Schoenberg and Igor Stravinsky, it meant discarding the conventional musical language of tonality and creating brand new modes of musical expression characterized by dissonance and forceful new rhythms.

During the first decade of the 20th century, Modernism was propelled by a mood of excitement and confidence. Never had the possibilities for the future seemed brighter. As events would soon show, this confidence was entirely unfounded. The Austrian novelist, Stephan Zweig was one of the most popular writers in the world in the 1920s. In his autobiography, *Die Welt von Gestern* (*The World of Yesterday*), he captured the misplaced optimism of the time:

Never was my love for this old world of ours stronger than in those final few years before the First World War, never were my hopes for the unification of Europe and my belief in its future greater than at this time. For we thought we glimpsed the red of a new dawn, but in truth, it was the fiery glow of a world about to be consumed by fire.[29]

---

[29] Stephan Zweig, *The World of Yesterday*, pg. 192

CHAPTER TWO: IMPRESSIONISM A NEW ART EMERGES

Impressionism first appeared in the late 19th century in France, growing out of an interaction between artists who were angered by the rigid standards of the government-sanctioned art establishment. The accepted academic style at the time was Neoclassicism, exemplified by the *Death of Marat* by Jean Jacques David. Content was rigidly regulated and subject matter was expected to be based on historical events, mythology, and religion.[30] Man was to be presented as an ideal, nature was to be celebrated and romanticized. The academic style was realistic, but not the realism we see and experience in our everyday lives. Rather it was realism as imagined through the prism of a quest for classical perfection.

In the beginning, the Impressionists were only connected to one another socially. They gathered, along with other painters, sculptors, writers, musicians, and performers, in the cafes that had begun to spring up in Paris in the 1850s and 60s, in the period after Napoleon III declared himself emperor. What they had in common was simply a passion to paint and to succeed as artists. Most of them had repeatedly been rejected by the Academy, and they were struggling for recognition. They rejected the idealized, classical portrayal of nature required by the Academy. Instead, they were fascinated by the reality of nature as it really is, or at least, as it is actually perceived by the viewer.

---

[30] *The Death of Marat*, for instance, commemorated a murdered hero of the French Revolution, Jean-Paul Marat, a radical journalist and politician. He was assassinated by Charlotte Corday, who plunged a five inch kitchen knife into his chest while he was taking a medical bath for a debilitating skin condition. David's painting glorifies Marat, portraying him in the style of a Christian martyr, his face and body bathed in glowing light.

Ever since the Renaissance, artists attempted to portray the natural world by means of perspective, a technique by which the illusion of three-dimensional space is created on a flat surface. This is accomplished by using a set of lines which converge on a single imaginary point on the horizon. The 1482 fresco, *Christ Giving the Keys to St. Peter*, by the Italian Renaissance painter Pietro Perugino, illustrates this technique vividly.[31] In the center foreground, we see Christ and Peter, surrounded by the apostles and other important persons on either side. Other smaller figures are seen behind them, standing on a set of lines which converge on a central point in the distance (hidden behind the building in the center), giving the illusion of depth and three-dimensional space.

Pietro Perugino, *Christ Giving the Keys to St. Peter* (1482)
(public domain)

---

[31] Perugino was commissioned by Pope Sixtus IV to paint the fresco in 1480 as part of the decoration of St. Peter's Basilica in Rome. Superstition held that, in the selection of a new pope, the Cardinal who was housed in the cell directly under the fresco (an honor bestowed by lot) would be elected pope. Records show that it worked at least three times.

But perspective is merely an illusion, not the reality of nature as it truly is. In the real world, for instance, we do not stand in a static environment, on a grid of infinitely receding lines. For the French Impressionists, the "reality of nature" was a question of perception – a phenomenon of transient sensations of light, perceived by the eye and interpreted by the mind. From this point of view, the best that an artist can hope for is to capture on canvas his own impression of what he sees. Claude Monet wrote, "My only merit lies in having painted directly in front of nature, *seeking to render my impressions before the most fleeting moments*."[32] For painters like Monet, nature was not solid or fixed, but something ephemeral and fluid, always in a state of transition.

Look again at *Christ Giving the Keys to St. Peter*. Look carefully at the human figures. Though they are recognizable as human beings, they are in no way realistic. Wearing brightly colored clothing, standing in stiff, artificial poses, they are almost like cartoon figures. They are idealized, almost symbolic representations of human beings. Now, look at the environment in which they are placed. It is unnaturally clean and brightly lit. We recognize the people, the buildings, the trees, by a kind of conceptual shorthand, but in actual reality, no scene matching this one ever existed, or ever could exist. We are looking at a conceptualized, idealized scene.

For the Impressionists, idealized scenes like this did not reflect reality as it is actually perceived. Once again, Nietzsche had already explored this philosophical ground. In his 1873 essay, *On Truth and Lie in the Nonmoral Sense*, he wrote:

---

[32] Laura Anne Kalba, *Color in the Age of Impressionism: Commerce, Technology, and Art*

> Every concept originates through equating the unequal. One leaf is never exactly like another, and so the concept of "leaf" is formed through an arbitrary abandonment of these individual differences, forgetting the disparities. And it awakens the idea - as if there existed in nature, in addition to leaves, the "leaf", a sort of primal form, after which all leaves were woven, marked, measured, colored, curled, and painted – though by an unskilled hand, so that no examples turned out correctly and reliably as the faithful image of the primal form.[33]

Nietzsche is mocking the Classical notion of ideal forms promoted by Plato. Nietzsche says that the idealized concept of "the leaf" is an illusion – in reality there exist only particular instances of real and individually varied leaves.

The Impressionists agreed with this sentiment. Renoir said, "Nature abhors regularity".[34]

It was not just that the Impressionists wanted to avoid idealized objects. They were not really concerned with objects themselves at all. They were far more interested in capturing the transient effects of the atmosphere surrounding the objects. Monet said, "I want to paint the air which surrounds the bridge, the house, the boat… the beauty of the air."[35]

---

[33] David B. Allison, *Reading the New Nietzsche*, pg.78

[34] Robert L. Herbert, Impressionism: *Art, Leisure, and Parisian Society*, pg. 192

[35] John House, *Monet: Nature Into Art*, pg. 221

Between 1890 and 1891, Monet devoted nearly thirty paintings to the subject of haystacks standing near his home in Giverny.[36] The actual haystacks belonged to Monet's neighbor, a farmer. Monet happened to notice the way the light changed on the haystacks at different times of the day. He asked his step-daughter to bring him two canvases so that he could attempt to catch the effect of the changing light. He soon discovered that the light changed too quickly and asked for more canvases. His step-daughter loaded as many as she could carry into a wheel-barrow and brought them to him. This became Monet's daily routine – paints, easels, and unfinished canvases carried back and forth between the field and Monet's studio. The titles of the individual haystack paintings that resulted from this operation are revealing: *Haystacks in the Morning, Haystacks at the End of Summer, Haystacks in the Morning Snow, Haystacks in the Sun, Haystacks in the Mist*, etc.

If the point is not yet clear, Monet was not especially interested in painting haystacks – he was attempting to capture the atmosphere surrounding the haystacks. The haystacks themselves were unimportant, only an occasion for "painting the air".

THE FIRST IMPRESSIONIST EXHIBITION

The *Académie des Beaux-Arts* (The French Academy of the Fine Arts) was created in Paris in 1816[37], its purpose being to protect French culture from corruption.

---

[36] I have visited Monet's home in Giverny and can recommend a photo op standing in front of the haystack which has been conveniently placed near his home for just such a purpose.

[37] The Academy in Monet's time was the result of a merger between three institutions with much older roots: the *Académie de peinture et de sculpture* (Academy of Painting and Sculpture, founded 1648), the *Académie de musique* (Academy of Music, founded in 1669) and the *Académie d'architecture* (Academy of Architecture, founded in 1671).

The Academy was sponsored by the government and set the standards for French art. Each year it held a juried exhibition. To be accepted for this exhibition was more than simply a badge of honor, it was required for anyone wishing to pursue a serious career in art.

The Academy routinely rejected submissions by Monet and others in his circle because they painted in a non-conventional style not approved by the Academy. In response, Monet and a group of like-minded artists, referring to themselves by the unwieldy name, "Anonymous Society of Painters, Sculptors, Engravers, etc.", staged their own exhibition, beginning on April 9, 1874. There were 165 works shown, with 30 artists participating.

The artists in this exhibition had no intention of revolutionizing art history or creating a movement. Since most of them had been rejected by the Academy, this was the only realistic way for their work to be seen and, hopefully, sold. These artists were the equivalent of indie filmmakers today, struggling against the studio system.

It was not the style, but the content of the artwork that represented the most significant departure from the dictates of the Academy. Instead of choosing subjects from history or Classical mythology, these artists looked to the world around them for subject matter. They painted peasants, working-class people, nondescript, ordinary-looking individuals engaged in everyday activities. They painted mundane landscapes as they actually saw them, rather than in an idealized form. Some of the artists and works on display were:

Portraits in a New Orleans Cotton Office, by Edgar Degas depicts the New Orleans cotton business run by the artist's uncle, who can be seen in the foreground, examining the raw cotton for quality. Degas' brother can also be seen reading the newspaper. This was the first painting by Degas to be purchased by a museum (also the first Impressionist to be distinguished in this way), and it marked a financial turning point in his career as an artist.[38]

The Absinthe Drinker, also by Edgar Degas, was harshly criticized, not because of its style, but because of its subject matter: a young woman, sitting alone, drinking in a café. The woman stares into space, a pale drink on the table before her[39]. Her surly companion stares in another direction, rumpled hat on his head, and pipe in his mouth. Although the painting appears to be a spontaneous scene, it was actually staged. Degas convinced two of his friends to act as models for the painting. Ellen André was an actress and an artist's model; Marcellin Desboutin was an engraver and artist.

Their reputations suffered as a result of the painting and Degas was forced to defend them by publicly declaring that they were not really alcoholics.

Dahlias, by Paul Cezanne, is a surprisingly conventional work from an artist who would later be called a "post-impressionist", creating more radical works that would set the stage for some styles of modern art in the 20th century.

---

[38] Dega's painting depicts the moment when his uncle Michel Musson's cotton brokerage business went bankrupt in an economic crash, according to Michael McMahon of the Pittsburgh Post-Gazette. The firm was swamped by the postwar growth of the much larger Cotton Exchange. In the painting, Degas' brother Rene reads *The Daily Picayune*, which carried the bankruptcy news.

[39] Absinthe was known at the time as "*La Fée Verte*", the green fairy. It was highly addictive and known to cause hallucinations, and for this reason (and because of its popularity) it was eventually banned in Europe and America.

However, the most controversial piece in the exhibition was a painting by Claude Monet, *Impression, Sunrise*. Monet chose the title at the last moment, as an afterthought. Nevertheless, it would furnish the name for the entire movement. In Monet's painting, the center of attention is a small circle of a reddish, orange sun barely penetrating the hazy, blueish sky. The sun's reflection on the water is marked by strokes of thickly applied paint which seem to stand out from the surface of the canvas. In fact, the overall technique seems to be defined by quick brushstrokes and an avoidance of mixing colors to create gradations.

It was this practice - the use of rapid brushstrokes, and entire paintings completed in one session - that caused the most controversy. It was seen as an insult to the meticulous and time-consuming brushwork of traditional Academy-trained artists, who often spent weeks or more on a single work. To many viewers, Monet's *Sunrise* seemed, by comparison, careless and unfinished.

The 62-year-old art critic, Louis Leroy, was shocked by what he saw. His review was published under the title, "The Exhibition of the Impressionists." He wrote sarcastically, "Impression – I was certain of it. I was just telling myself that, since I was impressed, there had to be some impression in it... and what freedom, what ease of workmanship! Wallpaper in its embryonic state is more finished than that seascape."[40]

However, at least one critic seemed to understand what the artists of the 1874 exhibition were trying to achieve. Jules-Antoine Castagnary wrote, "If one wishes to characterize and explain them with a single word, then one would have to coin the word, impressionists. They are impressionists in that they do not render a landscape, but the sensation produced by the landscape."[41]

---

[40] Christoph Heinrich, *Monet*, pg.32

Louis Leroy had used the word "impressionist" as a term of derision. Within a year, however, the label had lost its negative connotation and had entered into common usage as an apt description of the new art form.

SYMBOLIST POETRY

The Symbolist movement in 19th century France was the literary counterpart to French Impressionist painting, and its ideas provided inspiration to the Impressionist painters.

Symbolist poets sought to assemble moments of experience and perception into a kind of verbal collage, using symbols rather than direct descriptions. For them, the symbol was not necessarily tied to a single specific idea with a concrete, fixed meaning. Rather, a particular image might suggest a variety of things which may be only obliquely connected. Instead of attempting to clarify, they tried merely to suggest a tone or a mood in order to approach an indescribable condition.

Symbolism as a literary movement originated in 1857 with the publication of Charles Baudelaire's *Les Fleurs du mal* (*Flowers of Evil*). Baudelaire lived during a politically turbulent time in French history which seemed to mirror the turmoil of his personal life. Baudelaire was born in Paris in 1821. After his father died in 1827, his mother quickly married a French general for whom Baudelaire had nothing but contempt.

As a young man, he went to great lengths to defy his stepfather in every imaginable way, squandering his inheritance and living a self-indulgent, bohemian lifestyle.

---

[41] Jules Castagnary, *Le Siecle*, April 29 1874

Baudelaire was enraged when Louis Napoleon began a major public works project aimed at rebuilding and modernizing large sections of Paris, destroying many ancient and medieval parts of the city in the process. Motivated by disgust and despair, fueled by drugs and inspired by his own obsessive fantasies about the disappearing "old" Paris, Baudelaire began writing the poetry which would eventually comprise *Les Fleurs du mal*.

Throughout the work, Baudelaire seems fascinated by correspondences between the malignant and the beautiful. In fact, one of the poems in the collection is called *Correspondences*. This poem, which would become a foundational text for the Symbolist movement, establishes correspondences between objects in nature and the archetypes and symbols that populate the psyche.

Nature is a temple whose living colonnades
Breathe forth a mystic speech in fitful sighs,
Man wanders among the symbols in those glades
Where all things watch him with familiar eyes.

Like dwindling echoes gathered far away
Into a deep and thronging unison
Huge as the night or as the light of day,
All scents and sounds and colors meet as one.

Perfumes there are as sweet as the oboe's sound,
Green as the prairies, fresh as a child's caress,
— And there are others, rich, corrupt, profound

And an infinite pervasiveness,

> *Like myrrh, or musk, or amber, that excite*
> *The ecstasies of sense, the soul's delight.*[42]

Like the Impressionists, Baudelaire offers fleeting sensations and suggestions rather than conventional descriptions. His poem is filled with appeals to the "ecstasies of sense": of sound ("dwindling echoes gathered far away...sweet as the oboe's sound"), of scent ("like myrrh, or musk, or amber"), or of sight ("huge as night or as the light of day...green as the prairies").

Baudelaire was fascinated by Edgar Allan Poe and translated many of Poe's works into French. He saw Poe's dark imagery as a way of highlighting the tragedy and mystery of human existence. He even borrows Poe's iconic cat for use in *The Flowers of Evil*, using it as an erotic metaphor for the simultaneous allure and danger of women.

In his last years, Baudelaire was suffering from a number of physical conditions, exacerbated by stress, excessive drinking, and his long-term use of opium. He suffered a massive stroke in 1866 and spent his final months in a partially-paralyzed condition before his death in Paris in 1867. His ideas directly influenced the French Impressionist painters through Edouard Manet, whom Baudelaire befriended in 1858[43], and the later Symbolist poets like Stéphane Mallarmé and Paul Verlaine.

In 1886, nearly twenty years after the death of Charles Baudelaire, Symbolism officially became a movement with the publication of the *Symbolist Manifesto* in the French newspaper, *Le Figaro*. This peculiar document, composed by Jean Moréas, declares that the Symbolists are against "plain meanings, declamations, false sentimentality and matter-of-fact description".[44]

---

[42] Charles Baudelaire, *The Flowers of Evil*, translation by James McGowan, pg. 18

[43] Baudelaire can be seen, fashionably dressed, at the far left of Manet's painting, *The Music in the Tuileries* (1862)

In his manifesto, Moréas names several "approved" Symbolist poets, beginning with Baudelaire and including Stéphane Mallarmé, who would come to be regarded as one of the most important French writers of the latter 19th century.

Mallarmé was born in Paris in 1842, and as a young man, chose not to follow in his father's footsteps as a civil-servant, but instead to pursue languages. His early influences included Victor Hugo, and of course, Baudelaire, in whose memory Mallarmé wrote the poem, *The Tomb of Charles Baudelaire*.

> *The buried temple empties through its bowels,*
> *Sepulchral sewer spewing mud and rubies,*
> *Abominably some idol of Anubis,*
> *Its muzzle all aflame with savage howls.*
>
> *Or if the recent gas the wick befouls*
> *That bears so many insults, it illumines*
> *In haggard outline an immortal pubis*
> *Flying along the streetlights on its prowls.*
>
> *What wreaths dried out in cities without prayer*
> *Of night could bless like that which settles down*
> *Vainly against the marble of Baudelaire*
>
> *In the fluttering veil that girds her absence round,*
> *A tutelary poison, his own Wraith,*
> *We breathe in always though it bring us death.*[45]

---

[44] Rosina Neginsky, *Symbolism, Its Origins and Its Consequences*, pg. 556

[45] Stéphane Mallarmé, *The Tomb of Charles Baudelaire*, from *Collected Poems*.

Mallarmé wrote that the goal of poetry was to "depict not the thing, but the effect it produces,"[46] and that "everything that is sacred and wishes to remain so must envelop itself in mystery."[47] In his poetry, he follows his own recommendations, making extensive use of symbol and metaphor. His complex language is full of elusive ambiguity.

In later life, Mallarmé proved to be an influential figure, not only because of his writing but for hosting a regular Tuesday evening meeting in his home on the Rue de Rome in Paris which became a hub of Parisian intellectual life. These meetings were frequented by artists of all kinds, who gathered to discuss poetry, art, music, and philosophy. Among those in attendance at one time or another were writers like Paul Valéry, Oscar Wilde, Paul Verlaine, and W.B. Yeats, the painters Renoir, Monet, Degas, and Whistler, as well as the sculptor Rodin.

Among the intellectual notables of the world of art and literature who regularly attended Mallarmé's Tuesday meetings was a young composer, Claude Debussy, for whom the ideas of Mallarmé were gospel.

IMPRESSIONIST MUSIC: CLAUDE DEBUSSY

Claude Debussy was born in Paris in 1862 and began studying music at the Paris Conservatoire at the young age of ten. He won the coveted Prix de Rome prize in 1884, and consequently spent two years in Italy.

Upon returning to Paris in 1887 he began to associate with the Symbolist poets and became a regular participant in Mallarmé's Tuesday meetings.[48]

---

[46] Lloyd Austin, *Poetic Principles and Practice: Occasional Papers on Baudelaire, Mallarmé...*, pg. 59

[47] Marian Zwerling Sugano, *The Poetics of the Occasion: Mallarmé and the Poetry of Circumstance*, pg. 197

[48] J. Peter Burkholder, *A History of Western Music*, pg. 791

Paris, in the late 19th century, was the very center of the European art world and Debussy was involved with all of it. His real quest, however, was for a truly modern musical language that was distinctly French, purged from German influence. Though Debussy was an admirer of Wagner's *Tristan and Isolde*, he disliked the German propensity for emotional angst and noisy bombast, as exemplified by his contemporaries, Strauss and Mahler. To this end, Debussy immersed himself in French painting and poetry, working out musical analogies to Impressionist art and Symbolist poetry.

Debussy made a specialty of devising strategies of aimlessness, working to dissolve the traditional grammar of music, attempting to reflect the sense of floating ambiguity that characterizes Impressionist art and the poetry of the Symbolists.

Debussy was greatly aided in his quest for a new musical aesthetic by a chance encounter that occurred during the 1889 Paris World's Fair, where, under the shadow of the newly constructed Eiffel Tower, Debussy first heard the otherworldly music of the Javanese gamelan. The gamelan is an orchestra of bronze gongs tuned to unique musical scales that cannot be reproduced on Western instruments. Debussy was enchanted by this music and returned day after day to take it in.

His enthusiasm is evident in what he wrote to a friend, describing Javanese music as being "able to express every nuance of meaning, even unmentionable shades," making the chord progressions of western tonal music, by comparison, seem like "empty phantoms."[49]

---

[49] Brenda Lynne Leach, *Looking and Listening: Conversations between Modern Art and Music*, pg. 122

Debussy applied this influence to his own music in a number of ways. He began by eliminating or masking cadences. In traditional music of the common practice period, cadences are like punctuation in writing, and serve the same purpose: like commas and periods, they divide musical ideas into distinct, easily identifiable phrases, bringing a musical phrase to a temporary halt.

This is an example of a traditional cadence. If you play it at the piano, you will understand its function immediately: plop, plop, plop, and everything stops. For Debussy, under the influence of the flowing, fluid music of the Javanese gamelan, this kind of interruption in the flow of music was no longer desirable. By eliminating cadences like this, Debussy was able to achieve the kind of static, timeless quality that he so admired in the music of Indonesia.

In addition to the elimination of cadences, Debussy began to use unusual, exotic scales as well. By so doing, he was able to blur any sense of traditional tonality.

This is the whole-tone scale (G, F, Eb, Db, B).[50] Unlike the traditional major scale, it contains no half-steps, only whole-steps (or whole tones, hence the name). Because it has no half-steps, it has no "center of gravity" - no single note seems more important than any other. Because of this characteristic, it seems to "float" - it is aimless, directionless. It also approximates the sound of the slendro scale, common to gamelan music, which probably explains Debussy's attraction to it.

His 1907 work for piano entitled *Cloches a travers les feuilles* (*Bells Through the Leaves*) from *Images, Book II* for piano uses exactly these notes in its opening passage. It is almost certainly meant to evoke the sound of the Javanese gamelan.[51]

PRELUDE TO THE AFTERNOON OF A FAUN

Prélude à l'après-midi d'un faune (*Prelude to the Afternoon of a Faun*) is Claude Debussy's most important work. It is a composition for orchestra, first performed in Paris on December 22, 1894. The title refers to a poem by Stéphane Mallarmé, *Afternoon of a Faun*, which was the inspiration for Debussy's orchestral work.

The Afternoon of a Faun is considered to be Mallarmé's finest work and a landmark in the history of French Symbolist poetry. Written between 1865 and 1867, the final text was published in 1876. It describes the sensual experiences of a faun who has awakened from an afternoon nap and, in a dreamlike monologue, begins to recount his encounters with several nymphs during the morning.

---

[50] This example is an incomplete whole-tone scale containing only five tones to highlight its similarity to the Javanese slendro scale which is a five-note scale. The complete whole-tone scale would include the note "A".

[51] For another striking and beautiful illustration of Debussy's propensity for gamelan imitation, listen to his piano solo, *Et la lune descend sur le temple qui fut*, approximately one minute into the piece (right after the series of large, parallel chords).

Mallarmé believed that the reader should never be given anything directly, that he should be forced to pull the meaning out of the words. While recognizing that his manner of writing made the work nearly impenetrable, Mallarmé nevertheless believed that this was the highest form of art. The poem opens with these words:

> *Save from my flute, no waters murmuring*
>
> *In harmony flow out into the groves;*
>
> *And the only wind on the horizon no ripple moves,*
>
> *Exhaled from my twin pipes and swift to drain*
>
> *The melody in arid drifts of rain,*
>
> *Is the visible, serene and fictive air*
>
> *Of inspiration rising as if in prayer.*

The "faun" of Mallarmé's poem is a half goat, half man, Pan-like creature[52], and his flute is probably best imagined as an ancient Greek aulos, which fits the "twin pipes" described in the poem.

Debussy was intimately acquainted with Mallarme's poem and he went to great lengths to evoke its mood, and even to make hidden references to the structure of the poem. (The poem is 110 lines – Debussy's Prelude is 110 measures).

Debussy asked Gustave Doret, a young man still in his twenties, to conduct the orchestra at the premiere. As Doret examined the score in Debussy's small apartment, he was impressed by the innovative structure of the work, and by the unusual instrumental effects that were called for.

---

[52] See the paintings of the faun by Hungarian painter Pál Szinyei Merse for a clear image of this creature.

At first, the players did not understand the music – it was unlike anything they had ever heard. Eventually, however, over the course of many rehearsals, a feeling of intimate collaboration between the musicians and the composer began to develop.

The first performance took place in Paris, on December 22, 1894, and was attended with great anticipation - Mallarmé himself was in the audience. When the conductor raised his baton, the audience was absolutely silent.

The piece begins by invoking the very music which the faun plays in the poem. For this flute solo, Debussy makes use of a chromatic scale which, like the whole-tone scale, creates a sense of ambiguity by clouding any sense of traditional tonality.

This flute solo might logically be assumed to be the primary theme of Debussy's Prelude. In the Classical tradition, this theme would then be developed and transformed. However, Debussy, like Monet and Mallarmé, is turning away from the traditional practices of his art and using his musical discourse to convey a more fleeting and elusive impression. The flute is answered by horns, accompanied by harp glissandos, contributing to the dreamlike atmosphere. The flute solo appears again, this time surrounded by delicate, shimmering strings.

In the middle section of the piece, the orchestra crescendos into a full-blown love song, representing the amorous longings of the faun.

The strings play long, flowing melody lines which have more in common with Indian ragas than the symmetrically balanced phrases of traditional European melodies. Eventually, the sound dies away and the flute repeats the opening melody as the orchestra dissolves into silence.

The initial performance was met with thunderous applause and calls for encore, which were only quieted when the orchestra agreed to play the entire work a second time.[53]

In later years, many analysts would point to Debussy's *Prelude to the Afternoon of a Faun* as the birth of modern music. [54]

---

[53] Harvey Lee Snyder, *Afternoon of a Faun: How Debussy Created a New Music for the Modern World*

[54] Pierre Boulez is supposed to have said this. He is quoted in the *Anthology for Musical Analysis: The Common-Practice Period*, by Charles Burkhart, pg. 379, and in *Music in the 20th Century*, by Dave DiMartino, pg. 168. He should know - as a conductor, Boulez is regarded as one of the most authoritative interpreters of Debussy's music.

CHAPER THREE: PRIMITIVISM - THE OLD IS NEW

"Paris is always a good idea," or so Audrey Hepburn is supposed to have said. And this is doubly so in Spring, if we can believe the Vernon Duke song, "April in Paris". But on May 29, 1913, Paris was unseasonably hot, with temperatures reaching 85 degrees. Nevertheless, by late afternoon a crowd had begun to gather outside the swanky new Théâtre des Champs Elysées where the Ballets Russes was to perform that evening. "There, for the expert eye, were all the makings of a scandal," recalled French poet, Jean Cocteau, then only 24 years old. He described the scene: "A fashionable audience...outfitted in pearls, egret hairdresses, and plumes of ostrich...a thousand nuances of snobbery, super-snobbery, and counter-snobbery."[55] They were drawn by the hopeful prospect of an outrage.

Their anticipation was not without reason. The Ballets Russes had established a reputation for simultaneously charming and shocking Parisian audiences ever since they first arrived in 1909. Igor Stravinsky, the young Russian composer who had thrilled audiences with his colorful collage of Russian folk songs and modernist harmonies in *Petrushka* in 1911 and *The Firebird* in 1910, was rumored to have created a provocative new work set in pagan Russia. Vaslav Nijinsky, the choreographer, had caused a minor scandal himself only a few months previously, with his blatantly erotic portrayal of the faun in Debussy's *L'Après-midi d'un faune*[56]

---

[55] Alex Ross, *The Rest is Noise*, pg.74

[56] Ivan Hewett, *The Rite of Spring 1913: Why did it provoke a riot?*, The Telegraph, May 16, 2013

Advance publicity for the brand new work, *Le Sacre du Printemps* (*The Rite of Spring*), was extravagant, promising that the audience would experience an art not confined by space and time.[57] Seat prices doubled.

As the house lights dimmed, a single bassoon began to play a folk-like melody in its extreme upper register. So peculiar was the sound that the famous composer Camille Saint-Saëns, after asking a companion to identify the instrument that was playing, reportedly remarked, "If that's a bassoon then I'm a baboon!"[58] As the music progressed, dissonant strands of melody intertwined like vegetation bursting out of the earth.

The audience at first listened in silence, but as the density and dissonance of the music increased, hisses and catcalls began to be heard, quickly escalating into what Stravinsky called "a terrific uproar".[59] Writer Gertrude Stein, who was in the audience, described the scene:

> One literally could not hear the sound of music. Our attention was distracted by a man in the box next to us flourishing his cane, and finally, in an altercation with the man in the next box, his cane came down and smashed the opera hat that the other had just put on in defiance. It was all incredibly fierce.[60]

---

[57] Modris Ecksteins, *Rites of Spring: The Great War and the Birth of the Modern Age*

[58] Kim Willsher, *Rite that caused riots: celebrating 100 years of The Rite of Spring*, The Guardian, May 27, 2013

[59] Paul Griffiths, *Modern Music, A Concise History*, pg. 41

[60] Alex Ross, *The Rest is Noise*, pg. 75

The reviews were uniformly hostile. The composer Giacomo Puccini called it, "the work of a madman ... sheer cacophony". *Le Figaro*'s critic, Henri Quittard wrote, "A laborious and puerile barbarity."[61] A more detailed account was offered by the American writer, Carl Van Vechten:

> I attended the first performance in Paris of [Stravinsky's] anarchistic ballet, *The Sacrifice of Spring*, in which primitive emotions are both depicted and aroused by a dependence on barbarous rhythm... a certain part of the audience, thrilled by what it considered a blasphemous attempt to destroy music as an art, and swept away with wrath, began very soon after the rise of the curtain to whistle, [and] to make cat-calls...others of us who liked the music and felt that principles of free speech were at stake, bellowed defiance.[62]

The riot that occurred at the premiere of Stravinsky's *Rite of Spring* would eventually come to be seen as indicative of the provocative nature of twentieth century art in general – it became almost a metaphor for the relationship between the modern artist and the public. Musicologist Daniel Albright calls this "the defining moment of Modernism – not just music, but in all the arts" and credits it with establishing "the gold-standard for twentieth century artistic scandals."[63] But before analyzing Stravinsky's music in an attempt to discover what the first audience found so disconcerting, we should step back and get a broader view of the movement that this work came to symbolize.

---

[61] Kim Willsher, *Rite that caused riots: celebrating 100 years of The Rite of Spring*, The Guardian, May 27, 2013

[62] Piero Weiss and Richard Taruskin, *Music in the Western World, A History in Documents*, pg. 441

[63] Daniel Albright, Putting Modernism Together, pg. 136

PRIMITIVISM

In general, Primitivism simply means a fascination with the primitive. As an art movement, Primitivism may refer either to the deliberate borrowing from (or appropriation of) primitive motifs or to simply making indigenous people the subject of a work of art.

During the Enlightenment, arguments about the supposed superiority of the "simple" life of indigenous people were used mostly as a rhetorical device for criticizing negative aspects of European civilization. Knowledge of and interest in so-called "primitive" people was based on reports from European explorers like Captain Cook and Columbus who had encountered previously unknown native cultures on their voyages to the Americas and the South Pacific islands.

During the 18th and 19th centuries, as Africa and Asia were colonized by the European powers and contact with indigenous peoples grew, Europeans developed an ambivalent attitude towards the native cultures which they encountered. In general, they belittled the colonized peoples with words like "primitive" or "savage". But in time, many Europeans began to rethink their assumptions about the inherent superiority of Western civilization.

Perhaps no one expressed this ambivalence better than the novelist Joseph Conrad. He was born Józef Teodor Konrad Korzeniowski in 1857 in Berdichev, Polish Ukraine, a part of Poland then under Russian control. When he was only five years old, his parents were sent to Northern Russia because of suspected anti-government activity, where they soon died due to the harsh conditions.

Conrad was sent to live with an uncle who eventually permitted him, at age sixteen, to go to sea. Attaching himself to the French merchant marine, he made voyages to the West Indies and South America. After being severely wounded in a duel at age twenty, he left France for England.[64]

Conrad signed on to a British freighter and rose steadily through the ranks until, at the young age of 29, he became master of his own ship at which time he adopted the name Joseph Conrad and became a British citizen. He sailed to Australia, Borneo, Malaysia, South America, and the islands of the South Pacific, and during these long voyages began to write.

In 1890, he was sent to Africa as part of the Belgian Colonial service with an assignment to sail up the Congo River. Before 1850, very few Europeans had dared to travel beyond the coasts of equatorial Africa. The few who attempted it usually succumbed to disease. Conrad was no exception - he became so ill with fever and dysentery that he was forced to return home. His disturbing personal experience became the inspiration for his most important work, *Heart of Darkness*, written in 1899.

In this remarkable novella, Conrad examines the ambiguous nature of what it means to be "primitive" and to be "civilized". On the surface, the story simply depicts a journey up the Congo River, into the heart of Africa (presumably the "heart of darkness" to which the title refers) in search of the mysterious ivory trader, Mr. Kurtz. But as the story progresses, another question emerges: what happens when an apparently civilized man is immersed in the primitive?

Though the narrator continually refers to the Africans as "savages", his description betrays an undisguised fascination with the accoutrements and trappings of primitive culture:

---

[64] Though he is today recognized as a master of the English language, when he first arrived in England he knew only a few words.

> Dark human shapes could be made out in the distance, flitting indistinctly against the gloomy border of the forest, and near the river two bronze figures, leaning on tall spears, stood in the sunlight under fantastic headdresses of spotted skins, warlike and still in statuesque repose. And from the right to the left along the lighted shore moved a wild and gorgeous apparition of a woman. She walked with measured steps, draped in striped and fringed cloths, treading the earth proudly, with a slight jingle and flash of barbarous ornaments. She carried her head high, her hair was done in the shape of a helmet; she had brass leggings to the knee, brass wire gauntlets to the elbow, a crimson spot on her tawny cheek, innumerable necklaces of glass beads on her neck; bizarre things, charms, gifts of witch men, that hung about her, glittered and trembled at every step.[65]

On one level, *Heart of Darkness* could be read as a critique of colonial Europe, which hypocritically called the colonized people "savages" while displaying an infinitely greater savagery in its own treatment of them. Mr. Kurtz, the seemingly enlightened European, is described as "an emissary of pity, and science, and progress", but who, intoxicated with power, turns himself into a god, to be worshiped by the Africans he ruled.

Yet, on a deeper level, Conrad is also describing a Freudian journey into the true heart of darkness, a journey into the primitive depths of the self, which, contrary to the superficial veneer of civilization, is, at its core, every bit as primitive and savage as the natives condescendingly referred to in those terms.

---

[65] Joseph Conrad, *Heart of Darkness*, pg. 70

The mystery of Kurtz is that of a self whose overt morality is merely a rationalization of the desire to dominate. Consequently, the dividing line between "civilized" and "primitive" becomes dangerously blurred and uncomfortably ambiguous. In the end, Conrad's story about an encounter with an alien civilization, like Freud's, becomes a journey of self-discovery, a disquieting mirror in which the reader is forced to examine himself.

> [These] men were – No, they were not inhuman. Well, you know, that was the worst of it – your suspicion of their not being inhuman. It would come slowly to one. They howled and leaped, and spun, and made horrid faces, but what thrilled you was just the thought of their humanity – like yours – the thought of your kinship with this wild and passionate uproar.[66]

Conrad clearly sensed a mysterious power at work in what he deemed to be the primitive and he hinted that this same power also lay suppressed and dormant within modern man.

But he was not the first to hold this point of view. In the eighteenth century, Giambattista Vico had argued that primitive man was actually closer to the sources of poetry and artistic inspiration than civilized man. He wrote that the history of mankind is the history of ideas and can be divided into three ages: the age of gods, the age of heroes, and the age of men.

---

[66] Ibid, pg. 40

Vico suggests that in the earliest age, the age of gods, ancient man, unencumbered by science and rationality, understood the visible world through imagination alone, using the language of myth and metaphor - the very language of poetry. According to Vico, with each successive stage in the development of reason, came a proportional decrease in the power of imagination, and a consequent decline in the power of poetic language.

For a group of adventurous artists at the turn of the century, the quest for this primal source of imagination led them to the art of primitive cultures from which they, at first, sought an infusion of inspiration and energy, and which they, finally, directly imitated.

Like the Impressionists, these "primitivist" artists rebelled against the schools of academic painting, which prescribed a rigid curriculum based on copying the idealized classical forms as presented in Renaissance perspective painting. They rejected the precisely delineated forms of the academy and used bright "unnatural" colors. Like the Impressionists, they favored quick brushstrokes and cultivated an unfinished look.

Primitivist artists welcomed the common complaint that their paintings looked as if a child could have done them. For them, this merely confirmed the authenticity of their self-expression and validated their quest to draw on the deepest sources of creative power.

The first modern primitivist painter was Paul Gauguin, who gave up a career at the stock exchange to become a painter, and then gave up his wife and family when he found he could no longer support them. He moved to rural Brittany in northwest France to immerse himself in the simple life and ancient superstitions of the peasants.

When Brittany proved to be not "savage" enough for his tastes, he then relocated to colonial Tahiti, where he lived for ten years, painting brightly colored scenes of lush vegetation and beautiful native women.

The Tahiti visited by Gauguin had long since lost its Garden of Eden-like innocence, thanks to a century of colonization – now alcoholism and prostitution were rampant. Nevertheless, Gauguin idealized the women of this culture so foreign to his own, women who seemed to have a primitive connection to spirituality which the ultramodern French painters of his day found irresistibly appealing.

Paul Gauguin, *Arearea* (1892) (Photograph by author)

"Emotion first, understanding afterwards" was Gauguin's favorite saying. For him, this meant expressive rather than realistic images, startling rather than accurate colors, and scenes that defied rational explanation.

He wrote that "God does not belong to the scholar or the logician. He belongs to poets, to the dream."[67]

By turning away from civilization and from reason, Gauguin was attempting to rediscover the primordial source of imagination about which Vico had speculated.

HENRI MATISSE – KING OF THE BEASTS

Partly in response to Gauguin, a number of painters sought out primitive subjects and techniques. One of these was Henri Matisse. Born on the last day of 1869, Matisse took up painting in 1890 when his mother bought him a box of paints while he was recovering from appendicitis.[68] After years of struggle, a breakthrough came in 1905, when he and other like-minded artists were allowed to show their work at the Salon d'Automne.

Viewers were stunned by the bright, unnatural colors and the deliberately unrefined manner of execution. The critic Louis Vauxcelles gave a mocking name to the group, calling them "wild beasts" (*fauves*) in his review. As their leader, Matisse was called *le roi des fauves* – the "king of the beasts"[69] and art historians were given a convenient name for this art: *fauvism*.

What was it about these paintings that so provoked Vauxcelles? As an example, take a look at *Woman with the Hat* (1905) by Matisse. There is nothing unusual about the subject: a lady (the wife of Matisse), seated in a formal, posed position, head turned towards the viewer, wearing a hat which might have seemed extravagant if the wearer were seen walking down the street, but perhaps not out of place in a work of art where anything goes.

---

[67] Norbert Lynton, *The Story of Modern Art*, pg. 20

[68] Edward Lucie-Smith, *Lives of the Great 20th Century Artists*, pg. 16

[69] ibid

It was the way Matisse portrayed her that seemed to be an affront to the viewer (and possibly to Matisse's wife as well).

His colors seemed outrageous and even absurd. Her hair appears to be red on one side and green on the other.[70] Her face is painted yellow, streaked with pale purple, green, and blue. Behind her is a riot of bright color, all rendered with brushstrokes that must have seemed hurried and careless.

Despite negative reviews, important collectors now began to buy Matisse's work, including the wealthy Russian industrialist Sergei Shchukin, who in 1909 commissioned Matisse to paint a large work to decorate the spiral staircase in his mansion, the Trubetskoy Palace, in Moscow. To fulfill this commission, Matisse created *The Dance*, a stark, even primitive portrayal of five women dancing in a circle. The uncanny quality of this work seems to evoke a sense of the primal in viewers.

It has been called forbidding, menacing, tribal, ritualistic, even demonic.[71] Drum beats almost seem to be heard while observing the ecstatic dancers frozen in their dynamic poses.

In 1910 Matisse completed *Music*, the companion to *The Dance*, designed to hang with its companion piece over the spiral stairs of Shchukin's mansion. In contrast to the frenzied energy of *The Dance*, a solemn stillness pervades *Music*. Five men are shown, all but one seated on the ground. Two are playing musical instruments.

The canvas shows evidence of numerous revisions (one of which was the painting-over of the male genitalia at the request of the patron) – unlike *The Dance*, for which Matisse made preparatory sketches, and even a preparatory painting, *Music* was created directly on the canvas.

---

[70] This, of course, would not be out of place at all today, but in 1905 it seemed quite bizarre.

[71] https://www.henrimatisse.org/the-dance.jsp

Both paintings convey a stark sense of the primitive, both in the manner of execution and their subject matter. As art historian Norbert Lynton puts it, "We feel that we are lifted out of our civilization into some prehistoric age and are witnessing the earliest dancing, the beginnings of music."[72]

PICASSO AND AFRICAN ART

Though Maurice Vlaminck, one of the fauves, had been collecting primitive art since at least 1905,[73] it was probably Matisse that introduced his friend Picasso to African art. Matisse describes noticing some African statuettes in a shop window: "I was struck by their character, their purity of line.

I bought one and showed it to Gertrude Stein, whom I was visiting that day. Then Picasso arrived and he took to it immediately."[74]

Norbert Lynton has observed that it is strangely appropriate that it would be Matisse, "king of the beasts", who first responded to the work of "distant tribesman". He explains the attraction that African art held for these sophisticated Parisian artists:

> They saw these carvings as intensely dramatic objects, forbidding initially because of the distortion of face or figure but soon revealing potent harmonies within their strange idiom and even an attractive and convincing element of naturalism.[75]

---

[72] Norbert Lynton, *The Story of Modern Art*, pg. 34

[73] Jack D. Flam, *Matisse and the Fauves* from *Primitivism in the 20th Century*, pg. 213

[74] Arianna Huffington, *Picasso, Creator and Destroyer*, pg. 90

[75] Norber Lynton, *The Story of Modern Art*, pg. 30

Before long Picasso was spending time in the Ethnographic Museum of Scientific Expeditions housed at the time in the Trocadero Palace in Paris. It was a transforming experience for him. As he recalled later,

> All alone in that dusty museum, with masks, dolls...dusty manikins [sic]...I was all alone. I wanted to get away. But I didn't leave. I stayed. I understood that it was very important: something was happening to me...The masks weren't just like any other pieces of sculpture. Not at all. They were magic things...They were against everything. I understood. I was against everything too. They were weapons. To help people avoid coming under the influence of spirits again, to help them become independent. They are tools. If we give spirits a form, we become independent...[76]

After his experience at the Ethnographic Museum, Picasso returned to his studio where he had been working on a very large canvas. This was a work he originally intended to call *The Brothel of Avignon*, but would later be known as *Les Demoiselles d'Avignon*. So impressed was Picasso by what he had seen at the Trocadero, he immediately painted images of African masks over the faces of two of the women in this painting.

Picasso may have concluded that these alterations were too extreme - he did not immediately show the painting, except to a few friends, most of whom reacted negatively. Gertrude Stein, perhaps for the only time in her life, was silent.[77]

---

[76] Arianna Huffington, *Picasso, Creator and Destroyer*, pg. 90

[77] Kymberly N. Pinder, *Race-ing Art History: Critical Readings in Race and Art History*, pg.253

Matisse was outraged, not by Picasso's daring appropriation of African imagery, but by the thought that his own work might be overshadowed by "Picasso's hideous whores".[78] Even Picasso's dealer, Ambroise Vollard blurted out, "It's the work of a madman".[79]

It is possible that these negative reactions may have created doubts in Picasso's mind about the work. Or it may be possible that he had contemplated reworking *all* the faces with African masks. But whatever his private motives, he rolled it up, and put it away, and there it remained for nearly a decade until It was first exhibited publically in 1916. Nevertheless, Picasso continued to experiment with the incorporation of African masks into his paintings.

While previous artists, like Gauguin, had explored primitive themes, it was not until Picasso's *Demoiselles d'Avignon* that the aesthetic of primitive art itself began to have a real influence on modern art.[80]

STRAVINSKY'S *RITE OF SPRING* AS MUSICAL PRIMITIVISM

What was it about Stravinsky's *Rite of Spring* that its first audience found so provocative?

Some authors argue that the whole story of the "riot" is exaggerated, perhaps deliberately so, by Diaghilev as a promotional gimmick designed to increase ticket sales.[81] Others argue that it was the stilted choreography rather than the music that provoked the hostility of the audience.[82]

---

[78] John Richardson, *A Life of Picasso*, pg. 45

[79] Joshua Wolf Shenk, *Powers of Two: Finding the Essence of Innovation in Creative Pairs*, pg.169

[80] William Rubin, *Primitivism in 20th Century Art*, pg. 7

[81] Author Modris Eksteins seems to take this position in his *Rites of Spring: The Great War and the Birth of the Modern Age*

[82] Paul Griffiths, in *Modern Music: A Concise History from Debussy to Boulez*,

But it seems clear that something very much like a riot did, in fact, take place in the Théâtre des Champs Elysées on May 29, 1913. The descriptive word that comes up most often in the first-hand accounts is the word "primitive", revealing the fact that the first audience clearly perceived what was being conveyed by the music.

Stravinsky's *Rite of Spring* is an example of musical primitivism for three important reasons. The first reason is the subject matter: a human sacrifice in the prehistoric world of pagan, pre-Christian Russia. The second reason is the musical content: as musicologist Richard Taruskin has convincingly demonstrated, Stravinsky quotes freely from primitive Eastern European and Russian folk melodies throughout the *Rite of Spring*.[83]

The third reason is technique: Stravinsky makes use of harmonies and rhythms deliberately designed to evoke a sense of primitive power and violence.

In his autobiography, Stravinsky said that the idea for the *Rite of Spring* flashed through his mind in 1910 while he was working on the *Firebird*: "There arose a picture of a sacred pagan ritual: the wise elders are seated in a circle and are observing the dance before death of the girl whom they are offering to the god of Spring in order to gain his benevolence."[84]

---

writes, "Probably the audience was reacting as much to Nijinsky's choreography, 'a very labored and barren effort', in Stravinsky's view, as to the score..." (pg. 41)

[83] Richard Taruskin, *Music in the Early Twentieth Century*

[84] Boris Mikhailovich Yarustovsky, *Foreword* to *The Rite of Spring in Full Score*, pg. vii

Stravinsky discussed his idea with Nicholas Roerich, an expert in Russian folk art and ancient rituals.[85] Roerich told Stravinsky about pagan Russian festivals such as *Semik*, a spring festival in which wreaths are cast on the water to predict the future, and *Kupala*, a midsummer festival when images of the sun god Yarilo were burned in effigy. Young men leapt over the fire after which they abducted brides for themselves from among the eligible females of the tribe. Stravinsky and Roerich planned the scenario of the *Rite of Spring* based on these two festivals.[86]

There are, in fact, several stratagems employed by Stravinsky in the musical score that seem designed to induce tension and to ratchet up the discomfort of the listener. In the beginning, all seems well.

This is the opening melody of the *Rite of Spring*, played by a solo bassoon. It is a simple, folk-like melody which can easily be played on the white keys of the piano. It is repeated three times, clearly establishing the key of C. However, in bar 10, the English Horn plays this melody:

---

[85] Roerich was also an artist and a mystic, and his art became the basis of the original stage setting for *Rite of Spring*.

[86] *Music of the Early Twentieth Century* by Richard Taruskin

In contrast to the bassoon melody, which was a C major, "white-key" melody, this English Horn melody is a pentatonic modal melody which could be played entirely on the black keys of the piano. By superimposing these two conflicting melodies, the "white-key" melody against the "black-key" melody, Stravinsky is setting up an environment in which the listener is being acclimated, at the very beginning of the work, to a bitonal harmonic world, in which two conflicting tonalities will exist simultaneously. In the *Introduction* section of the *Rite of Spring* this conflict is very subtle and the tension it produces is only slightly unsettling, but by section two, *The Augurs of Spring*, it erupts with rampaging ferocity.

This section is one of the most memorable in the *Rite of Spring*, and is perhaps the clearest evidence of Stravinsky's primitivist intent. The dissonant chord played by the strings is repeated relentlessly, some two hundred times. Though the pulse is steady and persistent, the accents fall at uneven and unpredictable moments, creating a ruthless, violent effect. In his book *The Rest is Noise*, Alex Ross illustrates this accent pattern in a verbal way so that the reader can experience for himself the rhythmic discombobulation created by Stravinsky's accent pattern:

> one two three four five six seven eight
>
> one *two* three *four* five six seven eight
>
> one *two* three four *five* six seven eight
>
> *one* two three four five *six* seven eight[87]

As if this music alone were not shocking enough, onstage the dancers "trembled, shook, shivered, stamped, jumped crudely and ferociously, circled the stage in wild khorovods."[88] If there was indeed a riot at the premiere of the *Rite of Spring*, this is surely the moment when it erupted. But the rhythm alone is only half of the musical story. Here is the chord which is repeated two hundred times by the strings, with irregular, violent accents:

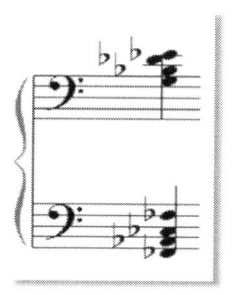

In this piano reduction, the harmonic content of the chord can be more easily understood. The lower half of the chord is a simple major chord built on F-flat (equivalent to an E major chord, enharmonically speaking). The upper part of the chord is another simple chord: a dominant seventh chord built on E-flat.

It should be pointed out that there is nothing shocking or modern about either the upper or lower parts of this chord if heard alone.

---

[87] Alex Ross, *The Rest is Noise*, pg. 75

[88] ibid

But when they are combined, they create a supremely harsh dissonance, producing the highest degree of tension imaginable. This is the harmonic counterpart to the bitonality which Stravinsky introduced in the intertwining melodies of the introduction: two conflicting key areas which are heard simultaneously.

The *Rite of Spring* is a work of extraordinary sophistication and compositional craftsmanship, and despite (or because of) the scandal surrounding it, Stravinsky suddenly found himself a celebrity in the world of art music and a hero of Modernism. And though he would go on to produce many important works in the twentieth century, he would never again return to the violent rhythmic force that made the *Rite of Spring* the perfect symbol of Primitivism.

BÉLA BARTÓK AND HUNGARIAN FOLK SONGS

Primitivism in the early twentieth century was not merely a movement based on the tribal culture of Africa and Oceania. It also drew upon folk sources, "folk" referring to the "common people", in contrast to the cultured or sophisticated. There were numerous "folk" movements prior to the twentieth century which exalted the mythology of the common people as being untainted by civilization and having a mystical connection with the land.

Some composers were attracted to what they considered the unspoiled vigor of folk songs. One of these was the Hungarian composer Béla Bartók, who is now regarded as one of the first ethnomusicologists because of his thorough and systematic study of Hungarian folk music.

Bartók's journey into ethnomusicology began in 1904 when he overheard a young nanny singing Transylvanian folk songs to the young children in her care. He was fascinated by what he heard and determined to try to understand this unusual music.

Along with fellow composer Zoltan Kodaly, Bartók began to travel to isolated, rural towns and villages of Hungary and Romania in search of what he called "peasant songs" (or "folk songs" as they are referred to today by more polite modern ethnomusicologists) which he recorded on an early Edison phonograph machine.[89] These songs, sung by ordinary people, were recorded and preserved by Bartók, who later carefully transcribed them in traditional musical notation, in order to systematically analyze their idiosyncrasies. He said, "to handle folk tunes is one of the most difficult tasks…One must penetrate it, feel it, and bring out its sharp contours…"[90]

Through his musical analysis, Bartók was able to absorb the characteristics of these folk songs, and then make use of them in his own music. As an example, listen to the *Dance Suite*, which Bartók composed in 1923, written on commission in celebration of the 50 year anniversary of the merging of Buda, Pest, and Óbuda into a single city.[91]

The *Dance Suite* is filled with melodies and rhythms which Bartók created by imitating the characteristics of authentic folk music he had previously studied. Bartók explained that

> the aim of the whole work was to put together a kind of idealized peasant music – you could say an invented peasant music – in such a way that the individual movements of the work should introduce particular types of music. Peasant music of all nationalities served as a model: Magyar, Rumanian, Slovak, and even Arabic. In fact, here and there is even a hybrid of these species"[92]

---

[89] Many of these field recordings still exist and can be heard in various places on the Internet.

[90] Elliott Schwartz, *Contemporary Composers On Contemporary Music*, pg. 76

[91] Halsey Stevens, *The Life and Music of Bela Bartok*, pg. 64

[92] László Somfai, *Béla Bartók: Composition, Concepts, and Autograph Sources*, pg. 18

Bartók's *Dance Suite* contains moments of rhythmic ferocity (especially in the second movement), which, along with his melodies derived from folk sources, make it, like Stravinsky's *Rite of Spring*, an example of musical Primitivism.

CHARLES IVES AND MUSICAL QUOTATION

The American composer Charles Ives made use of a variety of what could broadly be termed "folk" sources: popular songs of his day, patriotic Civil War-era songs[93], marches, revival hymns, and ragtime, all stirred into a seemingly incongruous mix that often defies description.

Unlike Bartók who analyzed his folk sources in order to create melodies of his own, Ives preferred quotation – transplanting entire melodies, intact, into his own compositions. Often these unrelated melodies appear in conflict with one another – different keys and contradictory rhythms appear simultaneously, creating a kind of crazy quilt collage of sound which, nevertheless, is strangely consistent with itself.

Ives explained this unusual musical practice by recounting a memory from his childhood:

> As I remember some of the dances, as a boy, and also from father's description of some of the old dancing and fiddle playing, there was more variety of tempo than in the present-day dances. In some parts of the hall a group would be dancing a polka, while in another, a waltz, and perhaps something else going on in the middle. Some players in the band would, in an impromptu way, pick up with the polka, some with the waltz, or a march.

---

[93] Ives was intimately acquainted with songs from the Civil War because his father, George Ives, was a bandmaster in the war, the youngest bandmaster in the Union army. His band was also reported to be one of the best. (www.charlesives.org)

> Sometimes the change in tempo and mixed rhythms would be caused by a fiddler who was getting a little sleepy, or by another player who had been seated too near to the hard cider barrel. Whatever the reason for these changes and simultaneous playings of things, I distinctly remember catching a kind of music that was natural and interesting, and which was decidedly missed when everybody came down on the same beat again.[94]

There are many works by Charles Ives which display his propensity for musical borrowing. His *Symphony No. 3* (1908), for which he won the Pulitzer Prize in 1947,[95] could be described as a musical recollection of the many religious revival meetings held in the countryside around Danbury, Connecticut, where he was raised.

The thematic material of each movement is based entirely on hymns: *O for a Thousand Tongues to Sing, What a Friend We Have in Jesus, There is a Fountain Filled with Blood,* and *Just as I am Without One Plea*.[96]

As an example of Ives-style sound collage, my personal favorite is his *Ragtime Dance No. 4* (1904), in which the sacred and the profane collide in a kind of surreal, rowdy, burlesque, tent-revival extravaganza: ragtime rhythms, wild marching band outbursts, and a tender rendition of *Bringing in the Sheaves* all jostle for position in this short, but exciting little piece.

---

[94] Stuart Feder, *Charles Ives, "My Father's Song": A Psychoanalytic Biography*, pg. 248

[95] Ives, who was then 74 years old, and financially secure after many successful years in the insurance business, gave the prize money away. "Prizes are for boys and I'm all grown up." (Jon Paxman, *A Chronology Of Western Classical Music 1600-2000*, pg. 591.)

[96] Paul C. Echols, liner notes from *Charles Ives, Symphony No. 3*, Michael Tilson Thomas, Concertgebouw Orchestra

Charles Ives was never consciously part of any particular movement. He was a hard-headed, independent-thinking, New England Yankee individualist. Nevertheless, much of his music fits under the broad umbrella label of Primitivism because of his continual use of early American folk and popular material in his works.

It is ironic that artists in the early twentieth century, so self-consciously modern, should embrace and draw inspiration from the primitive. As Daniel Albright observes, commenting on this odd phenomenon of opposite extremes converging, "in the domain of Modernism, *The Flintstones* and *The Jetsons* are always the same show." [97]

---

[97] Daniel Albright, *Putting Modernism Together*, pg. 143

CHAPTER FOUR: EXPRESSIONISM THE ART OF ANGST

IMPRESSIONISM'S EVIL TWIN

The term "Expressionism" is thought to have been coined in 1910 by the Czech art historian Antonin Matejcek, who intended the term to mean the opposite of Impressionism.[98] Whereas the French Impressionist painters, with their pleasant subjects, delicate colors and shimmering images, sought to portray the beauty of the outward world, the Expressionists, according to Matejcek, struggled to express the dark inner life, often through harsh and unpleasant subject matter.

Expressionism was, for the most part, a uniquely German phenomenon. It sprang out of the turbulent artistic, social, and psychological climate existing in Germany at the turn of the century - it grew out of the same intellectual environment as Freud's studies in hysteria and the unconscious. The Expressionists, like Freud, were fascinated by the inner workings of the mind, and in order to communicate the tension and anguish of the human psyche, they attempted to shock their audience with deliberately distorted images.

The Norwegian painter Edvard Munch was an important source of inspiration for the Expressionists. His disturbing, emotionally charged works opened up new possibilities for introspective expression. Munch is well known today primarily for his famous painting, *The Scream* (1893). In this work, all of the elements of the composition are designed to evoke a sense of extreme discomfort on the part of the viewer: the grotesquely unnatural and ambiguous individual (is it male or female?), the hands clasped to the sides of the head in a posture of shocked horror, and the bizarre, nightmare landscape, unlike anything in the real world.

---

[98] Daniel Albright, *Modernism and Music, an Anthology of Sources*, pg. 259

Munch's painting has become a recognized icon of the anxiety and uncertainty of the modern world, just as da Vinci's *Mona Lisa* is an emblem of the calm serenity of the world of the Renaissance. Ironically, *The Scream* is so well-known today that its impact is muted by its overwhelming familiarity.[99] To get a fresh sense of the power of Munch's imagery, take a look at his *Evening on Karl Johan Street* (1892). Like *The Scream*, this painting is all about anxiety, but of a more subtle and possibly more disturbing kind. The viewer confronts a night-time city street. The pale faces of the pedestrians, dressed in formal attire (or is it funeral attire?), appear vacant and zombie-like. A darkened figure walks alone in the opposite direction, separated from the crowd and from the viewer. The image is permeated with a suggestion of the alienation of urban life.

Edvard Munch, *Evening on Karl Johan Street* (1892) (public domain)

---

[99] Merchandise based on *The Scream* is available in an astonishing variety of forms: as an action figure, a mouse-pad, a pair of socks, a t-shirt, a jigsaw puzzle, a book cover, a rub-on tattoo, and a fidget spinner, to name only a few.

Munch understood the feeling only too well. In the 1890s, he had left Norway, seeking wider recognition. He traveled restlessly throughout Germany and Scandinavia, often living in extreme poverty.[100] In 1894 he was discovered by friends wandering the streets of Berlin, having been turned out of his room for non-payment, and having eaten nothing for three days.

However, by 1905 Munch's work was, at last, beginning to become better known within Germany and he was spending much of his time there, bringing him in direct contact with the Expressionists, for whom his work provided vital inspiration.[101]

DIE BRÜCKE

The artists' group *Brücke* (The Bridge) was established in Dresden on June 7, 1905, a date that is regarded as the birth of Expressionism. The group's name was inspired by a passage in Nietzsche: "Man is a rope tied between the animal and the Superman, a rope over an abyss…what is great about man is that he is a bridge and not a goal."[102] For the artists themselves, the name signified an eagerness to cross over into a new, unexplored future.

The founding members were Ernst Ludwig Kirchner, Fritz Bleyl, Erich Heckel, and Karl Schmidt-Rottluff. It is curious to note that, in forming this group, they were all abandoning architecture for art. Only Kirchner had received any art training at all, and that for only a short period.

---

[100] Munch was frequently isolated and alone, troubled by mental illness, plagued by thoughts of death, and at various times in his life he found it difficult to part with his paintings, selling them only when absolutely necessary. (Hilton Kramer, *The Age of the Avant-Garde*, pg. 104)

[101] Edward Lucie-Smith, *The Lives of the Great 20th Century Artists*, pg. 12

[102] Carl Jung, *Nietzsche's Zarathustra: Notes of the Seminar Given in 1934-1939*, pg. 49

> Kirchner and his friends wanted to be artists, to live like artists, even more than to produce works of art...Kirchner, Heckel, and Schmidt-Rottluff lived together in a somewhat poverty-stricken way that was probably not forced on them by lack of money. Their paintings decorated their rooms, they made some of the furniture themselves in an emphatically primitive way. Girlfriends served as models, and sunshine and youthful energy as inspiration.[103]

The Brücke artists were attracted to the artistic style of medieval woodcuts, especially by German artist Albrecht Dürer. They admired the vitality of this art, with its strong, austere lines and non-naturalistic portrayal of its subject matter.

They imitated the woodcut style using a modern version of the technique called the linocut.[104] One of their first productions was a linocut print featuring a manifesto by Kirchner announcing the aims of the group:

> With faith in development and as a new generation of creators and connoisseurs, we call together all young people. As young people ourselves, we carry the future and want to create for ourselves freedom of life and movement against the long-established power of our elders. Everyone who conveys his creative energy directly and authentically belongs with us.[105]

---

[103] Norbert Lynton, *The Story of Modern Art*, pg. 36

[104] The linocut is a printing process which involves carving an image into a block or sheet of linoleum which is then inked and pressed onto paper or fabric. Linoleum as a floor covering had been used since the 1860s and the linocut process had been used in Germany for creating wallpaper before the *Brücke* artists adopted it.

[105] Norbert Lynton, *The Story of Modern Art*, pg. 34

Like Picasso and Matisse in France, Kirchner was fascinated by primitive art. He was quite familiar with the African and Oceanic collection at the Dresden Ethnographic Museum and he transmitted this enthusiasm to the rest of the group.[106]

In general, the early art produced by the Brücke group has a rough-hewn character, makes use of overly bright colors reminiscent of the *Fauves*, and favors images with suggestively sexual themes.

> They painted nudes, landscapes, and nudes in landscapes. The intensity of the colours bore out the force of their desires and pleasure. The models were very youthful, shameless and mocking. Forms were defined by just a few lines, interspersed with red or yellow patches worthy of Van Gogh and Munch.
>
> Outlines hardened when the group started taking an interest in art from Africa and Oceania examples of which they saw in the ethnographic museums of Dresden and Berlin.[107]

DER BLAUE REITER

Der Blaue Reiter (*The Blue Rider*) formed in 1911 in Munich as a loose association of painters led by Wassily Kandinsky and Franz Marc, later joined by Paul Klee.

The name *Blaue Reiter* was possibly adopted in reference to a 1903 painting by Kandinsky called *The Blue Rider*, in which a cloaked rider on a speeding horse rushes through a rocky landscape.

---

[106] ibid

[107] Philippe Dagen, *Die Brücke: Origins of Expressionism* from *The Guardian*, May 8, 2012

The rider in this painting is wearing a blue cloak and the horse seems to be casting a blue shadow. For Kandinsky, who was strongly influenced by Theosophy,[108] the color blue was associated with spirituality.[109]

Kandinsky was a highly educated man who had taught law and economics in Russia before giving up this promising career at age thirty in order to become an artist. He enrolled in the Munich Academy but was not immediately accepted, so he began studying art on his own.

Before leaving Russia he happened to see an exhibition of works by Monet. For Kandinsky, it was a revelation. He was especially moved by Monet's *Haystacks*.

> That it was a haystack the catalogue informed me. I could not recognize it. This non-recognition was painful to me. I considered that the painter had no right to paint indistinctly. I dully felt that the object of the painting was missing. And I noticed with surprise and confusion that the picture not only gripped me, but impressed itself ineradicably on my memory. Painting took on a fairy-tale power and splendor.[110]

The *Blaue Reiter* group in Munich represents a very different kind of Expressionism from the *Brücke* group in Dresden. The purpose of the *Blaue Reiter*, according to Kandinsky, was to assimilate all expressive art forms, including children's art, primitive art, folk art, along with music and literature of all kinds.

---

[108] Virginia Hanson, *H. P. Blavatsky and the Secret Doctrine*, pg.217

[109] Lisa Florman, *Concerning the Spiritual—and the Concrete—in Kandinsky's Art*, pg. 188, footnote 58

[110] John Sallis, *Shades--of Painting at the Limit*, pg. 67

"I dreamed of painters and musicians in the front rank" of the *Blaue Reiter* movement, Kandinsky wrote. "The harmful separation of one art from another, of 'art' from folk art, children's art, 'ethnography', the stout walls erected between what were to my eyes closely related, often identical phenomena..."[111]

To achieve this purpose, Kandinsky and Marc published an almanac in 1912 entitled *Der Blaue Reiter*. It contained essays and illustrations, mostly concerned with art, but also including music. The general thesis was that the art world lacked something that the world of music had successfully evolved: a generally agreed underlying theory. Therefore, the best course of action was to take a broad survey of all sorts of art and discover what was essential and permanent and what was temporary and nonessential.

The almanac contained fifty illustrations of European folk art, several pages of children's drawings, and more than fifty reproductions of modern art, including works by Kandinsky and Marc, but also examples of the new art in France: Matisse's *Music* and *Dance*, and works by Picasso. There were images from the Dresden artists Kirchner and Heckel. In addition, there were sixteen illustrations of masks, figures, and other objects made by primitive peoples from various parts of the world. There were two articles concerned with new ideas in music: one on a new work by Scriabin, and another by Arnold Schoenberg on the relationship between music and text.

EXPRESSIONISM IN AUSTRIA

Expressionism in Austria is principally represented by two major figures: Oskar Kokoschka and Egon Schiele.

---

[111] Donald E. Gordon, *German Expressionism, from Primitivism in 20th Century Art*, pg. 374-375

Although they were essentially rivals, they both concentrated on the same subject matter: sexuality and death. Sexually charged imagery and provocative body language were used by both artists for psychological effect, to shock the psyche and challenge the facade of complacency and conformity that dominated Viennese culture.

Schiele had a scandalous reputation in Vienna. His studio was overrun by young girls who were the willing subjects of his drawings, some of which were extremely erotic in nature. In 1911 Schiele left Vienna with a young model, seventeen-year-old Wally Neuzil, who was living with him at the time. The pair ended up in Krumau but were forced to leave by the strong disapproval of the townsfolk. They then moved to Neulengbach where Schiele's studio soon became the gathering place for under-aged girls and delinquent children of the neighborhood.

In 1912 Schiele was arrested and charged with seducing a girl below the age of consent. Though the charge was eventually dropped, he was convicted of exhibiting an erotic drawing in a place accessible to children (the disgusted judge even burned one of Schiele's drawings in the courtroom, in a dramatic demonstration of his distaste). During his imprisonment Schiele made the most of his time, creating several self-portraits inscribed with self-pitying comments.[112]

---

[112] "I do not feel punished, rather purified," and "To restrict the artist is a crime." (Edward Lucie-Smith, *Lives of the Great 20th Century Artists*, pg. 87)

Oskar Kokoschka reveled in his own reputation for scandal. He considered himself a writer as much as an artist, and wrote two plays, *Sphinx und Strohmann* (*The Sphinx and the Scarecrow*) and *Mörder, Hoffnung der Frauen* (*Murderer, the Hope of Women*), both of which are filled with violence, and both of which, as was no doubt fervently hoped for, caused a scandal when publically performed. The poster announcing the performance of *Mörder, Hoffnung der Frauen* was designed by Kokoschka and features original artwork by him. The raw, primitivist style of the art, which depicts a ghastly, pale woman and bloody, flayed man hints at the barbarism and violence of the performance.

In 1911, Kokoschka began a passionate love affair with Alma Mahler, the widow of the great composer. However, two years later their relationship was beginning to unravel, as evidenced by this strange story: "Having traveled together to Naples, they visited an aquarium where Kokoschka watched an insect sting and paralyze a fish before devouring it, immediately associating the scene with the woman by his side".[113]

The story has an even more bizarre postscript: after Alma ended their relationship, Kokoschka commissioned doll-maker Hermine Moos to create a life-size replica doll of Alma Mahler, "complete and lifelike in all details."[114] The artist sent Moos drawings and exact measurements, along with detailed instructions concerning fabrics and materials to be used. Kokoschka was somewhat disappointed by the finished product (its "skin" appears to be a layer of feathers – Kokoschka claimed it was "a polar-bear pelt, suitable for a shaggy imitation bedside rug").

---

[113] Ibld, pg. 82

[114] ibid

Nevertheless, he made several drawings of the doll in different positions and clothing – he even took photographs of it.[115] In the end, his obsession with Alma Mahler ran its course and he disposed of the doll in a way that might be expected from an eccentric Expressionist artist:

> Finally, after I had drawn it and painted it over and over again, I decided to do away with it. It had managed to cure me completely of my Passion. So I gave a big champagne Party with chamber music, during which my maid Hulda exhibited the doll in all its beautiful clothes for the last time. When dawn broke—I was quite drunk, as was everyone else—I beheaded it out in the garden and broke a bottle of red wine over its head.[116]

EXPRESSIONISM AND THE GREAT WAR

After the outbreak of World War I in 1914,[117] the intense colors and jagged angles of the Expressionists seemed suddenly appropriate and timely.

Initially, many of the Expressionist artists viewed the war in a positive light, anticipating the overthrow of the hated middle-class with its restrictive values and stifling moral code. However, as more and more artists enlisted or were drafted, the first-hand experience of war shattered their optimism, and in some cases, their minds as well. Many of these artists-turned-soldiers created works which reflected their experiences, bringing viewers face to face with the horrors of the front line.[118]

---

[115] Anyone who is curious may find these photographs easily by means of a Google search.

[116] Sadie Stein, *My Fair Lady* from *The Paris Review*, February 17, 2015

[117] Incidentally, the man whose assassination precipitated the war, Archduke Franz Ferdinand, after viewing the works of Oskar Kokoschka in 1911 remarked, "This man's bones ought to be broken in his body!" (Edward Lucie-Smith, *Lives of the Great 20th Century Artists*, pg. 82)

[118] As examples, see *Shock Troops Advance Under Gas*, as well as other horrific works by Otto Dix

Oskar Kokoschka used the influence of his friend and protector Adolf Loos to get himself appointed Lieutenant in an exclusive regiment. Nevertheless, he was seriously wounded – suffering a head injury and a bayonet wound to the lung – before being taken prisoner. He survived the war, despite the severity of his wounds.[119]

Egon Schiele was drafted in 1915 and assigned to a detachment guarding Russian prisoners of war, later becoming a clerk in a prison camp for Russian officers. The war somehow seemed to enhance Shiele's reputation as an artist. He was asked to take part in several exhibitions designed to enhance Austria's image with the neutral powers. For one of these he produced a poster design which resembled the Last Supper with himself in the place of Christ.[120]

Schiele died less than a month before the end of World War I, not from the violence of war, but from the Spanish influenza, which was then rampant in Europe.[121]

The *Blaue Reiter* artist, Franz Marc, was drafted into the German Army and served in the cavalry. He was later transferred to a military camouflage unit where he painted canvas covers for artillery using a pointillist technique, in styles "ranging from Manet to Kandinsky".[122] The German government eventually drew up a list of important artists to be withdrawn from positions of danger. Marc was on the list, but before he received the reassignment order, he was killed at the Battle of Verdun, struck in the head by a shell fragment.[123]

---

[119] Edward Lucie-Smith, *Lives of the Great 20th Century Artists*, pg. 82

[120] The *Forty Ninth Secession Exhibition Poster*

[121] Edward Lucie-Smith, *Lives of the Great 20th Century Artists*, pg. 87

[122] John Windsor, *General Patterns Army*, from *The Independent*, August 3, 1996

[123] Edward Lucie-Smith, *Lives of the Great 20th Century Artists*, pg. 75

At the outset of the war, Brücke founder Ernst Ludwig Kirchner became, in his words, "an involuntary volunteer". As he recounted later, "military life was not for me".[124] In 1915 he was declared unfit for duty and discharged. At about this same time he painted *Self-Portrait as a Soldier*. It is a disturbing work with unnaturally bright colors and odd angles. In the background is a nude model and a canvas covered in blood-red colors. In the foreground is the artist, wearing his military uniform and displaying the stump of a freshly severed hand, evidently reflecting Kirchner's not unrealistic fear of battlefield wounds (or perhaps, fear of losing his capacity to create art?). Nevertheless, he portrays himself coolly smoking a cigarette, indifferently looking toward the viewer with blank, expressionless eyes. Kirchner survived the First World War, but would meet his unhappy end before the subsequent war got underway.

EXPRESSIONISM IN LITERATURE

Franz Kafka was born in 1883 into a German-speaking Jewish family in Prague, in what was then the Kingdom of Bohemia, but today is called the Czech Republic.

Though not officially affiliated with any Expressionist group, he nevertheless exemplifies many of the characteristics of Expressionism in his writing.

The Expressionist painters avoided any portrayal of objective, outward reality in their art, aiming instead to convey a subjective "expression" of an inward, psychological reality. Likewise, Kafka, in his writing, creates a surreal, dream-like world in which the isolated protagonist is confronted with bizarre and absurd predicaments.

---

[124] Ibid, pg. 68

His stories are not about objective happenings in the real world. They are subjective explorations of a whole range of psychological themes, especially alienation, existential anxiety, guilt, and frustration.

Kafka wrote many short stories and a few novels. In addition, he liked to create shorter aphorisms and parables. One of these miniature works will serve to illustrate Kafka's style and technique.

> It was very early in the morning, the streets clean and deserted, I was walking to the station. As I compared the tower clock with my watch I realized that it was already much later than I had thought. I had to hurry - the shock of this discovery made me unsure of the way - I did not yet know my way very well in this town. Luckily, a policeman was nearby. I ran up to him and breathlessly asked him the way. He smiled and said: "From me you want to know the way?" "Yes," I said, "since I cannot find it myself." "Give it up! Give it up," he said, and turned away with a sudden jerk, like people who want to be alone with their laughter.[125]

This tiny story, as short as it is, nevertheless displays some of the most distinctive characteristics of Kafka's prose. The first is the surreal and dreamlike atmosphere so typical of Kafka's stories.

The second is the pervasive sense of alienation: the protagonist finds himself alone in an inexplicably deserted city. The third characteristic is anxiety: it is the typical nightmare scenario – the narrator realizes that he is late, but seems to be unable to remedy the situation. The fourth characteristic is absurdity: the policeman behaves in an incongruous and baffling way, as though privy to an inside joke to which only the protagonist is excluded.[126]

---

[125] Franz Kafka, *The Complete Stories*, pg. 456

[126] There is not sufficient space here to describe or analyze Kafka's longer writings, but they are his best works: *The Trial* and *The Castle* should be read by everyone.

Obviously Kafka is not attempting to relate a real event taking place in the world of external reality. Instead he is conveying an inward psychological condition of angst, confusion and alienation. In this sense, his work shares much in common with the aims of the Expressionist painters.

EXPRESSIONISM IN FILM

Expressionism had a tremendous impact on films appearing in Germany in the 1910s and 1920s. In the rush of excitement and enthusiasm that accompanied initial German victories at the beginning of the war, many theater owners, responding to the mood of patriotic fervor, vowed to withdraw all French and English films. This sentiment was made government policy in 1916 when the German government officially banned all foreign films. Consequently, German film companies were forced to increase production in order to fill demand. At the beginning of the war, in 1914, only twenty-four German films were released. By 1916 the number had risen to 130.

During the postwar period, due to inflation and the devastated economy, budgets for films were small. Producers compensated by creating less expensive set designs with wildly non-realistic, geometrically absurd angles, along with designs painted on walls and floors to represent lights, shadows, and objects.

The gloomy themes of Expressionism resonated as never before in the pessimistic atmosphere of postwar Germany, and film producers began to draw on these morbid, disturbing ideas which seemed to correspond to the public mood. Consequently, the plots and stories of the early Expressionist films often dealt with madness, insanity, betrayal and other similarly dark subjects.

Expressionist film production in Germany reached a fever pitch in the 1920s, with some film companies offering new releases only weeks apart. Some of these memorable films include:

The Cabinet of Dr. Caligari (1920) in which the mysterious Dr. Caligari uses a somnambulist to commit murders in the villages he visits. The action takes place in a bizarre nightmare world of jagged lines and impossibly angular geometric shapes.

Nosferatu (1922), originally titled *Nosferatu: a Symphony of Horror*, this film is an icon of Expressionism. It is a retelling of Bram Stoker's *Dracula*, the name change necessitated because Stoker's heirs refused to sell the film rights to the studio. After the film was produced Stoker's heirs sued successfully and demanded that all copies of the film be destroyed. Luckily, some copies survived and the film has become an eerie classic of Expressionism.

Metropolis (1927) is set in a dystopian future in which mankind is divided into two classes: the wealthy ruling class, living in the upper city, and the poverty-stricken working class, living in the lower city. While those living in the wealthy upper city spend their days in indolent luxury, the miserable inhabitants of the lower city are doomed to a life of toil, operating the machines that keep the city going. The angular, crooked skyline, and the mood of chaos, tension and intensity are hallmarks of Expressionist art.

EXPRESSIONISM IN MUSIC

Arnold Schoenberg was born in 1874 into a middle-class Jewish family in Vienna. As a musician he was largely self-taught, a fact which may account for some of his originality as a musical thinker. Evidently, Schoenberg felt that musical composition was simply a natural part of learning about music because he began composing at a very early age, putting into compositional practice whatever he discovered.

He made himself at home in Viennese musical circles at the turn of the century and as early as 1904 placed an advertisement in the *New Musikalische Presse* seeking composition pupils.[127] One of the first to respond was Anton Webern, who would remain a Schoenberg disciple for life and would, in the future, become an important and influential composer in his own right.

Schoenberg was personally acquainted with the Austrian Expressionist artists Oskar Kokoschka and Egon Schiele, both of whom painted portraits of the composer.[128]

He also became friendly with the older and more established Viennese composers, Strauss and Mahler, who found Schoenberg's early compositions to be interesting and encouraged, even defended his musical experiments. At the premiere of Schoenberg's First String Quartet, for instance, when laughter and catcalls erupted, it was Mahler who stood to applaud Schoenberg, nearly getting into a fistfight with one of the troublemakers.[129]

While these early works of Schoenberg were harmonically daring in many ways, they still remained solidly within the stylistic confines of precedents established by Wagner, Strauss, and Mahler. In fact, so clear was the influence of Wagner, that Schoenberg's own brother-in-law, Alexander Zemlinsky, after hearing Schoenberg's 1899 *Verklärte Nacht*, remarked that it sounded like the score of *Tristan and Isolde*, but "smeared while the ink was still wet."[130]

---

[127] Alex Ross, *The Rest is Noise*, pg. 46

[128] Schoenberg actually took up painting himself and made several Expressionist self-portraits.

[129] Ibid, pg. 53

[130] James McCalla, *Twentieth-Century Chamber Music*, pg.3

Then in 1909, Schoenberg began a frenzy of inspired creative activity, perhaps sparked by an emotional crisis caused by marital infidelity on the part of his wife, Mathilde. In a short space of time, he wrote three works that were radically different from anything he had done before (or that anyone had done before), creating his *Three Pieces for Piano*, *Five Pieces for Orchestra*, and the solo drama, *Erwartung* (*Expectation*). They are highly expressionistic – moods change suddenly from dark, languid introspection to a flurry of turbulent excitement. In an uncanny way, these compositions call to mind the work of the Vienna Expressionist painters, as if a painting by Egon Schiele had somehow sprung to life as a musical composition.

This connection is not accidental – Schoenberg himself conceived of this music in painterly terms. In a letter to Alma Mahler, he wrote that she should listen to his music for "colors, noises, lights, sounds, movements, glances, gestures."[131]

In these works, Schoenberg crossed a musical threshold. Finally leaving behind the models of Wagner, Strauss, and Mahler, he left behind any sense of tonality as well. For this reason, these works, and those that followed have commonly been described as "atonal"[132] since they were written with no regard to tonality whatsoever.

---

[131] Alex Ross, *The Rest is Noise*, pg. 62

[132] But not by Schoenberg himself. He hated the word because he thought it wrongly implied "no tones". But despite Schoenberg's fussy objections, it is an apt description for his new system which is "not tonality", or "contrary to tonality".

The system of tonality, the set of assumptions that governed musical practice since the time of Bach, is based on the notion of a hierarchy of pitches, with the "center of gravity" being the "tonic" pitch. Of the twelve possible notes within an octave, those that are consonant with the tonic pitch are considered to be stable, and those that are dissonant (not consonant) with the tonic pitch, are considered to be unstable. Consonance is the norm, and dissonance is a temporary disruption of that norm, creating momentary tension which must be resolved back to consonance.

In Schoenberg's new system of atonality, this musical world is turned upside down. There is no longer a hierarchy of pitches - all twelve possible tones within the octave are treated more or less equally and dissonance has become the new norm. Schoenberg celebrated the new role of dissonance in his music, referring to it in Lincolnesque terms, as the "emancipation of dissonance."[133]

Schoenberg showed these revolutionary new works to both Strauss and Mahler but was met with puzzlement and disdain from the older composers. Mahler wrote that he could not translate the notes on the page into music.

Strauss remarked that Schoenberg would be better off "shoveling snow than scribbling on music paper."[134] But Schoenberg, having embraced this potent, new expressionistic musical force, could not turn back.

In 1912 he created a work which would come to be regarded as a masterpiece of atonality, *Pierrot Lunaire*. It was composed at almost exactly the same time Stravinsky was creating *Rite of Spring* and actually received its first public performance seven months prior to Stravinsky's famous work.[135]

---

[133] Arnold Schoenberg, *Style and Idea*, pg. 260

[134] Alex Ross, *The Rest is Noise*, pg. 53-54

Pierrot Lunaire is a musical setting of twenty-one Symbolist poems by Albert Giraud. Each poem is a rondel, a verse form originating in 14th century France, in which the first two lines of the stanza are treated as a refrain, repeated as the last two lines of the second stanza and the third stanza (which repeats only the first line of the refrain). As an example, here is the text of one of Giraud's *Pierrot* poems, the first in Schoenberg's set:

> 1. *Moondrunk*
>
> *The wine which through the eyes we drink*
>
> *Flows nightly from the moon in torrents,*
>
> *And as a spring-tide overflows*
>
> *The far and distant land.*
>
> *Desires terrible and sweet*
>
> *Unnumbered drift in floods abounding.*
>
> *The wine which through the eyes we drink*
>
> *Flows nightly from the moon in torrents.*
>
> *The poet, in an ecstasy,*
>
> *Drinks deeply from the holy chalice,*
>
> *To heaven lifts up his entranced Head, and reeling quaffs and drains down*
>
> *The wine which through the eyes we drink.*

---

[135] Stravinsky traveled to Berlin and was in the audience at an early performance of *Pierrot Lunaire*. He treasured his ticket and concert program from the event for the rest of his life. (Raphael Mostel, Arnold Schoenberg's *Pierrot Lunaire Marks Century*, from *Forward*, April 20, 2018)

Of the fifty *Pierrot Lunaire* poems written by Giraud, Schoenberg selected twenty-one, which he divided into three groups comprised of seven poems each. The main character is Pierrot, dreaming in a mad, moonlit world. In the first group, he sings of love, sex, and religion; in the second, violence, crime, and blasphemy; and in the third, of his return home, haunted by his past.

In the program notes prepared for the premiere, Schoenberg explained his thinking about the text by quoting the German Romantic poet Novalis:

> There are tales, like dreams, without coherence but with associations; poems like fragments made from the most diverse things, purely from melodious and beautiful words, but without any sense of coherence, comprehensible at most in a few strophes. This true poetry can have broadly at most an allegorical sense and, like music, an indirect effect.[136]

Schoenberg's musical settings of these poems are absolutely atonal and effectively convey the dark, nightmare world of the text. Musically, the settings of *Pierrot Lunaire* are each organized around a primary theme. In the first, *Mondestrunken*, Schoenberg uses the following idea:

This motive, or some variation of it, is heard repeatedly during *Mondestrunken*, and becomes a unifying theme for the movement.

---

[136] Bryan R. Simms, *The Atonal Music of Arnold Schoenberg*, 1908-1923, pg. 118

After forty rehearsals,[137] the premiere was held at the Berlin Choralion-Saal on October 16, 1912. The reaction was mixed, and there were some accusations of blasphemy in the text. Schoenberg responded that if the words had been set to more traditional music, "not a single one of [these critics] would give a damn for the words. Instead, they would go away whistling the tunes."[138] For most detractors, however, it was the music that was intolerable. One critic from an American newspaper wrote:

> Arnold Schoenberg may be either crazy as a loon, or he may be a very clever trickster who is apparently determined to cause a sensation at any cost. His *Pierrot Lunaire* is the last word in cacophony and musical anarchy...a musical, or rather, unmusical ensemble, consisting of piano, violin, viola, cello, piccolo, and clarinet...discoursed the most ear-splitting combinations of tones that ever desecrated the walls of a Berlin music hall. Schoenberg has thrown overboard all of the anchors of the art of music.
>
> Melody he eschews in every form; tonality he knows not, and such a word as harmony is not in his vocabulary...The remarkable thing about this whole farce is that Schoenberg is taken seriously. A musically cultured audience sits through such an atrocity with hardly a protest...He even has adherents who rally round his standard and swear by him, declaring that this is the music of the future. One music critic expressed the feelings of all sane musicians when he wrote: "If this is the music of the future, then I pray my Creator not to let me live to hear it again".[139]

---

[137] Kathleen Coessens, *Experimental Encounters in Music and Beyond*, pg. 101

[138] Michael Dervan, *Westport's awake to the sounds of chamber music*, from *The Irish Times*, September 10, 2014

[139] From *The Musical Courier*, New York, November 6, 1912, quoted by Nicholas Slonimsky in his *Lexicon of Musical Invective: Critical Assaults on Composers Since Beethoven*, pg. 153

If listening audiences and music critics (and even fellow composers like Strauss and Mahler) could not comprehend or appreciate Schoenberg's radical atonal music, the artist Wassily Kandinsky understood immediately. He wrote to Schoenberg, "You have realized in your work that which I...have so long sought from music. The self-sufficient following of its own path, the independent life of individual voices in your compositions, is exactly what I seek to find in painterly form."[140]

Within days of hearing Schoenberg's music, Kandinsky made a series of paintings inspired by what he had heard.[141] In these paintings, Kandinsky moved away from any form of representational art into pure abstraction.

Schoenberg and Kandinsky became close friends, exchanging letters in which they discussed modern music and art, and the importance of the subconscious mind as the creative source for art.

Kandinsky encouraged Schoenberg in his own painting, and the two even exchanged canvases. He also encouraged Schoenberg to contribute to the written almanac of the *Blaue Reiter* group.[142]

THE TWELVE-TONE SYSTEM: SEARCHING FOR ORDER

In his early atonal works, Schoenberg evidently composed on a kind of improvisational model. This seems clear from his own descriptions of his atonal music.

---

[140] Walter Frisch, *German Modernism: Music and the Arts*, pg. 118. Kandinsky was prompted to write after hearing Schoenberg's *First* and *Second String Quartets* and the 1909 *Piano Pieces*.

[141] Primarily *Impression III – Concert* (1911) which was inspired by Schoenberg's *Three Piano Pieces*.

[142] Roberta Smith, *Kandinsky and Schoenberg, Seen and Heard on Canvas*, from the *New York Times*, October 24, 2003

For instance, when he sent the score for his *Five Pieces for Orchestra* to Richard Strauss, he included an accompanying note explaining the music: "There is no architecture...just a vivid, uninterrupted succession of colors, rhythms, and moods."[143]

However, by the 1920s Schoenberg had begun to search for a way to bring structure to his atonal compositions. The old tonal system had evolved several formal devices which greatly aided the composer in building longer works of music. Schoenberg was searching for a similar way to provide unity and order while retaining flexibility in an atonal composition.

The solution he found can be best understood by first examining an ancient magical word square called "the sator square".[144]

```
S A T O R
A R E P O
T E N E T
O P E R A
R O T A S
```

The sator square is comprised of five Latin words, SATOR, AREPO, TENET, OPERA, ROTAS (roughly translated as "the sower Arepo keeps the work circling").

---

[143] Alex Ross, *The Rest is Noise*, pg. 58

[144] While there seems to be no evidence that Schoenberg was inspired directly by the sator square, it is known that his pupil, Anton Webern was well aware of it.

These words, each comprised of five letters, are arranged one over the other so that the letters form a square. Arranged in this way, it can then be read in four different directions, forward, backwards, from top to bottom, and from bottom to top.[145]

Schoenberg's twelve-tone system amounts to a musical version of the sator square. The procedure may be briefly summarized this way: An ordered set of pitches, containing all twelve tones available within an octave, may be presented, like the Latin words of the sator square, in four ways: forwards (the original row), backwards (retrograde), with inverted intervals (inversion) and with inverted intervals, backwards (retrograde inversion). In addition, all four versions of the tone row may be presented starting at any pitch level, producing twelve possible transpositions. This unique ordering of the twelve chromatic pitches is to be maintained throughout the composition, using part or all of one of the four permutations of the row for all musical content

"The method consists primarily of the constant and exclusive use of a set of twelve different notes," Schoenberg wrote."This means, of course, that no tone is repeated within the series and that it uses all twelve tones of the chromatic scale, though in a different order."[146] Schoenberg also offered some aesthetic advice about writing music with his new system: "In twelve-tone composition consonances… - in fact, almost everything that used to make up the ebb and flow of harmony – are, as far as possible, avoided."[147]

---

[145] Inscriptions of the sator square have been found in the ruins of Pompeii and numerous other places in the ancient world. It was also used in alchemy and thought to have magical properties (Walter O. Moeller, *The Mithraic origin and the meanings of the Rotas-Sator square*)

[146] Arnold Schoenberg, *Style and Idea*, pg. 218

[147] Ibid, pg. 207

His didactically cumbersome name for his new procedure was: *The Method of Composing with Twelve Tones Which are Related Only with One Another*, but it soon came to be referred to more simply as "the twelve-tone method".

C	B	E♭	G	A	A♭	E	F	B♭	G♭	D♭	D
D♭	C	E	A♭	B♭	A	F	G♭	B	G	D	E♭
A	A♭	C	E	G♭	F	D♭	D	G	E♭	B♭	B
F	E	A♭	C	D	D♭	A	B♭	E♭	B	G♭	G
E♭	D	G♭	B♭	C	B	G	A♭	D♭	A	E	F
E	E♭	G	B	D♭	C	A♭	A	D	B♭	F	G♭
A♭	G	B	E♭	F	E	C	D♭	G♭	D	A	B♭
G	G♭	B♭	D	E	E♭	B	C	F	D♭	A♭	A
D	D♭	F	A	B	B♭	G♭	G	C	A♭	E♭	E
G♭	F	A	D♭	E♭	D	B♭	B	E	C	G	A♭
B	B♭	D	G♭	A♭	G	E♭	E	A	F	C	D♭
B♭	A	D♭	F	G	G♭	D	E♭	A♭	E	B	C

(ORIGINAL → / ← RETROGRADE; INVERSION ↓ / ↑ RETROGRADE INVERSION)

When all of possible forms of the twelve-note row are arranged in a "matrix", it very much resembles the sator square, and functions in exactly the same way.

The twelve-tone row does not constitute the musical composition itself. It merely establishes the parameters within which the composer will work for the duration of a given composition. The idea is that by maintaining a constant set of intervals (relationships between pitches within the row sequence) the atonal composition will be infused with a kind of harmonic unity which will function psychologically like the old tonal system, providing an internal logic for the composition.

This is not to suggest that the listener will be able to perceive this internal logic. The twelve-tone row in a musical composition is like the steel framework of a modern building – even though it is not perceived, it nevertheless supports the outer structure.

PERSECUTION AND EMIGRATION

As early as 1921, Schoenberg began to personally experience anti-Semitic persecution - he and his family were asked to leave an Austrian hotel because of a "no Jews allowed" policy, forcing him to cut short a working vacation.[148] As the political situation in Germany deteriorated, anti-Semitism increased. In 1923 Schoenberg complained bitterly in a letter to Kandinsky:

> I have at last learned the lesson that has been forced upon me during this year, and I shall not ever forget it. It is that I am not a German, not a European, indeed perhaps scarcely a human being (at least the Europeans prefer the worst of their race to me) but I am a Jew.[149]

Adolf Hitler became chancellor of Germany on January 30, 1933. On March 1st, only days after the burning of the Reichstag,

Max von Schillings, the president of the Prussian Academy of Arts (where Schoenberg had been teaching a master class), announced that the Führer intended to "break the Jewish stranglehold on Western music".[150]

On April 7th the Nazi government issued the *Gesetz zur Wiederherstellung des Berufsbeamtentums* (*Law for the Restoration of the Professional Civil Service*) which banned Jews from holding university positions.[151]

---

[148] Bluma Goldstein, *Reinscribing Moses*, pg. 138

[149] Jeremy Eichler, *Modernist Prophets Of Disparate Arts*, from *The New York Times*, October 24, 2003

[150] Malcolm MacDonald, *Schoenberg*, pg. 71

Consequently, on May 30th the Prussian Ministry of Culture revoked Schoenberg's contract, but it was too late - Schoenberg was already gone.[152] Initially he traveled to Paris, but eventually made his way to the United States. The composer Milton Babbitt relates the following story about Schoenberg's arrival in America:

> Schoenberg arrived on the shores of this country, in New York, in October 1933...The man who went to meet him at the boat was named Lehman Engel. He couldn't speak German, and Schoenberg, who never learned to speak English very well, spoke very little English at that time. Lehman said, "Here is a little present for you," and gave him a message from some of his colleagues in this country...Schoenberg said, "Thank you," which he had learned to say, and Lehman said, "You're welcome." Schoenberg began to cry because he thought Lehman had meant, "You're welcome in this country."[153]

SCHOENBERG'S DISCIPLES

When Schoenberg began taking students in 1904, Anton Webern and Alban Berg soon became not only students but close associates and supporters of Schoenberg.[154]

---

[151] Tim Bergfelder, *Destination London: German-Speaking Emigres and British Cinema*, 1925-1950, pg. 232

[152] Malcolm MacDonald, *Schoenberg*, pg. 71

[153] Milton Babbitt, *Words About Music*, pg. 5

[154] This group, Schoenberg, Webern, and Berg (centered in Vienna) soon began to be called the "Second Viennese School", a reference to the "First Viennese School" comprised of Haydn, Mozart and Beethoven. As this idea began to circulate, Schoenberg acquired an air of authority, historical prestige, and an almost guru-like status.

Webern had already been studying music at the University of Vienna where he eventually earned his Ph.D. in musicology in 1906.[155] Before entering Schoenberg's orbit, Webern's music had been influenced by Wagner, Strauss, Mahler, and Debussy.

But he soon changed directions in a radical way, wholeheartedly embracing Schoenberg's methods with an enthusiasm that sometimes alarmed his teacher. Schoenberg confided to his diary that his students were always, "at my heels, trying to outdo what I offer…they always raise everything to the tenth power." [156]

Though Webern began to enthusiastically employ the methods of Schoenberg, the sound of his music was very different from that of his teacher. In contrast to Schoenberg's music, which tends to be dense with emotional turbulence and expressionist angst, Webern's music is extremely economical and austere. Webern is a miniaturist – his music is among the shortest and softest in the entire repertoire.

One hostile critic wrote that Webern's music is so soft and brief that it requires the utmost concentration. "Inevitably these faint rustlings, these tiny squeaks and titterings call to mind the activity of insects."[157] The impulse to go to the brink of nothingness was central to Webern's aesthetic. A joke circulated that Webern had introduced a new dynamic marking, *pensato* – don't play the note, only think it.[158]

---

[155] J. Peter Burkholder, *A History of Western Music*, pg. 826

[156] Bryan R Simms, *The Atonal Music of Arnold Schoenberg*, 1908-1923, pg. 113

[157] Warren Storey Smith, Boston Post, November 20, 1926 (from the *Lexicon of Musical Invective: Critical Assaults on Composers Since Beethoven* by Nicholas Slonimsky)

[158] Alex Ross, *The Rest is Noise*, pg. 63

In contrast to Webern, who gave the impression of a bookish professor, Alban Berg was handsome and outgoing, with an ironic sense of humor. He rarely engaged in the high-flown visionary rhetoric to which Webern and Schoenberg were prone.

> On one occasion, Berg had trouble keeping a straight face, when his comrade-in-arms Webern, at a rehearsal of his Quartet for violin, clarinet, tenor saxophone, and piano, Op. 22, told the saxophonist to play a descending major seventh "with sex-appeal". Berg feigned an asthma attack, fled outside, and burst into hysterical laughter.[159]

Like Webern, Berg employed Schoenberg's methods but aimed for very different results. Both Schoenberg and Webern were driven by a desire to create the "music of the future" and went to extreme lengths to avoid any musical sound that was even remotely reminiscent of the past.

Berg, on the other hand, did not seem to share their concerns, and he frequently incorporated consonances, scales, and chords drawn from traditional harmonic practice. Consequently, his music has a rich, almost romantic appeal quite unlike that of his fellow twelve-tone composers.

His best-known work is an opera entitled *Wozzeck,* which tells a grim story of a German soldier in World War I who loses his mind and murders his wife. Berg based *Wozzeck* on a drama by Georg Buchner called *Woyzeck.* Buchner's play is a pitiless meditation on alienation and degradation.

---

[159] Ibid, pg. 64

But in Berg's opera, the character of Wozzeck is handled more sympathetically, and at the climax of the opera, (spoiler alert) Wozzeck's death scene, Berg abandons atonality altogether and presents the audience with an interlude in the undisguised key of D minor, dripping with full-blown, emotion-laden Romanticism.

Berg explained that this reversion to tonality amounts to "a confession of the author who now steps outside the drama" to make "an appeal to humanity through its representatives, the audience."[160] This statement by Berg suggests that he consciously juggled tonality and atonality as needed to serve his story-telling ends. As Wozzeck's mind unravels, atonal dissonance proves to be a potent representation of his mental state, but in his death, Berg deploys the familiar musical language of the last century to arouse the pity of the audience.

The atonal and twelve-tone music of Schoenberg, Webern and Berg – full of nervous tension and psychological angst - proved to be the perfect analog to the art of the Expressionist painters.

Taking a wider view, Expressionism itself, whether in music, painting, literature, or film, proved to be an accurate mirror of the general atmosphere of unease and dread which gradually settled over Germany like a dark cloud in the 1920s and 1930s. As events would show, the disquieting sense of impending doom communicated by the Expressionists proved to be prophetic, both for the culture at large and tragically, for themselves personally.[161]

---

[160] Will Crutchfield, *Wozzeck Speaks To Us by Mixing Two Musical Modes*, from *The New York Times Archives*, 1989

[161] Schoenberg's students, Berg and Webern, both died in bizarre ways: Berg was stung by a bee which led to infection, blood poisoning, and ultimately to his death on Christmas Eve, 1935. Anton Webern was accidentally shot by an American soldier on September 15, 1945, long after the conclusion of hostilities. For a full accounting of Webern's death and possible attempted cover-up by the U.S. Military see *The Death of Anton Webern: A Drama in Documents*, by Hans Moldenhauer.

CHAPTER FIVE: FUTURISM - SPEED, NOISE, AND MACHINES

Would it ever occur to you to name your daughter Propeller? If so, you are either a punk musician or a Futurist painter. As a matter of fact, one of the Futurist painters by the name of Giacomo Balla was so excited by the new technology of the airplane that he did exactly that.[162]

In the early 1900s, a group of young, rebellious Italian writers and artists were determined to celebrate industrialization. They were exasperated by their sense that Italian culture was mired in the past. As they saw it, Italy was no longer on the cutting edge of cultural innovation but was instead complacently resting on previous artistic achievements dating back to the Renaissance. Their fervent hope was that the "Machine Age" would result in an entirely new global order - even a renewed consciousness for mankind. Unwilling to wait, they took matters into their own hands, publishing a manifesto in 1909 announcing a new movement that would emphasize "speed, technology, youth, defiance, and violence."[163]

Filippo Tommaso Marinetti was the author of the *Futurist Manifesto*, and could rightly be called the ringleader of the whole group. He was born in Alexandria, Egypt in 1876 to parents who had come to Egypt in 1865 to act as legal advisors for foreign companies taking part in a modernization program.

He studied at the Sorbonne in Paris, then traveled to Italy to study law, where he received a doctorate in 1899.[164] Ultimately, Marinetti decided against becoming a lawyer and chose instead to become a writer.

---

[162] John M. MacKenzie, *Popular Imperialism and the Military: 1850-1950*, pg. 219, footnote 82

[163] Rosemary K. West, *Italian Futurism: The First Modern Avant-Garde Movement*, pg. 1

Marinetti's was not the first manifesto of an artistic movement. The Symbolist poets had published one of their own in 1886. Symbolism, however, had already been in existence for thirty years when their manifesto appeared. Marinetti, true to his impetuous nature, could not wait - his manifesto proclaimed a movement that did not yet exist.[165]

The *Futurist Manifesto* appeared on February 20, 1909, on the front page of the leading French newspaper, *La Figaro*. It would have appeared earlier, but Marinetti delayed publication because of an unforeseen event that took place at the beginning of 1909. On January 2, two hundred thousand people were killed by an earthquake in Sicily. Marinetti recognized that this was perhaps not the ideal moment to startle the world with his manifesto, so he delayed publication until he was sure to get front page coverage.[166]

From its very first words, the reader is warned that the Futurist Manifesto will prove to be an unusual and puzzling piece of work: "We have been up all night, my friends and I...discussing right up to the limits of logic and scrawling the paper with demented writing."[167]

---

[164] Ibid, pg. 3

[165] Daniel Albright, *Putting Modernism Together*, pg. 99

[166] Geert Buelens, ed., *The History of Futurism: The Precursors, Protagonists, and Legacies*, pg. 13

[167] Filippo Tammaso Marinetti, *The Futurist Manifesto*

Before coming to any specific points however, Marinetti, in colorful surrealistic language describes himself and his fellow Futurists "standing alone, like sentinels in an outpost...alone with the engineers in the infernal stokeholes of great ships, alone with the black spirits which rage in the belly of rogue locomotives...we were suddenly distracted by the rumbling of huge double-decker trams that went leaping by, streaked with light...when suddenly the hungry automobiles roared beneath our windows."[168]

For Marinetti, the modern industrial city becomes "a kind of dream-space where...everything appears in a glamorous, artificial light."[169] His impatient enthusiasm for forward motion, though, is evident, even through the screen of his confusing, self-contradicting language:

> `Come, my friends!' I said. `Let us go! At last Mythology and the mystic cult of the ideal have been left behind. We are going to be present at the birth of the centaur and we shall soon see the first angels fly!'[170] ...we went up to the three snorting machines to caress their breasts. I lay along mine like a corpse on its bier, but I suddenly revived again beneath the steering wheel - a guillotine knife - which threatened my stomach. A great sweep of madness brought us sharply back to ourselves and drove us through the streets...crushing beneath our burning wheels, like shirt-collars under the iron, the watchdogs on the steps of the houses.[171]

---

[168] ibid

[169] Geert Buelens, ed., *The History of Futurism: The Precursors, Protagonists, and Legacies*, pg. 15

[170] It is impossible to know what Marinetti might have meant by his assertion that "mythology has been left behind" in the same sentence in which he hopes to be present "at the birth of the centaur", a mythological animal.

[171] Filippo Tammaso Marinetti, *The Futurist Manifesto*

One can only suppose that this bizarre, hallucinatory introduction must have been designed to acclimate the reader to the sense of frantic urgency in which the propositions are finally put forward.

Number One: "We want to sing the love of danger, the habit of energy and rashness".[172]

Number Two: "The essential elements of our poetry will be courage, audacity, and revolt."

In the third proposition, Marinetti calls for "movements of aggression", for "feverish insomnia", "the racers stride", "the slap and the blow with the fist".

In the fourth proposition, he declares that "the magnificence of the world has been enriched by a new beauty: the beauty of speed." [173]

Proposition number five continues his celebration of speed: "we want a hymn to the man at the wheel".

In proposition number eight, Marinetti incorporates the language of Einstein's recently unveiled theories about the interrelationship of time and space into his hyperbolic praise of speed: "Time and Space died yesterday. We are already living in the absolute since we have already created eternal, omnipresent speed."

Marinetti's language thus far has evidently been calculated to throw his audience into a frenzy. Into this boiling cauldron of verbal tumult, he tosses proposition number nine: "We want to glorify war - the only cure for the world - militarism, patriotism, the destructive gesture of the anarchists, the beautiful ideas which kill, and contempt for woman."

---

[172] Just in case the reader has not detected already the energy and rashness of the introduction.

[173] This, of course, was long before the word "speed" became a euphemism for amphetamines, though one imagines that Marinetti might have endorsed the drug as well.

This proposition is certainly the most controversial in the entire manifesto, especially in light of the rise of Mussolini and fascism. And what all this militarism has to do with Marinetti's "contempt for woman" is an unexplained puzzle.[174]

As if proposition number nine were not shocking enough, number ten declares: "We want to demolish museums and libraries, fight morality, feminism and all opportunist and utilitarian cowardice."

Marinetti's desire to break with the past is explicit and clear in this tenth proposition (if it was not already obvious in the previous nine). But it was his eleventh proposition that proved to be the most important in the Futurist Manifesto, in the sense that it paved the way for the artwork of his fellow futurists:

> We will sing of the great crowds agitated by work, pleasure and revolt; the multi-colored and polyphonic tides of revolutions in modern capitals: the nocturnal vibration of the arsenals and the workshops beneath their violent electric moons: the gluttonous railway stations devouring smoking serpents; factories suspended from the clouds by the thread of their smoke; bridges with the leap of gymnasts flung across the diabolic cutlery of sunny rivers: adventurous steamers sniffing the horizon; great-breasted locomotives, puffing on the rails like enormous steel horses with long tubes for bridle, and the gliding flight of aeroplanes whose propeller sounds like the flapping of a flag and the applause of enthusiastic crowds.[175]

---

[174] Though Marinetti thought it necessary to elaborate on this controversial and perplexing phrase in his 1911 *Le Futurisme*. He says that what he really meant was "hatred for the tyranny of love", by which he seems to mean romance and traditional marriage relationships.

[175] Filippo Tammaso Marinetti, *The Futurist Manifesto*

Despite the laughable content and histrionic character of Marinetti's futurist propositions, he was able to gather together as co-signers, a group of talented artists, among whom were: Luigi Russolo, painter; Carlo Carrà, painter and author; Umberto Boccioni, painter and sculptor, and Gino Severini, painter.

In fact, Marinetti's futurist prescriptions were realized almost immediately in specific paintings, like Boccioni's *The City Rises* (1910). In this work, the modern city is portrayed as a frenzied, almost electrically charged space in which the shapes of men and animals seem to vibrate with energy. The central focus of the painting is a group of men straining against a gigantic red horse whose blue collar looks more like a propeller, slicing the air. In the background, the chimneys and building scaffolds of the city are seen rising above the turmoil in the streets below.

In October of 1911, Boccioni, along with some of the other Futurists, traveled to Paris to see the new art that was emerging there, specifically the Cubism of Picasso and Georges Braque.[176] Picasso and Braque had been experimenting with this technique in Paris since 1910. Cubism features fragmented images which are rearranged as geometric shapes. At the time of its inception, Cubism was viewed as a kind of anti-Impressionism. Where Impressionism is characterized by hazy images and overly-bright colors, Cubism makes use of muted browns and hard lines.[177]

---

[176] Norbert Lynton, *The Story of Modern Art*, pg. 88

[177] Daniel Albright writes that "Impressionism looks like a binge and Cubism like a hangover." (*Putting Modernism Together*, pg. 117)

Boccioni, undoubtedly the finest painter among the Futurists, began immediately to make use of the new language of Braque and Picasso. In his *States of Mind, the Farewells* (1911), the influence of Cubism is evident, especially in the eye-catching numbers which echo the numeric figures in Picasso and Braque. In Boccioni's work, however, the Cubist aesthetic has been adapted to serve the Futurist taste in subject matter. Where Picasso and Braque painted Cubist portraits and still life images, Boccioni uses fragmentation and geometric lines to present a steam engine, in conformity with the Futurist taste for speed and machines.

As it happened, the Futurists' call for speed, violence, and for the overturning of the world, was to be answered in brutal and deadly ways the artists could not have foreseen. The *Futurist Manifesto* appeared on the brink of an era that the artists sensed, but did not fully anticipate. The "great crowds excited by work and pleasure" which Marinetti wrote about, turned out to be masses of soldiers dying in the trenches.

Sadly, before the decade had ended, Boccioni himself would be dead, caught up in the violence of World War I. When Italy joined the war in 1915, Boccioni volunteered for service. In 1916, during cavalry exercises with his regiment, he was thrown from his horse and trampled. He died the next day at the age of thirty-three.[178]

The Futurist painters loved the idea of speed. But how can the idea of speed be portrayed on a flat canvas? Artists since the Baroque era had portrayed dynamic action by freeze-framing a moment of motion, as in Bernini's *David* (1623), poised to throw the stone that will bring down Goliath. But the Futurists wanted to convey *dynamism itself*, not merely a frozen moment of dynamic action.

---

[178] Edward Lucie-Smith, *Lives of the Great 20th Century Artists*, pg. 56

Giacomo Balla[179] found a solution in his *Dynamism of a Dog on a Leash* (1912) by painting, in effect, several frames (so to speak) seen simultaneously. The language of photography is an apt way to speak of Balla's technique – he was, in fact, fascinated by photography and openly admitted that he was influenced by the analysis of motion provided by the multiple exposure technique of chronophotography.[180]

In his *Rhythms of the Bow* (1912)[181], the violinist's hand and bow are shown in multiple positions at the same time, conveying the idea of speed. In fact, speed is the only goal in a work like this. No emotional response is elicited from the viewer – we do not feel or imagine the music at all – we are simply invited to contemplate the phenomenon of speed.

Following the First World War, Futurism gained new members and assumed different formal qualities including *arte meccanica* (machine aesthetics). In 1922, Ivo Pannaggi and Vinicio Paladini articulated the principles of the *arte mechanica* idiom in their *Manifesto of Futurist Mechanical Art*. After the usual calls for complete rejection of the past, the authors come right to the point:

> Today it is the MACHINE that distinguishes our era. Pulleys and flywheels, bolts and smokestacks, all the polished steel and odor of grease (the perfume of ozone from power plants). These are the places we are irresistibly attracted to… We feel mechanically, and we sense that we ourselves are also made of steel, we too are machines, we have been mechanized by our surroundings.[182]

---

[179] The man who named his daughter "Propeller". He also had another daughter whom he named "Light".

[180] Chronophotography was a complex process of taking multiple successive photographs for the purpose of illustrating the mechanics of motion. It was invented and perfected in the late 19th century.

[181] Also known as *The Hands of the Violinist*.

Pannaggi's famous 1922 work, *Speeding Train*, illustrates their principles. The locomotive is a familiar Futurist symbol of modernity, motion, and machine. The painting depicts a powerful train barreling toward the viewer at a diagonal angle. The image suggests the artist's experience of observing the daily trains passing through the small coastal towns along the Adriatic (the blur of the moving cars, the clamorous noise of the motor, the ear-splitting scream of the whistle). The train itself is not portrayed realistically at all – it appears as a cylinder of highly polished metal, in motion against a geometrically divided background of brilliant color.

FUTURISM AND MUSIC

While the primary focus of Futurism was on the visual arts, some members of the movement became interested in new musical ideas as well.

Francesco Balilla Pratella published a manifesto in 1911, entitled *Futurist Music*. Pratella proposed a new music based on what he called a "chromatic atonal mode". Although he claims that his proposal is a "magnificent conquest by Futurism", the concept is actually very similar to the atonal ideas already being explored (with far greater skill) by Schoenberg in Germany. In 1913, Pratella introduced his music at a concert in Rome, playing a piece entitled *Musica Futurista*. While his fellow Futurists were delighted with the concert, it is generally agreed that Pratella's music did not live up to the rhetoric.[183] The music itself actually sounds quite conventional and even old-fashioned, the only slightly unusual feature being several runs up the whole-tone scale.

---

[182] Ivo Pannaggi and Vinicio Paladini, *Manifesto of Futurist Mechanical Art* from *Futurism: An Anthology*, edited by Lawrence Rainey, Christine Poggi, and Laura Wittman

[183] Benjamin Thorn, from *Music of the Twentieth-century Avant-garde: A Biocritical Sourcebook*, Larry Sitsky, ed.

Though Pratella's concert is said to have ended in a riot, Luigi Russolo, one of the original signers of the Futurist Manifesto was so inspired that he immediately wrote his own manifesto. Russolo was at first a futurist painter but gave up painting in order to devote himself to applying Futurist ideas to music.[184]

Russolo called his 1913 manifesto *L'arte dei Rumori* (*The Art of Noise*). His ideas were more extreme than those of Pratella, who had mostly concerned himself with new systems of pitch and rhythm. Russolo had no formal training in music, a fact which probably accounts for his more radical notions.

Russolo's manifesto envisions making music through the use of noise. His argument is based on a simple (and idiosyncratic) analysis of the history of music, which he sees as a steady progression from the simple and harmonious to the complex and noisy.

The ancient world, Russolo writes, was silent. As early, then medieval music appeared, it consisted of a simple melody line. As time passed, gradually other sounds were added, beginning with perfect consonances, "care taken," he writes, "to caress the ear with gentle harmonies."

"Today," writes Russolo, "music, as it becomes continuously more complicated, strives to amalgamate the most dissonant, strange, and harsh sounds. In this way, we come ever closer to the music of noise."

Russolo sees a parallel between the development of music and the "multiplicity of machines". He writes, "The machine today has created so many varieties and combinations of noise that pure musical sound – with its poverty and monotony – no longer awakens any emotion in the hearer."[185]

---

[184] Russolo's most famous painting is a bizarre work entitled, *Music*, in which a shadowy figure with a bad haircut is seen in the foreground playing some sort of keyboard with multiple hands and arms (presumably showing motion). Meanwhile, strange, mask-like multi-colored faces are converging on him from all sides while a blue swirl arises from the keyboard.

In order to realize the goals set forth in his manifesto, Russolo began to construct mechanical noise-producing instruments which he called "intonarumori" (noise-intoners). He envisioned six categories of sound: roars, whistles, whispers, screeches, percussive sounds, and animal or human voices. Each instrument consisted of an oblong wooden box with a large metal megaphone attached to amplify the sound. Inside, there were various mechanical devices used to generate the desired sounds by turning cranks, tapping stretched membranes and other means. Some had levers and wires to rattle pots or cardboard canisters filled with objects. One was used to imitate the starting of an automobile engine.

By 1914, an entire orchestra of intonarumori had been constructed and Russolo's first concert was scheduled in Rome. The performance, which took place on April 14, 1914, is legendary because of the public disturbance that ensued. Rotten fruit and vegetables were thrown at the performers during the concert and the event was topped off with the arrest of Marinetti and Russolo for having incited a riot.[186] The concert was reviewed for *L'Italia* by its music critic, Agostino Cameroni. Russolo was so irritated by what he read that he slapped Cameroni in public. Cameroni responded by having Russolo charged with assault.[187]

Undeterred, Marinetti and Russolo presented a series of twelve concerts in London in July of 1914.

---

[185] Luigi Russolo, *The Art of Noise*

[186] Thom Holmes, *Electronic and Experimental Music*, pg. 41

[187] Luciano Chessa, *Luigi Russolo, Futurist: Noise, Visual Arts, and the Occult*, pg. 133

A review in the Times of London likened the sounds to those of "a channel-steamer during a bad crossing". The critic suggested that it had been "unwise" for the musicians to proceed after the first piece was greeted with the "pathetic cries of 'no more' from all parts of the auditorium."[188]

Sadly, all of Russolo's instruments and performance scores were destroyed during the Second World War. However, a fragment of a 1913 score for 16 noise-intoners has since been discovered and recorded.[189]

MUSIC INFLUENCED BY THE FUTURISTS

George Antheil was born in America in 1900, and though not officially associated with any of the Futurist groups, his interest in non-musical machine and industrial sounds ties him with Futurist music in a philosophical sense.

Antheil made a name for himself in postwar Paris with works titled *Airplane Sonata* and *Sonata Sauvage*. He lived in a small, one-room apartment above Shakespeare & Company, the legendary bookstore owned by Sylvia Beach, who published Joyce's Ulysses. Antheil rubbed shoulders with the artistic and literary avant-garde in Paris: Igor Stravinsky, James Joyce, Ernest Hemingway, Gertrude Stein, Ezra Pound, Pablo Picasso, and Salvador Dali.

Antheil is best known for a work called *Ballet mecanique*, which was originally conceived as a work for 16 player pianos playing percussively, as machines, in addition to bells, xylophone, sirens, and three airplane propellers.

In a newspaper article, Antheil sounded very much like a Futurist when he called his *Ballet mecanique*, "the first piece of music that has been composed OUT OF and FOR machines..."[190]

---

[188] Thom Holmes, *Electronic and Experimental Music*, pg. 41

[189] Anyone with enough curiosity to do so can easily find recordings of the surviving score and, more interestingly, videos of performances by newly reconstructed *intonarumoris*.

Ballet mecanique was initially conceived as an accompaniment for a modernist film of the same name created by the French artist Fernand Léger and was scheduled to be performed with the film at its premiere.[191]

However, before completion, the director and composer disagreed over artistic differences (possibly over the practical inability of synchronizing sixteen player pianos with themselves and with the film). Consequently, the film and music were not properly joined together until the 1990s.[192] Antheil reworked the score and introduced it as a concert piece in Paris in 1926. The Paris premiere enraged some concert-goers, but their objections were drowned out by the cacophonous music.

Another composer who was influenced by the ideas of Futurism was Edgard Varèse. Born in Paris in 1883, he was subsequently raised in Italy where he received his first musical instruction. In 1903 he relocated again to Paris and became active in the modernist musical life of the city. There he met Strauss and Debussy and became acquainted with the Italian Futurists, including Luigi Russolo.

Like Russolo, Varèse was interested in noise sounds, but found Russolo's application to be unmusical and uninteresting. Varèse, in his own manifesto, criticized the Futurists for failing to synthesize noise with music: "Italian Futurists," he wrote, "why do you merely reproduce the vibrations of our daily life only in their superficial... aspects?"[193]

---

[190] Paul D. Lehrman, *Blast from the Past*, from Wired Magazine, November 1, 1999

[191] The film has no real narrative. It consists of a strange series of images of a woman in a swing, close-up shots of her mouth, of ordinary objects, and repeated images of human activities and machines in rhythmic movement.

[192] For a fascinating account of how the music and film were finally synchronized with the help of modern technology, see the article by Paul D. Lehrman, *Blast from the Past*, from Wired Magazine, November 1, 1999

In 1918, Varèse immigrated to the United States and became a citizen in 1927. Upon arriving in New York, Varèse fell in with a cosmopolitan group of artists – both expatriate and native – who were forging a distinctly American avant-garde.

Art critic Paul Rosenfeld identified these artists as the avatars of what he called "skyscraper mysticism", which he described in words that could have been written by Marinetti himself:

> …the forms and expressions of industrial civilization, in fierce lights, piercing noises, compact and synthetic textures; a feeling of immense tension, dynamism, ferocity, and also its fabulous delicacy and precision.[194]

The music Varèse created seemed to echo the sounds and rhythms of New York in the 1920s – the noise of traffic, the wail of sirens, the moaning of foghorns. Using percussion and traditional instruments to build huge masses of sound, unearthly harmonies and mechanical noise-producing devices, Varèse's music feels, at the same time both primitive and modern. The music critic Gillian Moore writes, "I often get the feeling when I'm listening to Varèse that this music has existed since the beginning of time: sounds seem to call out across the universe, to be at once audaciously futuristic and unutterably ancient."[195]

Perhaps no work of Varèse better represents his fascination with noise sounds than his work for percussion called *Ionisation*. In this work, the first "classical" work for percussion alone, Varèse wrote for 16 percussionists, who play 37 percussion instruments between them, including sirens and anvils.[196]

---

[193] Fernand Ouellette, *Edgard Varese*, pg. 39

[194] Alex Ross, *The Rest is Noise*, pg. 137

[195] Gillian Moore, *Edgard Varèse: in wait for the future*, from *The Guardian*, April 8, 2010

Marinetti had called for war in his Futurist manifesto, thinking that only the violence of war could propel the world into the future he imagined. Ironically, Futurism would prove to be one of the primary influences on an art movement which would be created by exiles fleeing from the war Marinetti had called for, and motivated by anti-war sentiments: Dada.

---

[196] The unique character of Varèse's music made him a magnet for young avant-garde musicians. Jazz saxophonist Charlie Parker used to follow Varèse around Greenwich Village begging for composition lessons. Rock guitarist Frank Zappa was also a fan of Varèse. In 1955, the then 15-year old Zappa, after locating the only copy of an album of Varèse compositions in his home town, was given an unusual birthday present by his parents – a long-distance phone call to New York City to speak with the composer. Unfortunately, Varèse was in Europe at the time, so Zappa spoke to the composer's wife instead.

CHAPTER SIX: DADA - THE ANTI-ART

The First World War erupted on June 28, 1914, when Archduke Franz Ferdinand, heir to the Austro-Hungarian Empire, was shot to death with his wife by a Bosnian Serb nationalist Gavrilo Princip in Sarajevo. The war was initially seen as a noble cause, and those who fought in it were, for the most part, motivated by national honor and patriotism. However, by the conclusion of the war in 1918, it was no longer seen in idealistic terms but universally viewed as an apocalyptic catastrophe. There were 20 million dead, and 21 million wounded. Over one-third of the working-age men of Europe were dead from either combat or disease.[197]

In addition to the human casualties of the war, the European art culture was turned upside down. For many artists and intellectuals, the war generated a profound sense of disillusionment and pessimism. Some, like George Grosz, responded to the war with cynical images, mocking all forms of government and religious leadership.[198]

The grim realities of industrial warfare led to a backlash against the patriotic propaganda and grandiose nationalism that had sparked the conflagration. In his 1929 book about his experiences in the war, *A Farewell to Arms*, Ernest Hemingway expressed his own bitterness towards the high-minded inspirational words that motivated men to fight and die:

> Abstract words such as glory, honor, [or] courage… were obscene beside the concrete names of villages, the numbers of roads, the names of rivers, the numbers of regiments and the dates.[199]

---

[197] Figures vary according to sources consulted.

[198] Jonathan Jones, *George Grosz's dada drawings show how the first world war upended art*, The Guardian, October 3, 2013

[199] Ernest Hemmingway, *A Farewell to Arms*, pg. 184

Robert Graves, in his autobiographical account of the First World War, explains how patriotism and religious belief became casualties of war:

> Patriotism, in the trenches, was too remote a sentiment, and at once rejected as fit only for civilians, or prisoners. A new arrival who talked patriotism would soon be told to cut it out.... Hardly one soldier in a hundred was inspired by religious feeling of even the crudest kind. It would have been difficult to remain religious in the trenches even if one had survived the irreligion of the training battalion at home.[200]

The survivors of the senseless slaughter of the First World War were left cynical and bitter, and it became common, especially among artists and writers, to embrace a nihilistic outlook on life.

Nihilism, as a word, comes from the Latin root word *nihil*, meaning "nothing". (The verb form is *annihilate*, "to bring to nothing".) As a philosophical proposition, Nihilism argues that life is without any objective meaning, purpose, or intrinsic value. A true Nihilist would argue that all values are baseless and therefore nothing can be known or communicated.[201]

While Nietzsche did not invent the word or the notion of Nihilism, he is the philosopher most often associated with it. In Nietzsche's view, the rise of science, rationalism, and skepticism after the Enlightenment led increasingly to the displacement of religious belief. But if religious faith finally disappeared (the "death of God", so to speak), Nietzsche believed that Nihilism would be the inevitable result.

---

[200] Robert Graves, *Goodbye to All That*, pg. 188-189

[201] Shane Weller, *Literature, Philosophy, Nihilism: The Uncanniest of Guests*, pg.16

In his 1901 book, *The Will to Power*, Nietzsche predicted the rise of Nihilism in the twentieth century:

> What I am now going to relate is the history of the next two centuries. I shall describe what will happen, what must necessarily happen: the triumph of nihilism.[202]

What Nietzsche predicted became reality for the embittered, cynical survivors of the First World War. In his unique poetic language, Nietzsche describes the sense of moral disorientation that would necessarily accompany the loss of religious faith which he foresaw:

> What were we doing when we unchained this earth from its sun? Whither is it moving now? Whither are we moving? Away from all suns? Are we not plunging continually? Backward, sideward, forward, in all directions? Is there still any up or down? Are we not straying, as through an infinite nothing? Do we not feel the breath of empty space? [203]

In the first months of the war, nationalistic fervor was nearly universal. Nevertheless, while some artists chose to serve in the military, and some died in the fighting, many others chose exile instead.

They simply refused to participate in what they saw as a monstrous waste of human life, prompted by nothing more than the whims of political leaders and would-be despots. These artists in exile, who emigrated either to nations that were safe, like America or to neutral nations, like Switzerland, created a nihilistic art movement motivated by disillusionment. They called it Dada.

---

[202] Nietzsche, *The Will to Power*, preface

[203] Nietzsche, *The Gay Science*, pg. 120

ZURICH – THE BIRTHPLACE OF DADA

Among the earliest exiles were a husband and wife theatrical team, Hugo Ball and Emmy Hennings. Hugo Ball was erudite, extremely well-read, and something of a scholar. He was described by those who knew him as ethereal, creative, and introverted.[204] He was also patriotic. When war broke out in August of 1914, he tried to enlist three times but was turned away because of poor health. His patriotic enthusiasm, however, evaporated after making an unauthorized visit to the Belgian front in November of 1914. What he saw there caused him such psychological trauma that he momentarily contemplated suicide.[205] Ball instead became a radical anti-war activist, organizing a series of meetings in Berlin which featured provocative anti-war performances, including strident poetry by himself and by a younger man whom Ball had befriended by the name of Richard Huelsenbeck, who liked to recite what he called *chants nègres*, poems intended to invoke the rhythm of African tribal songs presented to the beat of a drum.[206]

Eventually, Ball and Hennings fled to Zurich, using forged documents to avoid military inspection at the border. As a further measure against detection, Ball registered with the Zurich police under a false name. He was nevertheless arrested and briefly imprisoned by the Zurich authorities who charged him with falsifying documents. Without official papers, he was unable to obtain work, and soon the couple was destitute.

---

[204] Jed Rasula, *Destruction Was My Beatrice: Dada and the Unmaking of the Twentieth Century*, pg. 1

[205] Leah Dickerman, *Dada*, pg. 21

[206] ibid

In desperation Ball approached a Dutch seaman named Jan Ephraim, the owner of the Holländische Meierei Café, and proposed turning the café into an avant-garde artists' cabaret, arguing that it would attract intellectuals and draw a crowd. Ephraim was intrigued and agreed.

THE CABARET VOLTAIRE

On February 2, 1916, only three days before the scheduled opening, Ball placed an ad in a local paper inviting "young artists of Zurich, whatever their orientation, [to] come along with suggestions and contributions of all kinds."[207] Ball named the venue "Cabaret Voltaire" in reference to the 18th-century satirist Voltaire, whose novella, *Candide* mocked the idiocies of his own society. Ball said, "This is our *Candide* against the times."[208]

On the opening night, while Ball was frantically hammering together a stage and hanging futuristic posters, a group of Romanians arrived, bringing rolled up artworks and manuscripts. One of these was Tristan Tzara, who would later play a leading role in the Dada movement. On this opening night, Tzara, a small, dapper teenager, read poems which he produced from various coat pockets.[209]

Others appeared as well – a group of twelve Russian balalaika players squeezed onto the tiny stage. Several locals turned up wanting to try out unexceptional little poems – it was like a modern "open-mic" night.[210]

---

[207] Leah Dickerman, *Dada*, pg. 22

[208] ibid

[209] Jed Rasula, *Destruction Was My Beatrice: Dada and the Unmaking of the Twentieth Century*, pg. 3

[210] ibid

Hans Arp (also known as Jean Arp[211]) also happened to be there on the opening night. Arp was a German citizen. At the beginning of the war, he had fled to Paris to avoid conscription in the German army. The French, however, because of his German citizenship, suspected him of espionage, and after being interrogated he was advised to leave France. In 1915 he came to Switzerland to take advantage of Swiss neutrality. Nevertheless, after arriving, he received notice that he had been drafted into the German army and was ordered to report to the German consulate. Arp decided to feign insanity to avoid military service. Upon arriving at the consulate, he wrote the date in the first blank on his paperwork. He then wrote the date in every other blank as well, after which he drew a line at the bottom of the page and carefully added up all the numbers. He then took off all his clothes and handed in his paperwork.[212]

Pleased with the Cabaret's success on its opening night, Ball wrote to his old friend Huelsenbeck in Berlin, urging him to come to Zurich. Huelsenbeck was only too glad to escape from Germany where he was in danger of the draft. On February 11, Ball wrote in his diary, "Huelsenbeck has arrived. He pleads for stronger rhythm (Negro rhythm). He would prefer to drum literature into the ground."[213]

Huelsenbeck was an enthusiastic supporter of the Italian Futurist movement, and he brought with him the more aggressive tone of the Futurists.

---

[211] Arp was born of a German father and a French mother. When he spoke German he referred to himself as "Hans", and when he spoke French he referred to himself as "Jean".

[212] Leah Dickerman, *Dada*, pg. 23

[213] ibid

He proclaimed the view that the war had been primarily of Germany's making, thus demonstrating the hypocrisy of Germany's pretensions of intellectual and cultural greatness. This also reflected on other so-called civilized nations who, likewise, seemed hell-bent on mutual destruction.[214]

As the weekly performances got underway, the regular participants began to learn what each could bring to the show, and they tried for a little bit of everything. To begin the proceedings, Ball might play honky-tonk piano to set the mood. Then Emmy Hennings might appear and sing a tender ballad, or with the demeanor of a Madonna, do the splits. A few others might join her for a vaudeville skit, followed by a Maori tribal spell delivered by Tristan Tzara, wearing a monocle, while spinning and wiggling like a belly dancer. Then three performers might recite simultaneous poetry in three different languages. Huelsenbeck liked to recite his own poems, snarling aggressively while pounding on a drum and brandishing a riding whip. As Hans Arp reflected later, it was "total pandemonium".[215]

Huelsenbeck, in particular, longed for the primitive origins of mankind, and his poems plunged into the cauldron of primal forms, making liberal use of his invented faux-African lingo: "sokobauno, sokobauno, buruboo buruboo."[216]

A 1916 painting by Marcel Janco captures the frenzied atmosphere of the cabaret on a typical night. His rough Expressionist style conveys a sense of energy and excitement.

---

[214] Richard Sheppard, *Modernism - Dada – Postmodernism*, pg. 215

[215] Edward Lucie-Smith, *Lives of the Great 20th Century Artists*, pg. 143

[216] Huelsenbeck later published a book of these "African poems" entitled *Fantastic Prayers*. When he gave a copy to his mother, she burst into tears, fearing for his sanity. (Jed Rasula, *Destruction Was My Beatrice: Dada and the Unmaking of the Twentieth Century*, pg. 9)

Performers (Tzara can be identified by his monocle) are crowded onto a tiny stage, while a pianist (presumably Ball) seems lost in a private reverie. Patrons are seated at tables, some gesticulating towards the stage, some passed out in their seats. Modernist artwork covers the walls.

There was an air of roughness, unpredictability and even danger about the goings-on. It was nighttime entertainment in a seedy quarter of the city and brawls between drunken students were not uncommon. Because of the raucous music, windows could not be opened after 10:00 PM. In his memoirs, Huelsenbeck vividly recalled the coarse reality of the cabaret:

> Whenever someone opened the door, thick clouds of smoke would come pouring out, like the smoke that hovers over the fields during the burning of the harvest leavings...There were almost no women in the cabaret. It was too wild, too smoky, too way out.[217]

Despite the success of the cabaret, Hugo Ball began to privately worry about the increasingly frantic atmosphere. His diary entries during this period reflect his concern. On February 26, only three weeks after the opening, he wrote, "Everyone has become seized by an indefinable intoxication. The little cabaret is about to come apart at the seams and is getting to be a playground for crazy emotions."[218]

By March 2nd, the cabaret had become a staple of Zurich nightlife. Ball wrote, "Our attempt to entertain the audience...forces us to be incessantly lively...it is a race with the expectations of the audience..."[219]

---

[217] Richard Huelsenbeck, *Memoirs of a Dada Drummer*, pg. 9

[218] Hugo Ball, *Flight Out of Time, A Dada Diary*, pg. 51

[219] Ibid, pg. 54

On March 15 Ball confided to his diary, "The cabaret needs a rest. With all the tension, the daily performances are not just exhausting, they are crippling."[220]

On June 23, Ball wrote that he had invented a new form of poetry, "poetry without words", built solely of abstract phonemes. That night he presented a reading of one of these poems, while dressed in a cardboard costume – shiny blue cylinders that covered his legs, making it necessary that he be carried on and off stage, and a blue and white striped "witch doctor's hat". As he recounted later in his diary, it seemed as though he had reached back in time, as his voice took on the tone of liturgical singing: "I began to chant my vowel sequences in a church style…and I tried not only to look serious, but to force myself to be serious. For a moment it seemed as if there were a pale, bewildered face in my Cubist mask, the half-frightened, half-curious face of a 10-year-old boy, trembling and hanging avidly on the priest's words in the requiems and high masses of his home parish. Then the lights went out, as I had ordered, and bathed in sweat, I was carried off the stage like a magical bishop."[221] This proved to be a traumatic event for Ball and it was his last performance at the cabaret. He had become spooked and wary of whatever it was that they had unleashed.[222]

---

[220] Ibid, pg. 57

[221] Ibid, pg. 71

[222] Jed Rasula, *Destruction Was My Beatrice: Dada and the Unmaking of the Twentieth Century*, pg.xv

FROM CABARET TO DADA

The Cabaret Voltaire closed in July 1916. According to Huelsenbeck, Ephraim "told us we must either offer better entertainment, draw a larger crowd or shut down the cabaret."[223] There had evidently already been some discussion between Ball, Huelsenbeck, and Tzara prior to this point on the subject of extending the reach of the cabaret. Ideas included an international exhibition, a Voltaire Society, or a published anthology of some sort.

In the end, a publication was agreed upon, and on May 31, 1916, the one and only issue of *Cabaret Voltaire* was published, allowing readers to sample various aspects of the group's activities. There was an introduction by Ball and a chapter from his "fantastic novel", a catalog of one of the Cabaret Voltaire's exhibitions, and other contributions from modernists whose work had been shown at the Cabaret, including Marinetti, Kandinsky, and Picasso.[224]

Ball, however, had doubts about the entire publication enterprise. "In the end, we cannot simply keep on producing without knowing whom we are addressing…Can we write, compose, and make music for an imaginary audience?"[225] Tzara, on the other hand, was thrilled that the printed anthology now made the ideas and activities of the cabaret accessible to an audience much wider than the confines of the physical cabaret itself.

---

[223] Richard Huelsenbeck, *Memoirs of a Dada Drummer*, pg.17

[224] Leah Dickerman, *Dada*, pg.33

[225] Hugo Ball, *Flight Out of Time, A Dada Diary*, pg. 98

The selection of the word "Dada" as a name for the new movement seems to have been made by Hugo Ball during discussions with Tristan Tzara. In a diary entry dated April 18, 1916, Ball notes that he had discussed the word with Tzara on or before that date. "Tzara keeps on worrying about the periodical," he wrote. "My proposal to call it Dada is accepted."[226] Huelsenbeck offers an alternative recollection (one in which he plays a more crucial role). As he remembered it later, the name was chosen at random from a German-French dictionary during a visit with Ball, and that they had reveled in its primitive quality and infantile sound.[227]

DADA BECOMES A MOVEMENT

In an effort to create a more visible public identity, the group held its first "Dada evening" on July 14, 1916, in an old guild house on one of the city's main squares. It was something of a "greatest hits" revival from the Cabaret Voltaire, the cast of regulars recreated their now-familiar routines: Hennings read poems; Arp discussed paper collage; Ball, Huelsenbeck, Janco, and Tzara performed their simultaneous poem; chants nègres were recited while costumed and masked dances took place.[228]

After this first public "Dada evening" Ball began to distance himself from the group. He had always been somewhat ambivalent about the prospect of the activities of the cabaret becoming a broader movement. In 1917 he left Zurich for good, relocating to Bern where he took up a more traditional occupation as a newspaper editor, spending his free time writing about philosophy and religion.

---

[226] Ibid, pg. 63

[227] Leah Dickerman, *Dada*, pg.33

[228] Ibid, 35

After the departure of Hugo Ball, Tristan Tzara stepped into the leadership role of the Zurich Dada group. Tzara was quick to realize the potential power of the word Dada as a brand-name, and he seized the opportunity he now had to promote it with zeal and energy. Huelsenbeck wrote later that it was Tzara's "propagandistic zeal we have to thank for the enormous growth of Dada."[229] Under Ball's leadership, the activities of the Cabaret Voltaire had resembled a zany talent show more than a coherent art movement and Ball made no effort to articulate any specific theory or agenda. Now, with Tzara at the helm, principles and concepts that could be communicated to a wider audience began to emerge.

True to Modernist form, the first item on the agenda was to issue a manifesto. This Tzara did in 1918, publishing the manifesto on March 23rd and proclaiming it publically a few months later. It is simultaneously polemical and nonsensical. Here are a few sample quotations from the opening section of the manifesto:

> The magic of a word – Dada – which has brought journalists to the gates of a world unforeseen, is of no importance to us.
>
> I write this manifesto to show that people can perform contrary actions together while taking one fresh gulp of air; I am against action; for continuous contradiction, for affirmation too, I am neither for nor against and I do not explain because I hate common sense.
>
> DADA - this is a word that throws up ideas so that they can be shot down...
>
> DADA does not mean anything![230]

---

[229] Ibid.

[230] Tristan Tzara, *Dada Manifesto 1918*

Contrary to his insistence that Dada means nothing, Tzara proceeds to lay out some definite ideas about art. He criticizes Cubism and Futurism: "We recognize no theory. We are fed up with the Cubist and Futurist academies..."[231] But, like the Futurists, he reveals a similarly destructive agenda where the past is concerned: "Let each man proclaim: there is a great negative work of destruction to be accomplished. We must sweep and clean."[232] Finally, in the last paragraph of this puzzling and ostentatious document Tzara writes:

> ...abolition of memory: **DADA**; abolition of archaeology: **DADA**; abolition of prophets: **DADA**; abolition of the future: **DADA...Freedom: DADA DADA DADA,** a roaring of tense colors, and interlacing of opposites and of all contradictions, grotesques, inconsistencies: LIFE.

For the French-Spanish artist, Francis Picabia, the *Dada Manifesto* was a breath of fresh air. He wrote to Tzara, "Your manifesto expresses every philosophy seeking truth where there is no truth, only conventions."[233] Picabia had arrived in Switzerland in 1918, seeking treatment for neurasthenia,[234] but his reputation had preceded him. In fact, Tzara had become aware of Picabia long before Picabia knew anything of Dada.

---

[231] Ibid (As a matter of fact, Tzara even announced "the abolition of the future")

[232] ibid

[233] Marius Hentea, *TaTa Dada: The Real Life and Celestial Adventures of Tristan Tzara*, pg. 114

[234] Neurasthenia was a popular diagnosis in the late 19th century, covering a grab-bag of symptoms including headaches, muscle pain, weight loss, irritability, anxiety, impotence, depression, as well as lack of ambition, insomnia, and general lethargy. All of this was generally ascribed to "living too fast". (Julie Beck, *Americanitus, the Disease of Living Too Fast*, from *The Atlantic*, March 11, 2016)

Prior to his arrival in Switzerland, Picabia had been active in the avant-garde art scene in New York, mingling in the Alfred Stieglitz circle and socializing with Marcel Duchamp, not to mention the notoriety that accompanied having his work shown at the infamous 1912 Armory Show.

Picabia lived the fast-paced life of the New York artist to the extreme – smoking opium and drinking whisky every night, driving fast cars and even dodging bullets fired by a jealous husband whose wife PIcabia had seduced.[235]

Finally, Picabia's self-indulgent lifestyle caught up with him and he retreated to Switzerland to seek treatment and psychotherapy. When Tzara discovered that Picabia was in the country, he sent a letter introducing himself, along with gifts of poetry and Dada writings. Picabia reciprocated and soon became an integral part of the Zurich Dada circle. He brought with him the aesthetics and nihilistic outlook of the New York avant-garde and exerted a strong influence on the future direction of Dada as a movement.

THE ART OF THE ZURICH DADAISTS

Dada was never a formal "style" of art; it was a mental attitude with three primary characteristics. First, Dada was anti-war – it grew out of the activities of exiles from the First World War, appalled not only by the war itself, but by the very civilization that had produced it. They were especially contemptuous of naïve ideals of patriotism and nationalism which allowed the old men to send the young men off to certain death. "The beginnings of Dada were not the beginnings of an art," Tristan Tzara wrote later, "but of a disgust..."[236]

---

[235] Jed Rasula, *Destruction Was My Beatrice: Dada and the Unmaking of the Twentieth Century*, pg. 141-149

[236] André Breton, *André Breton: Selections*, pg. 12

Second, Dada was intentionally irrational. Confronted with a world that seemed to make no sense, the Dada artists responded with deliberate nonsense, subverting both the role of art and the artist. As Hans Arp explained, "Dada wished to destroy the hoaxes of reason and discover an unreasoned order."[237]

Third, Dada made use of mockery and parody. The Berlin Dada artists in particular ridiculed the social order, especially political leaders. Those in America, like Marcel Duchamp, derided the art establishment.[238] Hugo Ball, in his final performance at the Dada Evening on July 14, 1916, ridiculed the Zurich Dadaists themselves.[239]

The individual Dada artists displayed a wide variety of techniques and styles. For instance, during his years in Zurich, Arp specialized in collage. Desiring to distance himself from the French Cubists and the German Expressionists, Arp employed purely abstract images. His *Portrait of Tristan Tzara* (1916-1917) makes use of superimposed pieces of wood painted with various colors and kinds of paint. It is completely abstract, bearing no resemblance to the subject whatsoever. In contrast to the *Portrait of Tristan Tzara,* which employs naturalistic flowing lines, his *Rectangles Arranged According to the Laws of Chance* (1916-1917) implies a man-made quality. Arp chose paper squares randomly and assembled them in the order in which they were chosen.[240]

---

[237] Rosalind E. Krauss, *Passages in Modern Sculpture*, pg. 105

[238] In 1919 Duchamp painted a mustache and goatee on a print of the Mona Lisa, his new work, *L.H.O.O.Q*, letters which sound out in the French language, "She has a hot arse." (Jonathan Jones, *L.H.O.O.Q., Marcel Duchamp, The Guardian*, May 26, 2001

[239] Leah Dickerman, *Dada*, pg. 35

[240] Norbert Lynton, *The Story of Modern Art*, pg. 129

During the Zurich years, Picabia was involved with what he called "mechanomorphic" drawings, reflecting his fascination with American machines. In these blueprint-like drawings, Picabia used the shapes of gears, flywheels, and other mechanical parts to create portraits of friends, as well as purely abstract images. At an early meeting with the Zurich Dada group, Picabia reportedly smashed an alarm clock (an act which delighted the Dadaists), removed its mechanical parts, and after dipping them in ink, pressed them to a piece of paper, creating an image.[241] One of these clock images was featured on the cover of a subsequent *Dada* publication (the Tzara-edited successor to the Cabaret Voltaire anthology).[242]

DADA IN BERLIN

In January of 1917, Huelsenbeck left Zurich and returned to Berlin, bringing with him the ideas and techniques with which he had helped to establish Dada in Zurich. Berlin had changed significantly during his absence - from the proud capital of a warlike empire to the capital of a disillusioned nation facing defeat and material deprivation, now suspicious of its leaders and institutions. Huelsenbeck vividly described the scene in his memoir:

> Berlin was a city of tightened stomachers, of mounting, thundering hunger, where hidden rage was transformed into a boundless money lust, and men's minds were concentrating more and more on questions of naked existence... Fear was in everybody's bones.[243]

---

[241] Leah Dickerman, *Dada*, pg. 40

[242] Francis Picabia, *Réveil Matin (Alarm Clock)*, featured on the cover of *Dada 4-5*

[243] Richard Huelsenbeck, *En Avant Dada: A History of Dadaism*, pg. 39

On January 22, 1918, Huelsenbeck spoke at an "author's evening" held at the gallery of I. B. Neumann, delivering a speech entitled *Erste Dada-Rede in Deutschland* (*First Dada Speech in Germany*), in which he recounted the origins and innovations of the Zurich group, casting Dada as something brand new, "neither Futurism nor Cubism". He then read from his book, *Fantastic Prayers*, which he promised would "carry the coloring of this movement".[244]

Huelsenbeck succeeded in attracting the attention of like-minded artists who, in the subsequent weeks joined him in founding the "Club Dada". Among the early members were George Grosz, John Heartfield, Wieland Herzfeld, Raoul Hausmann, Hannah Höch, and Walter Mehring.

On April 12 Huelsenbeck presented his own manifesto. The venue was the meeting place of the Berlin Sezession (named for a group of breakaway artists who had "seceded" in 1898 from the city's art establishment) who were themselves hosting a retrospective exhibition honoring Lovis Corinth, twice president of the Sezession. Speaking before a packed house, Huelsenbeck launched into his presentation with an attack on Expressionism:

> Has Expressionism fulfilled our expectations of such an art, which should be a measure of our most vital concerns? No! No! No! Have the Expressionists fulfilled our expectations of an art that burns the essence of life into our flesh? No! No! No![245]

Using similarly overwrought language, laced with references to explosions, battle cries, and platitudes being torn to pieces, Huelsenbeck made his sales pitch for the Berlin Dada Club, concluding with a straightforward invitation to prospective new members:

---

[244] Richard Huelsenbeck, *Erste Dadarede in Deutschland*

[245] Richard Huelsenbeck, *Dada Manifesto, 1918*

> Dada is a CLUB, founded in Berlin, which you can join without commitments. In this club every man is chairman and every man can have his say in artistic matters.[246]

To round off the evening there were recitations of poetry (with dance) by George Grosz and a speech by Raoul Hausmann urgently expressing the need for the development of "new materials of painting".

Newspaper accounts describe the evening as tumultuous, and asserted that "the threat of violence hung in the air".[247]

> One envisioned Corinth's pictures torn to shreds with chair legs. But in the end, it didn't come to that. As Raoul Hausmann shouted his programmatic plans for Dadaist painting into the noise of the crowd, the manager of the Sezession gallery turned the lights out on him.[248]

Not long after the rambunctious April 12th meeting at which Hausmann called for "new materials" of painting, he hit upon the very form which would come to define the art of the Berlin Dadaists: photomontage.

The moment of inspiration came during a holiday excursion by Hausmann and Hanah Höch (with whom he was then romantically involved). As Höch recounted the story years later, she and Hausmann were amused by a photograph on the wall of a fisherman's cottage where they were staying near the Baltic Sea.

---

[246] ibid

[247] Brigid Doherty, essay on Berlin Dada, from *Dada* by Leah Dickerman, pg.88

[248] ibid

It depicted – fitted in among the pompous emblems of the Empire – five standing soldiers in five different uniforms…upon whom the head of the fisherman's son had five times been glued. This naïvely kitschy oleograph hung in many German rooms as a memento of the son's service as a soldier.[249]

Hausmann said, "It was like a thunderbolt: one could – I saw it instantaneously – make pictures, assembled entirely from cut-up photographs. In Berlin that September, I began to realize this new vision, and I made use of photographs from the press and the cinema."[250] As evidence of the success of the new technique, the "invention of photomontage" was also claimed by George Grosz, John Heartfield, and Johannes Baader.[251]

Whatever the merits of the competing claims of originality, photomontage soon became the primary means of expression by the Berlin Dadaists. One of Hausmann's most striking works is *Elasticum* (1920), in which he combined images, all evidently cut from advertisements, of tires, a speedometer, nuts and bolts and various bits of machinery, with images of Henry Ford, the American inventor of the assembly line, the father of mass-produced automobiles.

The work is aesthetically and thematically consistent, obviously assembled with a practiced sense of artistry.

---

[249] Ibid, pg. 90

[250] Ibid

[251] Ibid, pg. 93-96

By contrast, Hannah Höch's extraordinary masterpiece, *Cut with a Kitchen Knife Through Germany's Last Weimar Beer Belly Cultural Epoch* (1919), appears to be a deliberate jumble of unrelated images pulled at random from the popular culture of Weimar Germany. These cutouts seem not to be fitted together with the intention to make a new singular image from a collection of borrowed parts but simply pasted down, apparently without any consideration whatsoever. Nevertheless, Höch's photomontage graphically conveys the sense of confusion and social upheaval which characterized Germany after the war.

KURT SCHWITTERS AND MERZ

Kurt Schwitters pursued a course parallel to, yet independent from the Berlin Dada Club. He was a German academy-trained artist who, in his early career, adopted the style of the German Expressionists. However, in the social and economic turmoil that took hold of Germany after 1918, Schwitters completely changed his attitude about art. "What I had learned at the academy was of no use to me," he said. "Everything was wrecked anyway and what counted was to construct something from the fragments."[252] Schwitters turned from painting to collage, a technique that had been explored by Picasso and Braque in Paris, and Jean Arp in Zurich. For his particular style of collage, Schwitters used bits of garbage and debris which he found in the streets: an old bus ticket, bits of wood or string, a funnel, a crushed toy train, pieces of newsprint. He called his art "Merz".[253]

---

[252] Clive Frost, *Interview: Fragments of a Life*, from *The Independent*, April 10, 1999

[253] "Merz" is a fragment of the word "Kommerz-und Privatbank" (Commerce and Private Bank). Schwitters had torn these letters from an advertisement for use in an early collage. (Dietmar Elger, *Dada*, pg. 22)

Schwitters' choice of the word Merz as a brand-name for his art stemmed from a feud between the Berlin Dada group and the Sturm gallery in Berlin. The gallery's owner, Herwarth Walden, was the leading dealer in modern art in Germany, having built his reputation on the success of Expressionist and Futurist art. The arrival of Dada, therefore, threatened his status as the leading purveyor of avant-garde art, unless of course he now chose to promote Dada. The Berlin Dadaists, however, refused to deal with Walden because of his well-known association with Expressionism, the style that the Berlin group so vocally scorned. Consequently, in July 1919, when the Sturm Gallery offered Schwitters a prestigious one-man show, he adopted the name "Merz" to describe his art, which might otherwise be judged, on the basis of style and content, to be Dada. The show gave Schwitters national, even international publicity. Perhaps not surprisingly, when Schwitters applied for membership in the Berlin Dada Club, he was rejected by Huelsenbeck.[254]

In the end, this rejection made no difference at all. Kurt Schwitters turned his entire life into one long Merz project, creating Merz-drawings, Merz-paintings, Merz-poetry, and even turning his house in Hannover into a "Merz-bau" (which, sadly was destroyed in Allied bombing of Germany during World War II).

Schwitters found it necessary to escape from Germany during the years of Nazi rule, eventually making his way to Scotland, where he was promptly interned as an "enemy alien".[255] He was released seventeen months later and spent his last years living in England, impoverished and ignored by the British art establishment.[256]

[254] Dorothea Dietrich, essay from *Dada*, by Leah Dickerman, pg. 159

[255] David Galenson, *Kurt Schwitters' Art of Redemption*, *Huffington Post*, December 6, 2017

[256] Edward Lucie-Smith, *Lives of the Great 20th Century Artists*, pg. 140

He nevertheless continued to make collages from pieces of newspaper, found objects and discarded bits of rubbish. After his death, the sculptor Naum Gabo recalled that Schwitters would suddenly stop in the middle of a conversation, staring intently at the ground.

> Then he would pick up something which would turn out to be an old scrap of paper...He would carefully and lovingly clean it up and then triumphantly show it to you. Only then would one realize what an exquisite piece of color was contained in the ragged scrap. It needs a poet like Schwitters to show us that unobserved elements of beauty are strewn and spread all around us and we can find them everywhere...if only we care to look, to choose, and to fit them into a comely order.[257]

Schwitters died ignored and forgotten by the art world. But a later generation of artists, specifically Robert Rauschenberg and Richard Hamilton, would draw inspiration from Schwitters' work, sparking renewed interest and appreciation of his remarkable and highly personal art.

DADA IN NEW YORK

When Marcel Duchamp arrived in New York in 1915, he was no stranger to controversy or to provocation. His 1912 work, *Nude Descending a Staircase,* had scandalized the 1913 Armory Show, the exhibition which introduced modern art to America.

Duchamp was born in 1887 in Normandy, the son of a successful notary and one of six children – three boys and three girls. He began his career in art as an imitator of Cézanne but later adopted Cubism.

---

[257] David Galenson, *Kurt Schwitters' Art of Redemption, Huffington Post,* December 6, 2017

His *Nude Descending a Staircase* combined Cubism with the Futurist technique of revealing motion by painting simultaneous multiple frames. When it was submitted to the Salon des Indépendents, the hanging committee found it so unsettling that Duchamp was forced to withdraw it from consideration.[258]

Duchamp had better luck in 1913 when *Nude Descending a Staircase* was accepted for exhibition in the International Exhibition of Modern Art to be held at the National Guard Armory in New York City alongside works by Picasso, Matisse, and a host of other modern artists. The "Armory Show" was designed to be an introduction for Americans to the new experimental styles of the recent European painters, including examples of Impressionism, Fauvism, Cubism, and Futurism.

News reports and reviews of the Armory Show were generally hostile, filled with accusations of quackery, insanity, immorality, and anarchy. One former president, Theodore Roosevelt, reportedly "waved his arms and stomped through the galleries pointing at pictures and saying, 'That's not art!'"[259] However, one work was singled out for special scorn: Duchamp's *Nude Descending a Staircase*. One art critic said that it "resembled an explosion in a shingle factory".[260] Thanks to the controversy surrounding the work, Duchamp became an instant celebrity in the United States.

---

[258] Edward Lucie-Smith, *Lives of the Great 20th Century Artists*, pg.135

[259] Harold Rosenberg, *The Armory Show: Revolution Reenacted, The New Yorker*, April 6, 1963 P. 99

[260] Bennard B. Perlman, *Painters of the Ashcan School: The Immortal Eight*, pg. 210

In 1915, Duchamp, exempt from military service in France due to frail health, came to the United States, where he found himself at the center of a dynamic group of admiring young artists, including Francis Picabia, who would join the Zurich Dadaists in 1918, and Man Ray, the surrealist photographer. For Hans Richter, the German-born modernist painter and film-maker, Duchamp's nihilistic wit and intelligence were intoxicating:

> Duchamp's attitude is that life is a melancholy joke, an indecipherable nonsense, not worth the trouble of investigating. To his superior intelligence the total absurdity of life, the contingent nature of a world denuded of all values, are logical consequences of Descartes' statement, 'I think, therefore I am'.[261]

Even more important for Duchamp than this circle of young artists, was his introduction to the wealthy art patrons, Louise and Walter Arensberg, who hosted informal parties open to artists and intellectuals in their New York apartment on West 67th Street.[262]

---

[261] Hilton Kramer, *The Triumph of Modernism*, pg. 185

[262] "To term these gatherings a salon would be too polite. The use of recreational drugs was tolerated, but the narcotic of choice was alcohol. Evenings at Walter and Lou's lasted until quite late, and often got quite rowdy. At one, a guest mounted a flight of stairs, opened his trousers and urinated down the steps. This was cheered as an artistic statement and was said to have inspired Duchamp's 'Fountain,' which consisted of an inverted urinal... Though Lou Arensberg, who did not drink, tried to maintain a minimal amount of decorum by playing selections at her Steinway, she was often drowned out by shouts and noisy scuffles elsewhere in the apartment. Isadora Duncan was responsible for the loss of Walter's front teeth when, after much champagne, she seized him in a wild embrace, which sent him crashing, face first, to the floor. Parties often wound down at a neighborhood bar where, on at least one occasion, Arensberg was again flattened in a fist fight, and Duchamp received a nasty gash in the ear." (Stephen Birmingham, *Art That's Still Armed and Dangerous*, The New York Times, September 8, 1996)

The Arensbergs heavily subsidized Duchamp, providing him with a studio and offering to pay his rent in New York in exchange for a promised, but then incomplete work entitled *Large Glass*.[263] (In fact, Duchamp abandoned the *Large Glass* in 1923, deciding that it should remain "definitively unfinished".) [264]

After the *Nude Descending a Staircase*, Duchamp began to withdraw from the traditional act of painting more and more. At the same time, expressing a desire to relinquish control of his art, he began to incorporate elements of chance. In *3 Standard Stoppages* (1913-1914) he dropped three pieces of sewing thread, each one meter long, onto a canvas from a height of one meter, then fixed them in the irregular, unpredictable position in which they fell. He then cut out wooden templates to match the contours of each string, and offered the strings and matching wooden forms as the finished work of art. In the remarkable *Network of Stoppages* (1914), Duchamp used the templates from *3 Standard Stoppages*, each repeated three times, to form a kind of railway map, which he affixed to an old unfinished canvas.[265]

Duchamp soon abandoned painting altogether. Seeking an alternative to representing objects in paint, Duchamp began presenting objects themselves as art.

These "readymades", as he called them, challenged centuries of thinking about the artist's role as a skilled creator of original handmade objects. Instead, Duchamp argued, "An ordinary object [could be] elevated to the dignity of a work of art by the mere choice of an artist."[266]

---

[263] Larry Witham, *Picasso and the Chess Player: Pablo Picasso, Marcel Duchamp, and the Battle for the Soul of Modern Art*, pg. 112

[264] Martha Buskirk, ed. *The Duchamp Effect*, pg. 81

[265] Norbert Lynton, *The Story of Modern Art*, pg. 130-131

[266] Thomas Deane Tucker, *Derridada: Duchamp as Readymade Deconstruction*,

Duchamp expanded on this idea in his 1957 essay, *The Creative Act*, in which he argues that a work of art is ultimately defined, not by the intent and actions of the artist, but by the viewer, who "consecrates" the artist's product as "art". Since the artist "plays no role at all in the judgment of his own work," Duchamp asks,

> how can one describe the phenomenon which prompts the spectator to react critically to the work of art? ...This phenomenon is comparable to a transference from the artist to the spectator in the form of an esthetic osmosis taking place through the inert matter, such as pigment, piano or marble... the spectator experiences the phenomenon of transmutation: through the change from inert matter into a work of art, an actual transubstantiation has taken place, and the role of the spectator is to determine the weight of the work on the esthetic scale.[267]

Duchamp's essay is laced with sarcasm, ridiculing with subtlety and sophistication both the art establishment and the general viewing public.

His "readymades" illustrate his point perfectly: an artist may submit a painting over which he has labored for years or a common everyday object requiring no inspiration or labor at all – in the end, there is no difference because posterity, not the artist, establishes the value and significance of the work of art, in effect, negating the role of the artist entirely.

The first readymade submitted for exhibition was an ordinary snow shovel purchased at a hardware store on which Duchamp carefully painted the humorous title, "*Prelude to a Broken Arm – from Marcel Duchamp, 1915*".[268]

---

pg. 45

[267] Marcel Duchamp, *The Creative Act*, 1957

Duchamp's most famous (or infamous) readymade is entitled *Fountain*. It is a porcelain urinal on which Duchamp signed the name of a fictional artist, "R. Mutt". In 1917, while Duchamp was a member of the board of the Society of Independent Artists in New York, and without the knowledge of the board, he submitted the *Fountain* anonymously, under the name "R. Mutt". After much debate by the board, it was agreed that *Fountain* was not art and would not be shown. Duchamp promptly resigned from the board in protest.

The New York Dadaists attempted to create a controversy over the rejection. In the next issue of their publication, *The Blind Man*, there appeared an editorial (evidently written by Duchamp) entitled, "The Richard Mutt Case". It offers a revealing glimpse into the artistic philosophy of Marcel Duchamp:

> They say any artist paying six dollars may exhibit. Mr. Richard Mutt sent in a fountain. Without discussion this article disappeared and never was exhibited. What were the grounds for refusing Mr. Mutt's fountain: 1 Some contended it was immoral, vulgar. 2 Others, it was plagiarism, a plain piece of plumbing.
>
> Now Mr. Mutt's fountain is not immoral, that is absurd, no more than a bathtub is immoral. It is a fixture that you see every day in plumbers' show windows. Whether Mr. Mutt with his own hands made the fountain or not has no importance. He CHOSE it. He took an ordinary article of life, placed it so that its useful significance disappeared under the new title and point of view—created a new thought for that object. As for plumbing, that is absurd. The only works of art America has given are her plumbing and her bridges.[269]

---

[268] ibid

[269] Walter Kalaidjian, *The Cambridge Companion to American Modernism*, pg. 209

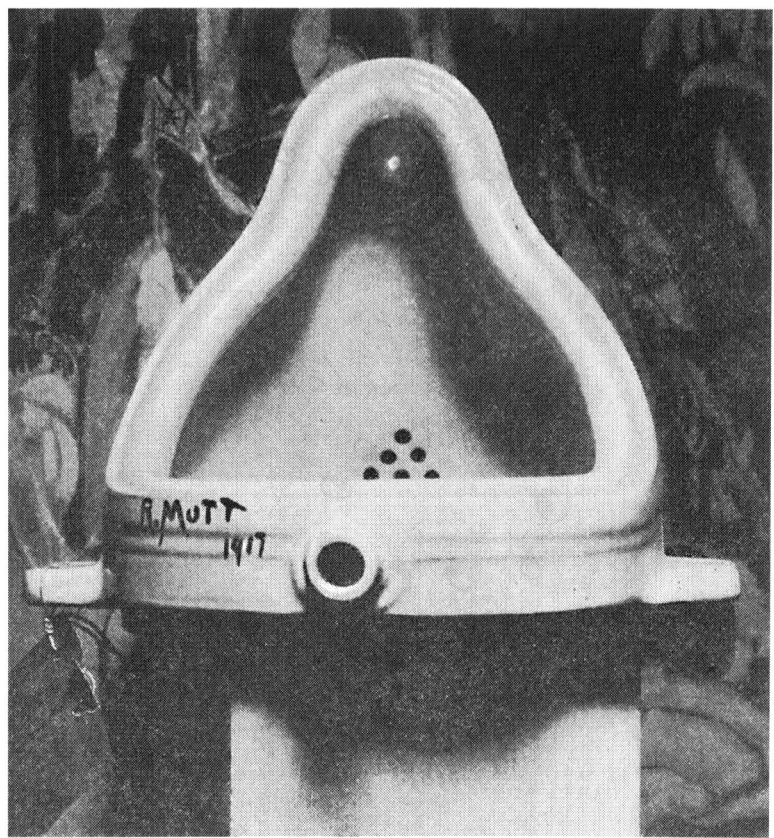

Marcel Duchamp, *Fountain* (1917) (public domain)

The original *Fountain* was photographed by Alfred Stieglitz and the photograph was published along with the editorial response to its rejection by the Society of Independent Artists. Unfortunately, the original work was lost, probably thrown out with the garbage by Stieglitz. Later, in response to enquiries by museum curators, Duchamp authorized replicas to be made in 1950, 1953 and 1963. Finally, in 1964, he authorized twelve more replicas (edition of eight with four proofs).[270]

---

[270] *Rogue urinals*, from *The Economist*, March 24, 2010

In an ironic, if belated, justification of Duchamp's sensibilities, a 2004 a poll of 500 art experts resulted in Marcel Duchamp's *Fountain* being named the most influential modern artwork of all time.[271]

---

[271] Louise Jury, *'Fountain' most influential piece of modern art*, from *The Independent*, December 4, 2004

CHAPTER SEVEN: NEOCLASSICISM CALLS TO ORDER

The First World War – the "war to end all wars" - represented the largest collective trauma the world had experienced up until that point. Artists responded to the war in various ways: German Expressionists attempted to capture the psychological angst that permeated society before and during the war. The Dadaists responded to the senselessness of the conflict by creating deliberately senseless art. However, by the conclusion of the war, the extreme experimentalism of the early 20th century no longer seemed to be an appropriate response to the authentic horrors of war. In the aftermath of the war, many artists turned away from the overt emotional turmoil of Expressionism and the cynical nihilism of Dada and embraced more reserved, traditional forms.

The Deluge (1920) is a painting by the British artist, Winifred Knights. The title, of course, refers to the story of the biblical flood. However, in view of the fact that the people in the image are clearly dressed in modern attire, the symbolism becomes clear – these are ordinary people fleeing from the cataclysm of the recent war. In fact, Winifred Knights has painted herself into the scene – she is the frightened woman in the right foreground. She was personally traumatized by what she experienced in the war, having witnessed the largest explosion on British soil during the conflict, in which 600 homes were destroyed and 73 lives were lost. Having experienced something of the actual horror of war firsthand, in her art she psychologically distances herself from the experience, first by presenting it in a metaphoric allusion to the biblical flood, and second, by the use of restrained imagery and muted cool colors.[272]

---

[272] Kathryn Hughes, *How painter Winifred Knights became Britain's 'unknown genius'*, from *The Guardian*, June 25, 2016

Winifred Knights, *The Deluge* (1920) (public domain)

In 1926 the French writer Jean Cocteau published a book of essays entitled *Call to Order*. The book included an inflammatory 1918 essay called *Cock and Harlequin*, in which Cocteau railed against the excesses of Modernism, calling for a return to order and simplicity: "A poet always has too many words in his vocabulary, a painter too many colors on his palette, and a musician too many notes on his keyboard."[273] In an oblique criticism of the music of Debussy, he wrote, "Enough of clouds, waves, aquariums, water sprites and nocturnal scents; what we need is a music of the earth, everyday music."[274]

In this 74 page manifesto, Cocteau argues for a new kind of modernism which would paradoxically be extremely classical. Cocteau's essay proved to be very popular and influential in that he seemed to capture the postwar climate that other artists, musicians, and writers were already sensing.

---

[273] William Oliver Strunk, *Source Readings in Music History, Volume 1*, pg. 1290

[274] Ibid, pg. 1292

At the beginning of the century, artists of all kinds had repudiated the rules of their craft and found themselves in possession of astonishing new freedoms. But when the optimism that had characterized their pre-war experiments in Modernism evaporated in the bitter aftermath of the First World War, many of these same artists now began to feel that stability was perhaps more important than freedom.[275]

This perceived need for stability was expressed in a desire for a new discipline, or even a return to the traditional disciplines of the past. Many of the artists who had been innovators of extreme avant-garde practices in the early years of the century, now turned to classical models of expression.

In February of 1917, Picasso traveled to Italy where he saw the celebrated collections of ancient sculpture at the Vatican, as well as Roman mosaics and paintings at Pompeii. This evidently inspired Picasso's competitive and cannibalistic instincts. Very soon afterwards, Picasso abandoned Cubism, with its fragmented portrayal of reality, and embraced a new, more realistic mode of painting, inspired by the traditional classical models he had seen in Italy.

Meanwhile, in Germany, G. F. Hartlaub, director of the Municipal Gallery in Mannheim began to observe a tendency on the part of German artists in the 1920s away from Expressionism and towards greater realism. In 1923 he coined a term for this neat, unemotional, apparently objective art, calling it *Neue Sachlichkeit*, or "The New Objectivity".[276] Hartlaub began to gather works that displayed these characteristics and in 1925 presented an exhibition called *Neue Sachlichkeit*.[277]

---

[275] Norbert Lynton, The Story of Modern Art, pg. 154

[276] Although "New Objectivity" has been the most common translation of *Neue Sachlichkeit*, other possible translations into English might plausibly be "New Matter-of-factness", "New Resignation", "New Sobriety", and "New Dispassion"

The New Objectivity was not a true movement – it was merely a convenient label shrewdly applied by a museum director to a trend he had observed.[278] In the same year as the New Objectivity exhibition, art critic Franz Roh published his *Nach Expressionismus: Magischer Realismus: Probleme der neuesten europäischen Malerei* (*After expressionism: Magical Realism: Problems of the newest European painting*) in which he celebrated the return to realistic imagery. (By "magical" he did not mean "supernatural", but rather that the objects of ordinary life seem new and strange when they become the focal point of a work of art.)

In an appendix, Roh published an insightful two-column comparison between Expressionist art and the new art which was beginning to appear, which he called "Post-Expressionist" art. [279]

---

[277] Norbert Lynton, *The Story of Modern Art*, pg. 156

[278] Ibid

[279] Anton Kaes, Franz Roh, *"Post-Expressionist Schema"* (1925), from *The Weimar Republic Sourcebook*

EXPRESSIONISM	POST-EXPRESSIONISM
ecstatic objects	plain objects
religioius themes	few religious themes
stifled object	explanatory object
rhythmic	representative
arousing	engrossing
excessive	rather strict, purist
dynamic	static
loud	quiet
summary	sustained
obvious	enigmatic
close-range image	long-range image
forward moving	also flowing backward
large size	many-columned
monumental	miniature
warm	cool to cold
thick coloration	thin layer of color
roughened	smooth
like uncut stone	like polished metal
work process preserved	work process effaced
leaving traces	
expressive deformation of objects	harmonic cleansing of objects
rich in diagonals	rectangular to frame
often actue-angled	parallel
working against edges of image	fixed within edges of image
primitive	civilized

As an illustration of the differences pointed out by Roh, look at a 1907 work by Ernst Ludwig Kirchner, *Erich Heckel and Otto Mueller playing chess*. Using Roh's table as a checklist, how many items in the Expressionism column does Kirchner's work match? Except for the first two items, ecstatic images, and religious themes, it matches the Expressionist list at nearly every point: it is dynamic, loud, thickly colored, rich in diagonals, working against the edges of the image, and primitive.

By contrast, look at an example of the "New Objectivity", the 1927 work, *On the Balcony*, by Georg Schrimpf. It is static, quiet, enigmatic, using cool colors, rectangular to the frame, and civilized.

Georg Schrimpf came to painting gradually, after working all sorts of jobs. He was entirely self-taught, and sketched constantly as a young man, learning his art by painting from nature and studying the old masters. With the outbreak of the First World War, the pacifistic Schrimpf went to great lengths to avoid service but ruined his health in the process.[280] His images are realistic, clear, simple, and ordinary, but at the same time, they create a sense of subtle unease because of their emotional detachment. For instance, in the work discussed above, *On the Balcony*, the shadows, and the fact that the figures are turned away from the viewer all contribute to a subtle sense of uneasiness about the meaning of the scene.

THE DARK SIDE OF CLASSICISM: HITLER, NAZIS AND ART

Hitler was an artist and had definite ideas about art. He was a classicist and detested Modernism. He admired the art of ancient Greece and Rome, which he considered to be the ultimate example of taste and craftsmanship, uncontaminated by Jewish influence.[281]

He judged modern art to be an act of aesthetic violence perpetrated by Jews against the German spirit.[282] When he came to power in January 1933, Hitler made cultural purification a top priority.

---

[280] Sergiusz Michalski, *Neue Sachlichkeit: Malerei, Graphik und Photographie in Deutschland 1919-1933*, pg. 74

[281] Sherree Owens Zalampas, *Adolf Hitler: A Psychological Interpretation of Hs Views on Architecture, Art, and Music*, pg. 73

[282] No one apparently pointed out to Hitler that, at least in Germany, very few modern artists were, in fact Jewish.

In September of 1933, the *Reichskulturkammer* (the Reich Culture Chamber) was established with Joseph Goebbels as Reich Minister for Public Enlightenment and Propaganda. The purpose of this chamber was to "stimulate the Aryanization of German culture and to prohibit atonal Jewish music, the blues, surrealism, cubism, and Dadaism."[283] By 1935 there were 100,000 members of the Reich Culture Chamber and Goebbels made it clear that only members of the Chamber would be allowed to be productive in cultural life.[284]

Some Expressionist artists sought accommodation with the new Nazi regime. Ernst Ludwig Kirchner, founder of *Die Brucke* and pioneer of German Expressionism, responded to pressure to resign from the Prussian Academy of Arts by writing the following letter:

> For more than thirty years I have struggled through my work for a new, strong, and authentic German art and will continue to do this as long as I live. I am neither a Jew nor a Social Democrat, nor otherwise politically active, and in general, have a clean conscience. I am therefore waiting patiently to see what the new government will do with regard to the question of the Academy and leave with confidence the question of my membership in your hands.[285]

---

[283] World Heritage Encyclopedia, *Art of the Third Reich*

[284] Jonathan Petropoulos, *The Faustian Bargain: The Art World in Nazi Germany*, pg.25

There was, in fact, some initial disagreement within the Nazi leadership on the subject of Expressionism. Some, including Goebbels, thought that forceful works of Expressionism exemplified the Nordic spirit. "We National Socialists are not un-modern;" Goebbels argued, "we are the carrier of a new modernity, not only in politics and in social matters but also in art and intellectual matters."[286] Others, including Goebbels' bitter rival, Alfred Rosenberg, were violently opposed to Expressionism. The matter was finally settled by Hitler himself, who declared that there would be no place for modernist experimentation within the Reich.[287]

HITLER'S CALL TO ORDER

On July 18, 1937, Hitler made a speech, officially opening the "Great German Art Exhibition" which showcased art approved by the Nazi regime. After some perfunctory remarks, he came straight to the point, first taking aim at artists influenced by Primitivism:

> It is either impudent effrontery or an inscrutable stupidity to exhibit to our own age works that might have been made ten or twenty thousand years ago by a man of the Stone Age. They talk of primitive art, but they forget that it is not the function of art to retreat backward from the level of development a people has already reached.[288]

Hitler then attacked the Expressionists more explicitly:

[286] Thomas Patteson, *Instruments for New Music: Sound, Technology, and Modernism*, pg. 136

[287] Jacob Phillips, *Dietrich Bonhoeffer's Discipleship and German Expressionism*, from *Modernism, Christianity and Apocalypse*, pg. 62

[288] *Hitler's Speech at the Opening of the House of German Art in Munich*, July 18, 1937

I must assume that the eyes of some men show them things differently from the way they really are. Are there really men who can see in the shapes of our people only decayed cretins? Who feel that meadows are blue, the heavens green, clouds sulfur-yellow? They like to say that they experience these things in this way.[289]

Hitler goes on to say that if these artists really do see things this way, then they are in need of medical or psychological treatment. However, he adds ominously, if they do not really mean it when they say they see things this way, then perhaps it is a matter for the criminal court.

According to Hitler, it is well known that modern art is neither liked nor appreciated by the ordinary man-in-the-street. However, the Führer says that when this same ordinary citizen passes through these state-approved galleries, he will draw a sigh of relief at the purification of art. These common folk, Hitler asserts, "will recognize in me [their] own counselor and spokesman."[290]

The state-approved art on display in the Great German Art Exhibition of 1937 was uniformly academic, neoclassical, and dull. In photographs of the event, even Hitler looks bored. However, a far more interesting exhibition was to open the very next day, just down the road: the now infamous "Entartete Kunst" (Degenerate Art exhibition), featuring works representing all the modernist styles: Expressionism, Cubism, Surrealism, Dada, and abstraction.

On one of the walls of the Degenerate Art exhibition was a quote from a 1935 speech by the Führer which summed up the now firmly-fixed attitude of the Nazi regime towards all modern art, especially Expressionism:

---

[289] ibid

[290] ibid

> It is not the mission of art to wallow in filth for filth's sake, to paint the human being only in a state of putrefaction, to draw cretins as symbols of motherhood, or to present deformed idiots as representatives of manly strength.[291]

Earlier in the year a commission headed by Adolf Ziegler had been assigned the task of purging German museums of unacceptable art. Some 600 of the works seized by Ziegler's commission appeared in the Degenerate Art exhibition, hung at crazy angles, with derisive slogans painted on the walls nearby.

The art was divided into different rooms by category - art that was blasphemous, art by Jewish or communist artists, art that criticized German soldiers, art that offended the honor of German women. One room which featured entirely abstract paintings was labeled "the insanity room" – the guidebook for this room read: "In the paintings and drawings of this chamber of horrors there is no telling what was in the sick brains of those who wielded the brush or the pencil."[292]

The idea of the exhibition was not just to mock modern art, but to encourage the viewers to see it as part of an evil plot against the German people, polluting "Aryan" culture with alien influences.

The curators went to some lengths to get the message across, even hiring actors to mingle with the crowds and criticize the exhibits.[293]

---

[291] Jason Farago, *Degenerate Art: The Attack on Modern Art in Nazi Germany, 1937 review – What Hitler dismissed as 'filth'*, from The Guardian, March 13, 2014

[292] *Guide to the "Degenerate Art" Exhibition* (1937), group 9

[293] Paul Vallely, *A glimpse inside the forgotten world of Nazi art*, from The Independent, October 7, 2007

One reviewer of the exhibition wrote, "These artists should be tied to their paintings so as to provide every German with the opportunity of spitting in their faces; not just the artists but also the directors of the museums who in a period of massive unemployment stuffed great sums in the mouths of these horrors."[294]

The exhibition was a tremendous hit with the German public. More than three million people came to see it in Munich and the other cities in Germany where it appeared later.[295] For the artists now declared to be degenerate, however, it was a devastating blow.

Ernst Ludwig Kirchner, leader of *Die Brucke* was denounced as a degenerate artist. The Nazis removed 639 of his works from public display in Germany. The following year he committed suicide by gunshot.[296]

Erich Heckel, another founding member of *Die Brucke* was denounced as a degenerate artist and prohibited from exhibiting his artwork. 729 of his works were confiscated from public collections. His studio and its contents in Berlin were destroyed during World War II. He survived the war and the Nazis and died in 1970.[297]

Franz Marc, founder of *Der Blaue Reiter*, though he was killed in action during World War I, and despite his decorated war record, was posthumously condemned as degenerate, and 130 of his works were removed from public collections.[298]

---

[294] ibid

[295] ibid

[296] Martin Edmond, *The Resurrection of Philip Clairmont*, pg. 142

[297] Klaus H. Carl, *German Painting*

[298] Starr Figura, Peter Jelavich, *German Expressionism: The Graphic Impulse*, pg. 250 – It must be added that Franz Marc's large painting, *Tower of Blue Horses* was removed from the Degenerate Art exhibition after protest by the League of German

Oskar Kokoschka, the Viennese Expressionist, was labeled a degenerate artist, and 417 of his works were confiscated from German museums. Having fled to Prague in 1934 to escape the Nazis, he responded to the Degenerate Art exhibition with defiance, creating a painting of himself called *Self-Portrait as a Degenerate Artist*. The following year he escaped again, this time to London. He spent his final years, from 1953 to 1980, in Switzerland.[299]

Georg Schrimpf, despite being part of the New Objectivity, and despite the realistic style of his painting, was nevertheless declared to be degenerate – probably due to the fact that he had joined the German Communist Party in 1919 (even though he had left the party in 1926 and had since been appointed to a teaching position by the Nazi regime). His works were banned from public display (though some Nazi leaders, including Rudolf Hess, owned works by Schrimpf).[300]

If the Nazi Degenerate Art exhibition strikes us today as a demagogic and wholly irrational exercise, it must be admitted that the disposal of their newly seized stockpile of degenerate art was entirely pragmatic.

After the show closed in 1939, 1000 paintings and 4000 watercolors – mostly works that were deemed political in nature - were publically burned.[301] The more important pieces, however, were sold on the international market, including works by Georges Braque, Marc Chagall, Paul Gauguin, Van Gogh, Modigliani, Matisse, Picasso, and Paul Klee, most going to American collectors.[302]

Army Officers based on Marc's honorable military service, including his death at Verdun.

[299] Frank Whitford, *Oskar Kokoschka, a life*, pg. 162

[300] Gen Doy, *Seeing and consciousness*, pg. 157

[301] The works that were burned were those assessed by the Nazis to be of little value in the international art market.

NEOCLASSICISM IN MUSIC

Neoclassicism in music implies an objective, emotionally detached style that depends on traditional tonality. As a movement, it was anti-Romantic, repudiating the emotional and subjective music of the late 19th and early 20th century. Perhaps it goes without saying that Neoclassicism was opposed to the twelve-tone music of Schoenberg as well.

When Jean Cocteau issued his "call to order" in 1918, he condemned the music of Wagner, Debussy, and Igor Stravinsky, mentioning these composers by name. Cocteau, in his attack on Modernism, was especially harsh in his criticism of Stravinsky: "he does not try to hypnotize us or plunge us into semi-darkness [like Wagner]; he hits us over the head."[303] It is surprising to note that the most visible spokesman for Neoclassicism in music was none other than the arch-modernist, Igor Stravinsky.

Stravinsky adopted the philosophy of Neoclassicism wholeheartedly, calling it "a wholesome return to [the] formal idea…"[304] Aligning Neoclassicism with the anti-expressionist mood of the time, Stravinsky wrote:

> I consider that music is powerless to express anything at all, whether a feeling, an attitude of mind, a psychological mood, or a phenomenon of nature. Expression has never been an inherent property of music. That is by no means the purpose of its existence.[305]

---

[302] Paul Vallely, *A glimpse inside the forgotten world of Nazi art*, from *The Independent*, October 7, 2007

[303] Jean Cocteau, *A Call to Order*, pg. 34

[304] Joan Peyser, *To Boulez and Beyond*, pg. 99

[305] ibid

A convergence of factors led to Stravinsky's embrace of Neoclassicism, not the least of which can be traced to events in his native Russia. In October of 1917, at the height of the First World War, a communist-led revolution took place in Russia. Ill-equipped and poorly led, the Russian army had suffered catastrophic losses in campaign after campaign against the armies of Germany. In addition to battlefield failures, governmental inefficiency, corruption, and riots over the scarcity of food made revolution all but inevitable.

The 1917 Communist Revolution deprived Stravinsky of his family's property in Russia, cutting him off from a formerly secure source of income. Other personal losses occurred at nearly the same time: his brother died in Russia, and the nurse who had tended to his family and children in Paris also died.

To add insult to injury, the Ballets Russes had been invited to go on tour in America, and Stravinsky, who very much wanted to go and conduct his own compositions, was not invited. Stravinsky summed up his dire situation:

> This period, the end of 1917, was one of the hardest I have ever experienced. The Communist Revolution, which had just triumphed in Russia, deprived me of the last resources that had still, from time to time, been reaching me from my country and I found myself, so to speak, face to face with nothing, in a foreign land and right in the middle of war.[306]

---

[306] Ibid, pg. 90-91

It was Serge Diaghilev, the impresario of the Ballets Russes who had lifted Stravinsky out of anonymity in 1909, who came to his rescue again. He commissioned Stravinsky to string together a group of pieces attributed to a little-known 18th-century composer named Pergolesi. This new ballet, to be entitled *Pulcinella*, was to be a period piece. Diaghilev had created the scenario from an 18th-century Neapolitan manuscript. Picasso was to design the sets, capturing the spirit of the time with his current neoclassical style, and Stravinsky was asked for nothing more than "stylish orchestration" of the period music of Pergolesi.

What Stravinsky did with the music that was furnished to him by Diaghilev was not exactly a "stylish orchestration" - a better description would be a distilled reiteration of the original music, filtered through Stravinsky's own personality.

Picasso, who designed the sets for *Pulcinella*, himself no stranger to artistic cannibalism, wrote, "We pick out what is good for us where we find it. When I am shown a portfolio of old drawings, for instance, I have no qualms about taking what I want from them."[307]

There is more than a little irony in Stravinsky's appropriation of Pergolesi – much of the music which Stravinsky reworked was not composed by Pergolesi at all. In fact, Pergolesi, who lived from 1710-1736, was himself the subject of fraud: because his music was so popular in his day (and even after his premature death), publishers sold under his name all kinds of different pieces of music which were not, in fact, written by him.[308]

Stravinsky admitted that he changed very little of the faux-Pergolesi music that was given to him.

---

[307] Ibid, pg. 92

[308] Daniel Albright, *Putting Modernism Together*, pg. 164

"The remarkable thing about *Pulcinella* is not how much but how little has been added or changed."[309] What exactly did Stravinsky do to the music? He seems to have retained the overall form of the original pieces, retaining both the melody and the bass line. His real work was to change the instrumentation and the internal harmonies, adding subtle dissonances and making other musical changes seemingly designed to remove all trace of expression or emotion from the music.

Pulcinella premiered in Paris on May 15, 1920, and was generally met with a favorable response from audiences. Critics, however, seemed puzzled and found it difficult to reconcile the newly neoclassical Stravinsky of *Pulcinella* with the formerly modernist Stravinsky of *The Rite of Spring*. Champions of the avant-garde viewed Stravinsky as a traitor.[310] On the other hand, those who viewed themselves as defenders of tradition, saw Stravinsky's treatment of Pergolesi's original work as "disrespectful" and a "sacrilege".[311]

One of those who saw Stravinsky's Neoclassicism as a betrayal of Modernism was Arnold Schoenberg, still living in Germany at the time. He responded in 1925 with a special piece for choir entitled *Three Satires* in which he mocks composers who

> ...nibble at dissonances, wanting to pass for modern, but who are too cautious to draw the consequences...I take aim at those who pretend to aspire "back to..." ...This backwards-rake, just now reborn, missed a lot in school and must therefore at once newly experience the tonic and the dominant.[312]

---

[309] Harry Haskell, *The Early Music Revival: A History*, pg.76

[310] Maureen A. Carr, *After the Rite: Stravinsky's Path to Neoclassicism (1914-1925)*, pg.28

[311] Ibid.

In the second of the *Three Satires*, Schoenberg's text ridicules Stravinsky directly:

> Who's this beating the drum?
>
> It's Little Modernsky!
>
> He's had his hair cut in an old-fashioned queue
>
> And it looks quite nice,
>
> Like real false hair –
>
> Like a wig – just like (at least Little Modernsky thinks so)
>
> Just like Father Bach![313]

Stravinsky admitted to friends that Schoenberg's attack hurt him deeply, much more than any attack in the press.[314] However, in spite of attacks by fellow composers like Schoenberg, he continued to explore Neoclassicism for the next thirty years.

Though his initial neoclassical work, *Pulcinella*, could be rightly described as a "cutting and pasting" of Pergolesi, Stravinsky was too much of an artist to continue merely cannibalizing music of the past. In his later neoclassical works, he displayed far more original and interesting examples of this aesthetic orientation.

---

[312] Joseph Auner, *A Schoenberg Reader: Documents of a Life*, pg. 187

[313] Ibid, pg. 188

[314] Joan Peyser, *To Boulez and Beyond*, pg. 99

One of Stravinsky's last works in the now fully-assimilated neoclassical style was a ballet entitled *Orpheus* (1948). In 1947 he was commissioned by the New York-based Ballet Society to write the music for a ballet, with sets to be designed by the modernist sculptor, Isamu Noguchi. In keeping with the anti-expressionistic character of Neoclassicism, the work is starkly unemotional. The strings play without vibrato, producing a cold and emotionally detached sound. The tempo is slow and austere with no rhythmic urgency at all. The opening bars evoke the world of the ancient Greeks, imitating the tones of the harp of Orpheus, playing descending four-note fragments, a subtle reference to the Greek conception of tetrachords.

Igor Stravinsky, *Orpheus* (1948)

In 1948, Stravinsky was seen as the living embodiment of Neoclassicism. The shock wave he had created twenty-eight years earlier by his conversion from primitivist Modernism to Neoclassicism was all but forgotten. As events would soon reveal, however, Stravinsky had one final surprise in store.

CHAPTER EIGHT: ART AND MUSIC IN THE SOVIET UNION: CREATIVITY UNDER THREAT OF VIOLENCE

Before the outbreak of the First World War in 1914, Russian artists traveled regularly in Europe. Some of them had long working periods in Paris and became a conduit of information and influence in Russia. European avant-garde movements of the early twentieth century, like Symbolism and Futurism, inspired similar groups in Russia. The Russian adaptations of these Western art movements were often less materialistic in their outlook, instead emphasizing spirituality and a quest for hidden realities. The motto of the Russian Symbolists reveals this tendency: "From reality to a more-real hidden reality".[315]

MALEVICH AND SUPREMATISM

Suprematism was a uniquely Russian art movement, the brainchild of an art theoretician named Kazimir Malevich. Malevich had earlier experimented with Cubism and other European avant-garde techniques, but in 1915, after painting a large black square on a white background, he proclaimed that he had arrived at a form of art superior to all the art of the past. In his subsequent manifesto, entitled From Cubism to Suprematism, he wrote that Suprematism would lead to a "supremacy of pure feeling or perception in the pictorial arts."[316]

For Malevich, Suprematism represented the search for the bare essentials of art, the "zero degree" of representation, the point beyond which the medium could not go and still be considered art.[317]

---

[315] Lincoln Ballard, Matthew Bengtson, *The Alexander Scriabin Companion: History, Performance, and Lore*, pg. 175

[316] Museum of Modern Art: *MoMA Highlights: 350 Works from The Museum of Modern Art*, New York, pg. 67

This is exactly how Malevich described his painting, the *Black Square*, with which he launched the Suprematist movement. In keeping with the Suprematists' emphasis on the surface texture, the image is rough, and the paint is cracked. As to the content, the *Black Square* has been variously described as "nothing", "void", "the abyss", "infinity",[318] and "most enigmatic, and most frightening painting known to man".[319]

Kazimir Malevich, *The Black Square* (1915) (public domain)

Malevich and the Suprematists were influenced by a group of literary critics called the Russian Formalists.[320]

---

[317] Svetlana Boym, *Another Freedom: The Alternative History of an Idea*, pg. 3

[318] Octavian Esanu, *Transition in Post-Soviet Art: The Collective Actions Group Before and After 1989*, pg. 85

[319] Tatyana Tolstaya, *The Square*, from *The New Yorker*, June 12, 2015

[320] Under Stalin, the term "formalism" became a negative kind of shorthand expression, meaning any sort of elitist art.

The Formalists were Malevich's contemporaries and were opposed to the idea that language is a simple, transparent vehicle for communication.

Rather, they proposed that there is a fundamental opposition between practical, ordinary language on the one hand, which is used simply to communicate, and poetic or literary language on the other hand, which offers readers a special, heightened experience. They promoted the idea that poetic language (and by extension, art) can serve to make the world fresh and strange - that art has the power to cause us to see the world in new ways. Suprematist abstract painting was aimed at doing much the same thing, by removing the real world entirely and leaving the viewer to contemplate what kind of image of the world is offered by, for instance, a black square.

TATLIN AND CONSTRUCTIVISM

In 1913 a young Russian painter named Vladimir Tatlin visited Picasso in Paris. It is not known what Picasso showed him, but during this period Picasso was creating sculptures, not carved from wood or stone, but assembled from a variety of available materials. Picasso's *Guitar*, for instance, was made of sheet metal and wire. When Tatlin returned to Russia, he began to create his own assemblages, made mostly out of metal.[321] Some were meant to hang in the corners of rooms, some attached to the ceiling, but in effect, they were hanging in space.[322]

---

[321] Tatlin appears to be the first artist to create purely abstract (nonobjective) sculpture. Picasso, at this time, was creating sculptural adaptations of his Cubist images which were, like his *Guitar*, tied to real-world objects. (Hilton Kramer, The Age of the Avant-Garde, pg. 152)

[322] Norbert Lynton, *The Story of Modern Art*, pg. 101-102

Tatlin's work was first shown at the same St. Petersburg exhibition at which Malevich launched Suprematism. Tatlin and the older Malevich nearly came to blows over disagreements about the merits of their respective approaches to art. Malevich was jealous of his self-proclaimed leadership of the avant-garde in Russia. Furthermore, his art was mystical and inward-looking, while Tatlin's constructions focused attention on the outward world.

Tatlin's most famous work was an ambitious project – a vast tower, 400 meters in height (100 meters taller than the Eiffel Tower), to stand across the river Neva in Petrograd. It was commissioned as a monument to the ideals of international socialism and seen as a Russian answer to the Eiffel Tower. Tatlin's design resembled a cross between a spiral ziggurat,[323] listing to one side, and an amusement park roller coaster.[324]

Tatlin and his assistants made a wooden model of the tower, which was shown in Petrograd and Moscow in 1920, and a smaller version which toured Russia during the following years, carried in procession through the streets like the statue of a saint. A stamp was even designed with the tower as a motif.[325]

Lenin, however, was unimpressed. According to one account, after Tatlin had explained the tower, "Lenin said nothing at all."[326] Tatlin's ambitious tower was never built.

---

[323] Svetlana Boym, *Another Freedom: The Alternative History of an Idea*, pg. 333

[324] Richard Kostelanetz, *A Dictionary of the Avant-Gardes*, pg. 604

[325] Norbert Lynton, *The Story of Modern Art,* pg. 106-107

[326] Andre Furlani, Guy Davenport: *Postmodernism and After*, pg. 82

THE SOVIET UNION

The Soviet Union grew out of the October Revolution of 1917, led by Vladimir Lenin, which overthrew a provisional government that had come into being after the abdication of Tsar Nicholas II.

In the year before the revolution, Lenin had been hiding in Zurich, living in an apartment across the street from the Cabaret Voltaire, where the Dadaists were launching their own revolution. There are even rumors that Lenin occasionally visited the club for a drink. There is no record of what he thought about the Dadaists.[327]

After the revolution, the Bolshevik Party, under the leadership of Lenin, was in charge of Russia. Their first governmental act was to sue for peace and begin to withdraw from the ongoing First World War.

However, the Bolsheviks were soon drawn into a bitter civil war against the remnants of the forces still loyal to the monarchy.[328]

Mikhail Guerman, in *The Art of the October Revolution*, describes everyday life during the early days under Lenin:

---

[327] Dominique Noguez, in a book entitled, *Lénine Dada*, suggests that "Lenin loved disguises and mystification", and that there is archival information to suggest that Lenin was involved in the Cabaret Voltaire, even to the extent of possibly writing some of Tristan Tzara's poems. (Hans Renders, ed., *Theoretical Discussions of Biography: Approaches from History, Microhistory and Life Writing*, pg. 31)

[328] Dennis and Ioffe Frederick White, *The Russian Avant-Garde and Radical Modernism*

> One...has to take into account the fact that in 1918, [Russia was] a country three-quarters occupied by counterrevolutionary and foreign troops. Hunger was chronic. There was not enough fuel. In the evenings, only a few street lamps burned. Cold rooms were lit by dim and flickering wick and kerosene lamps. Residents stood guard at the entrances to their homes to protect themselves from bands of looters roaming the cities. Lines formed before dawn at the shops...[329]

Taking into account these dire circumstances, Lenin had little time or inclination to bother much about art, one way or the other. Consequently, with the government distracted by military and economic issues, Russian modernists, for the moment, experienced a high degree of artistic freedom. This was soon to change.

After Lenin's death in 1924, a struggle ensued for political control at the top of the government. The eventual winner was Joseph Stalin who moved quickly to consolidate his authority. He exploited the cult of Lenin, positioning himself as the only lawful successor, while simultaneously moving away from Lenin's policy of collective leadership. Stalin quickly secured total power over the party and the country and established a one-man dictatorship.[330]

Throughout the 1920s, modernist art was gradually replaced in public exhibitions by the lifeless forms of idealized naturalism which, it was argued, would better serve the cause of Communism. In a 1927 exhibition in Moscow entitled "Ten Years of Soviet Art", neither Malevich nor Tatlin were represented.

---

[329] Catherine Walworth, *Soviet Salvage*, pg. 4

[330] Dennis and Ioffe Frederick White, *The Russian Avant-Garde and Radical Modernism*

Finally, the official state policy was publically enshrined in the decree, "On the Reconstruction of Literary and Art Organizations". Art styles deemed to be "alien elements", such as Cubism, were outlawed. In a 1932 meeting attended by Stalin himself, the term "Socialist Realism" was chosen for the new state-approved art. Finally, in 1934 four specific guidelines for Socialist Realism were laid out. Henceforth:

1. Art should be relevant to the workers, and understandable to them.

2. Art should depict typical scenes of the everyday life of the people.

3. Art should be realistic in a representational sense.

4. Art should be supportive of the aims of the State and the Party.[331]

The new policy of Socialist Realism effectively killed off Modernism in the Soviet Union and forced the artists themselves to choose between artistic conviction and survival. Kazimir Malevich chose survival. His 1934 work, *Woman Worker*, conforms to the four dictates of Socialist Realism - it is a bland, unremarkable painting of a smiling peasant woman.

Malevich died the next year, 1935, at age 56. Fortunately, even though his earlier work was banned, it was not completely erased from history. Some of his modernist paintings were smuggled out of the Soviet Union, one rolled up and disguised as an umbrella.[332]

---

[331] Johannes Bach Rasmussen, *Travel Guide: Traces of the Cold War Period : the Countries Around the Baltic Sea* , pg. 190

[332] Laura Cumming, *Malevich review – an intensely moving retrospective*, from The Guardian, July 19, 2014

Vladimir Tatlin was held up to ridicule in an exhibition held in 1933 in which his work was shown under the label, "Formalist Excesses".[333] Official Soviet critics remarked that Tatlin was "no artist whatsoever".[334]

In the last years of his life, Tatlin lived in obscurity. His only known work during this period consists of illustrations for children's books (before their authors disappeared in Stalin's purges) and nondescript landscapes used as backdrops for theater productions in the Socialist Realist style. When he died in 1953 from food poisoning, his passing was virtually ignored in the official press.[335]

Stalin was adept in the use of terror in the management of Soviet artists. A few examples will serve to illustrate his technique. In 1930 he called the popular satirical writer Mikhail Bulgakov on the telephone to say that he had heard a rumor that Bulgakov was thinking of leaving the Soviet Union. Bulgakov replied that no Russian writer could live outside his homeland.

Stalin seemed pleased with this answer and said that the ban on Bulgakov's works would be lifted and that the two of them should talk again. Stalin never spoke to Bulgakov again, and the ban was reimposed. Bulgakov was naturally terrified, expecting disaster at any moment. He died in 1940 at the age of 48.[336]

---

[333] Svetlana Boym, *Architecture of the Off-Modern*, pg. 13 – This was the predecessor to Hitler's Degenerate Art exhibition.

[334] ibid

[335] Svetlana Boym, *Ruins of the Avant-Garde from Tatlin's Tower to Paper Architecture*, an essay from Julia Hell, ed., *Ruins of Modernity*, pg. 66

[336] *Facing off Stalin*, from The Economist, March 11, 2004

Osip Mandelstam, a well-respected Russian poet, was arrested and sent to the gulag for writing a poem, "Stalin Epigram" (1933) in which he referred to Stalin as a "slayer of peasants."[337] In 1934 Stalin called Mandelstam's friend, Boris Pasternak on the telephone and cryptically remarked, "We old Bolsheviks never deny our friends." Stalin then hung up and left Pasternak wondering what he meant, but fearing the worst.[338]

Mandelstam would die on the way to the gulag. His widow, Nadezhda, wrote in her memoir, *Hope Against Hope*, that Stalin had invented a new species of fear:

> The fear that goes with the writing of verse has nothing in common with the fear one experiences in the presence of the secret police. Our mysterious awe in the face of existence itself is always overridden by the more primitive fear of violence and destruction.[339]

The Russian composer, Dmitri Shostakovich came to know this fear first-hand.

STALIN AND SHOSTAKOVICH

Shostakovich was born on September 25, 1906. Even from an early age, he showed an astounding aptitude for music. In 1919, at the young age of 13, he was admitted to what was then called the Petrograd Conservatory, where he made a favorable impression on the head of the institution.

His *First Symphony*, written at age 19, was an international success, prompting a congratulatory letter from Alban Berg, who heard it performed in Vienna.[340]

---

[337] Steven Poole, *The Stalin Epigram by Robert Littell*, from *The Guardian*, June 11, 2010

[338] *Facing off Stalin*, from The Economist, March 11, 2004

[339] Richard Murphy, *Poetry and Terror*, from *The New York Review of Books*, September 30, 1976

[340] Solomon Volkov, *Testimony, The Memoirs of Dmitri Shostakovich*, pg. 45

The success of his *First Symphony* procured for the young Shostakovich a commission for a composition celebrating the tenth anniversary of the Revolution, a work which became his *Second Symphony*. His *Third Symphony* (subtitled *The First of May*) followed the same pattern, full of symbolic celebration of the Communist Revolution.[341]

As a result of his increasing success and growing fame, Shostakovich was asked to create music for the emerging Soviet film industry. The turgid plots of these films are entirely predictable and reflect the dictates of Socialist Realism: *The Golden Mountain* and *The Counterplan* unmask capitalist bosses and wreckers of industry. In the film, *Alone*, a Leningrad schoolteacher travels into Siberia where greedy, landowning peasants are obstructing a Soviet experiment.

Stalin personally oversaw the Soviet film industry. According to Shostakovich,

> Stalin had his own projection room at the Kremlin, and he watched films at night. That was work for him, and like all criminals, he worked at night…Stalin was in charge one hundred percent.
>
> If he ordered a film made, they made it. If he ordered them to stop shooting, they stopped shooting…If Stalin ordered a finished film destroyed, they'd destroy it.[342]

Stalin approved *The Golden Mountain*, *The Counterplan*, and *Alone* for wide release in 1931 and he is known to have loved the music Shostakovich composed for *The Counterplan*. It was probably at this time that Stalin first became personally aware of Shostakovich.[343]

---

[341] Boris Schwarz, *The New Grove Russian Masters 2*, pg. 176

[342] Solomon Volkov, *Testimony, The Memoirs of Dmitri Shostakovich*, pg. 249-251

[343] Alex Ross, *The Rest is Noise*, pg. 224

Stalin was not completely uncultured where music was concerned. He attended the Bolshoi ballet, he listened to classical music and liked to sing folk songs. He had definite opinions about music as well - he monitored every recording made in the Soviet Union, writing terse, one-word reviews on the album sleeves: "good", "so-so", "bad", and "rubbish".[344]

Once the parameters of Socialist Realism were codified in 1934, all artists, including composers, were expected to conform. As Shostakovich would soon discover, the application of these directives was subject to the interpretation and whim of Stalin.

ENEMY OF THE PEOPLE

Shostakovich's first contribution to the new regime of Socialist Realism was an opera entitled *Lady Macbeth of the Mtsensk District*. The story was derived from a novella by Nikolai Leskov and centers on Katerina Izmailova,

> ...the wife of a provincial merchant and mill-owner, who takes a lover from among her husband's workmen. She murders both her father-in-law and her husband before being deported to Siberia. There she also kills her lover's new mistress and finally herself.[345]

The opera was premiered on January 22, 1934, in Leningrad, then two days later in Moscow. It was praised as a "major achievement of socialist construction", which "could have been written only by a Soviet composer brought up in the best traditions of Soviet culture."[346] By 1936, the opera had given 83 performances in Leningrad and 97 in Moscow. It had also attracted international attention from New York, Stockholm, London, Zurich, and Copenhagen.[347]

---

[344] Ibid, pg. 220

[345] Tim Ashley, *Too scary for Stalin*, from *The Guardian*, March 26, 2004

[346] Boris Schwarz, *The New Grove Russian Masters 2*, pg. 177

On January 26, 1936, Stalin went to see *Lady Macbeth of the Mtsensk District* for himself. The 29-year-old Shostakovich was in the audience, but any hopes he might have harbored of being congratulated by the dictator evaporated when Stalin and his entire entourage ostentatiously stood up and left during the third act.

Two days later, an editorial appeared in *Pravda*, the official Communist Party newspaper, entitled, "Muddle Instead of Music". In this review, rumored to have been written by Stalin himself, *Lady Macbeth* was condemned as an artistically obscure and morally obscene work.[348]

"Singing is replaced by shrieking," the article read. "If the composer chances to come upon the path of a clear and simple melody, he throws himself back into a wilderness of musical chaos – in places becoming cacophony." The past success of the opera was attributed to "tickling the perverted taste of the bourgeoisie with its fidgety, screaming, neurotic music".[349]

For Shostakovich however, the most troubling line in the editorial read, "It is a game of clever ingenuity that may end very badly."

Years later, when dictating his memoirs, Shostakovich still remembered the event vividly:

---

[347] Ibid

[348] Shostakovich himself was sure that Stalin had written it because it was so ungrammatical. "...the article appeared before the big purges. There were still some fairly literate people working at *Pravda*..." (Solomon Volkov, *Testimony, The Memoirs of Dmitri Shostakovich*, pg. 114)

[349] *Muddle Instead of Music*, *Pravda*, January 28, 1936

> On January 28, 1936, we went to the railroad station to buy a new Pravda. I opened it up and leafed through it – and found the article 'Muddle Instead of Music'. I'll never forget that day – probably the most memorable in my life. That article on the third page of Pravda changed my entire existence. It was written without a signature, like an editorial – that is, it expressed the opinion of the Party. But it actually expressed the opinion of Stalin, and that was much more important…The opera was taken off the stage…Everyone turned against me…There was a phrase in the article saying that all this could end very badly. They were all waiting for the bad end to come…Everyone knew for sure that I would be destroyed. And the anticipation of that noteworthy event – at least for me – has never left me. From that moment on I was stuck with the label 'enemy of the people', and I don't need to explain what the label meant in those days.[350]

For Shostakovich, the aftermath of his public censure was not only psychological – it was real and material as well. Many of his former friends ignored him and some fellow-composers even denounced him. Performances dwindled and income dried up.

In an attempt to remedy his situation, Shostakovich went to see a much admired and decorated hero of the Red Army, a military leader named Tukhachevsky and asked him to write a personal letter to Stalin, pleading his case. (Tukhachevsky was himself an amateur musician and had been friendly to Shostakovich in the past).

---

[350] Solomon Volkov, *Testimony, The Memoirs of Dmitri Shostakovich*, pg. 113-115

Unfortunately for Shostakovich, Tukhachevsky was arrested only a few months later. After being tortured, he signed his name to a confession, admitting to his part in a non-existent plot to overthrow Stalin. When the confession was retrieved decades later, it was stained with blood. In reality, there was no evidence Tukhachevsky was ever plotting against Stalin – Stalin simply saw him as a dangerous rival – too independent and too charismatic – and had him liquidated.[351] However, the Tukhachevsky affair now made matters even worse for Shostakovich.

In 1937, Shostakovich was summoned for interrogation by the NKVD (predecessor of the dreaded KGB). He arrived at the appointed hour, not knowing why he had been called. The inspector, a man named Zanchevsky greeted him and engaged him in friendly conversation. Suddenly he asked, "Do you know Tukhachevsky?" Shostakovich acknowledged that he did. "What do you know about the plot to assassinate Comrade Stalin?"

At this point, Shostakovich fell silent. Zanchevsky said, "Dmitri Dmitryevich, this is very serious. You must remember. Today is Saturday. I'll sign your pass and you can go home. But on Monday noon, you must be here."

Shostakovich related later to his friend and fellow-composer, Veniamin Basner, "I understood this was the end...I told my wife I probably wouldn't return. She even prepared a bag for me - the kind prepared for people who were taken away. She put in warm underwear. She knew I wouldn't be back."

On the following Monday Shostakovich returned at noon. He gave his name to a soldier at the door, who consulted a long list. Unable to find his name, he finally asked, "Who are you here to see?"

---

[351] Igor Lukes, *Czechoslovakia between Stalin and Hitler: The Diplomacy of Edvard Beneš in the 1930s* , pg. 95

Shostakovich gave him the name of the interrogator, Zanchevsky. The guard replied, "He won't be able to see you today. Go home. We'll notify you." Later that night Shostakovich discovered that Zanchevsky himself had been arrested on the previous day.[352]

Unable to defend himself, Shostakovich suffered in silence, finally coming to the conclusion that his only recourse was to respond with his music. Years later, when dictating his memoirs to Solomon Volkov, Shostakovich said, "The majority of my symphonies are tombstones. Too many people have died and were buried in places unknown to anyone, not even to their relatives.

It happened to many of my friends. Where do you put the tombstone for Tukhachevsky? Only music can do that for them."[353]

At the time of his public condemnation in *Pravda*, Shostakovich was at work on his *Fourth Symphony*. It was to be his most ambitious up until that time, filled with nervous energy, tension, and dissonance. However, taking into account his present situation and the prevailing political climate, he was advised that it would be a wiser course for him to simply withdraw the symphony. He withdrew the *Fourth Symphony* - it would not be heard publically until 1961.

---

[352] This story appears in Elizabeth Wilson's book, *Shostakovich: A Life*. A slightly different version was told by Veniamin Basner in the BBC 4 documentary, *Soviet Echoes*, and in the film by Larry Weinstein, *Shostakovich Against Stalin, The War Symphonies*. Because the story does not appear in Solomon Volkov's book, *Testimony, The Memoirs of Dmitri Shostakovich*, some have cast doubt on its validity. Conversely, Basner has doubted the authenticity of Volkov's book on the same grounds. I find the story entirely plausible and compelling, and have included it for that reason, drawing on and combining both Wilson's and Basner's accounts.

[353] Solomon Volkov, *Testimony, The Memoirs of Dmitri Shostakovich*, pg. 156

In 1937 Shostakovich instead unveiled his *Fifth Symphony*. On the surface, it seemed completely conventional, even following the traditional four-movement classical model. Like Beethoven's *Fifth Symphony*, it began in a gloomy minor key but ended in a heroic major key. Seemingly, it was a work anyone – even Stalin – could understand.

In an accompanying article published under the composer's name, he called the symphony, "My Creative Response" and described it as an apology for *Lady Macbeth* and the withdrawn *Fourth Symphony*. Government officials seemed willing to believe that Shostakovich had "seen the light", and was now rehabilitated.

The first movement of the *Fifth Symphony*, in keeping with the classical model, is in sonata form. But it is hard to miss the agonized tragedy of the music poured into this classical mold. Here is the first theme presented at the opening of the first movement:

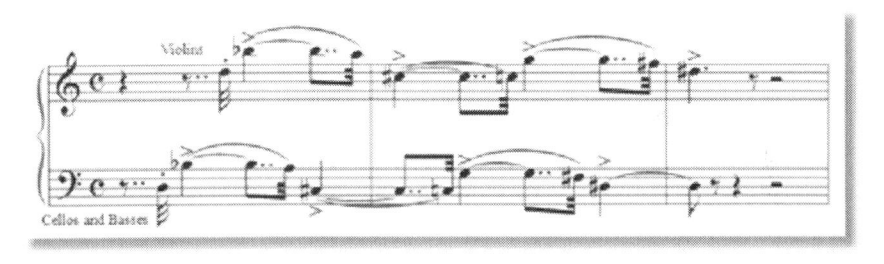

The painful, jagged melody of the opening retreats in measure five into a quietly pathetic melancholy:

Friends and supporters of Shostakovich understood that in his public statements repudiating his opera and his *Fourth Symphony* he was merely doing what was necessary in order to survive. They saw in his *Fifth Symphony* the victory of the lone artist over the state. The heroic fanfares of the last movement were interpreted by them as a sarcastic mockery of the forced rejoicing required by the government. Shostakovich's son, Maxim, said that his father confided to him that the message of the heroic final movement is the artist saying, "I am right. I will follow the way I choose."[354]

In the audience at the premiere of the *Fifth Symphony* were many who had lost friends and loved ones to Stalin's purges. For them, this music seemed to be a bold assertion of artistic will in the face of a repressive state. One listener was so gripped by the music that he stood to his feet. Soon others followed. At the conclusion, the ovation lasted a full thirty minutes.

One audience member wrote in her diary, "Everyone kept saying, 'That was his answer, and it was a good one.'"[355]

Shostakovich outlived Stalin by many years. At the time of Stalin's death on March 5, 1953, Shostakovich had produced no new work for nearly a decade, most likely due to the fact that he had been denounced for a second time in 1948. However, before the end of the year, on December 17, 1953, he premiered his *Tenth Symphony*. It is not clear when it was written, but Shostakovich himself claims that it was written after Stalin's death.

---

[354] Alex Ross, *The Rest is Noise*, pg. 234

[355] Ibid, pg. 236

> ...I did depict Stalin in music in my...Tenth [Symphony]. I wrote it right after Stalin's death, and no one has yet guessed what it is about. It's about Stalin and the Stalin years. The second part, the scherzo, is a musical portrait of Stalin... [356]

Armed with this insight from the composer, the *Tenth Symphony* can clearly be heard as a frightening glimpse of life under a totalitarian dictatorship. The first movement is dark and brooding and conveys a powerful sense of hopelessness and foreboding. The second movement is a musical picture of a rampaging monster, trampling and destroying everything in its path. The third movement is more relaxed but still warily unsettling. The fourth movement begins in the low strings, reminiscent of the darkness of the first movement, but as it gradually unfolds the energy increases and the mood brightens noticeably.

Shostakovich wrote fifteen symphonies in all. His last, the *Fifteenth Symphony* (1971) is one of his most puzzling and seems to have been deliberately designed to force his listeners to ask questions. It opens with a glockenspiel solo (the only symphony in the orchestral repertoire to do so), and it quotes directly from Rossini's *William Tell Overture* in the first movement, but the reason for this quotation is unclear. Shostakovich himself seemed unable to explain it: "I don't myself quite know why the quotations are there, but I could not, could not, not include them."[357]

---

[356] Solomon Volkov, *Testimony, The Memoirs of Dmitri Shostakovich*, pg. 141

[357] Wendy Lesser, *Music for Silenced Voices: Shostakovich and His Fifteen Quartets*, pg. 245

After the long, slow second movement and the short third movement comes the biggest puzzle of all: In the final movement Shostakovich quotes Wagner's famous theme of unfulfilled longing and death from *Tristan and Isolde*, but again, the meaning is not at all clear. The symphony draws to a close with a strange coda, which music journalist Tom Service interprets as

> a musical transliteration of the hum and clatter of hospital machines, the faceless whirring and bleeping that are the grim accompaniments of disease, decline, and death in medical institutions - sounds that Shostakovich was already familiar with at this stage in his life.[358]

This strange explanation is unsettlingly plausible. A lifelong smoker, Shostakovich was in poor health at this stage in his life and died from lung cancer on August 9, 1975.

---

[358] Tom Service, *Symphony guide: Shostakovich's 15th*, from The Guardian, September 23, 2013

CHAPTER NINE: ART AND MUSIC IN POSTWAR EUROPE

The Second World War ended in Europe on May 8, 1945, when the unconditional surrender of Germany was accepted by the Allies. Four months later, on September 2nd representatives of the Emperor of Japan signed surrender documents on board a U.S. warship in Tokyo Bay.

The surrender of Japan came after two of its cities had been destroyed by the newly developed atomic bomb, Hiroshima on August 6th, and Nagasaki on August 9th. The atomic bomb had been created in strict secrecy. However, after its use, the implications became clear to the entire world: What happened to Hiroshima and Nagasaki could potentially happen to any city - no one was safe. Furthermore, the very existence of these powerful new weapons made the possibility of the total self-annihilation of mankind now seem quite plausible.

It is, therefore, no surprise that Existentialism became the dominant philosophy of the postwar era. Existentialism is a pessimistic philosophy that, like Nihilism, suggests that there is no objective truth and no objective meaning in life. It is characterized by a sense of disorientation and confusion in the face of a meaningless and absurd world. Jean-Paul Sartre was the primary spokesman for postwar Existentialism. Even a casual glance at his book titles, *Being and Nothingness* (1943), and *No Exit* (1944) provides insight into his point of view. Some of his well-known quotations express the bleakly cynical outlook of Existentialism in a short, aphoristic way: "Life has no meaning the moment you lose the illusion of being eternal," and "All human actions are equivalent and all are on principle doomed to failure."[359]

---

[359] Jean-Paul Sartre, *Essays in Aesthetics*, pg.

Sartre was able to find a pessimistic angle even on the recent Allied victory over the Third Reich: "Once you learn the details of victory, it is hard to distinguish it from defeat."[360]

Europe after the Second World War seemed to confirm Sartre's assessment - despite the Allied victory, it was a devastated wasteland – its cities lay in ruins and its surviving citizens lived on the brink of starvation. German writers began to use the term *stunde null* to describe this time. The expression literally means "zero hour" and originally referred to midnight on May 8, 1945, the hour of Germany's surrender. But it came to be understood in a broader sense as "a time without a past", representing a break with both the recent Nazi past and by implication, a general sweeping away of cultural traditions in order to create a new society.[361]

ART IN POSTWAR EUROPE

Many of the leading artists from the first generation of Modernism had survived the war, among them Picasso and Matisse. At the outbreak of the Second World War, the American Embassy invited both Picasso and Matisse to come to the United States. Both refused.[362]

In the early 1930s, as the threat of war began to spread across Europe, Picasso's art increasingly began to reflect a preoccupation with violence and death.[363] His grisly, distorted, and tortured images during this period presented a vivid portrait of the cruel reality of war.

"I did not paint the war," Picasso said later, "but there is no doubt that the war is there in the pictures I painted then."[364]

---

[360] Utah Forum, Volume 8, pg. 46

[361] Stephen Brockmann, *German Literary Culture at the Zero Hour*, pg. 1

[362] Arianna Huffington, *Picasso: Creator and Destroyer*, pg. 250

[363] Lael Wertenbaker, *The World of Picasso*, pg. 132

Perhaps no wartime painting by Picasso captured the public imagination more than Guernica, created in 1937. The news of the destruction of the innocent population of this peaceful town in northern Spain jolted Picasso into a frenzy of creative fury.

After the war, Picasso became active in politics, and for a time used his art in support of Communism. He had joined the French Communist Party during the war while Paris was under Nazi occupation, partly as a way of expressing his disgust with the Nazi occupiers.[365] Picasso had hoped that the Communist cause would bring a significance and meaning into his life which had so far eluded him.[366]

In January 1951, still under the influence of his Communist infatuation, he painted *Massacre in Korea*, intended as a grand artistic protest against American involvement in the Korean War. However, it was too inconsequential to impress the Party leaders he had hoped to please, and it was too much like his earlier work to impress nonpartisan art critics. It seemed to be a disappointing repeat of techniques which now appeared tired and overused. For author James Lord, *Massacre in Korea* was evidence that Picasso's best days were behind him, and that as an artist, he was now basically irrelevant.

> Something has happened to Picasso. He is now a changed man...He surrounded himself with mediocre sycophants and third-rate artists, none of whom could remind him that moments of major attainment were no longer at hand.[367]

---

[364] ibid

[365] Jonathan Brown, *Picasso's Red Period*, The Independent, July 15, 2009

[366] Arianna Huffington, *Picasso: Creator and Destroyer*, pg. 364

[367] ibid

In short, in the years immediately following the war, Picasso no longer seemed to be at the forefront of modern art. Matisse after the war found himself in a similar position, but for different reasons.

In May 1940, as the German armies were beginning their invasion of France, Picasso was frantically making plans to escape Paris for the French countryside. On his way to the train, he met Matisse in the street. "Where are you going?" Picasso asked. "To my tailor," replied Matisse, blissfully unaware of the danger.[368]

Matisse had domestic problems which may explain his ignorance of larger events. At the time of the invasion, he had only recently separated from his wife of forty years and had been planning a trip to Brazil with his young assistant, Lydia Délectorskaya. Matisse's wife had suspected the artist of having an affair with his Russian assistant, and had demanded that she be fired. Matisse dutifully complied. Distraught, Délectorskaya attempted suicide by shooting herself in the chest; remarkably, she survived with no serious after-effects. Unimpressed, Matisse's wife divorced him anyway and moved out.

Délectorskaya promptly returned to Matisse and worked with him for the rest of his life, running his household, paying the bills, typing his correspondence, keeping meticulous records, assisting in the studio and coordinating his business affairs.[369]

---

[368] Ibid, pg. 253

[369] Michael Hodges, *The unbelievable story of Henri Matisse*, *The Daily Mail*, March 29, 2014

Upon hearing of the German invasion and the imminent fall of Paris to the Nazis, Matisse quickly cancelled his travel plans and left instead for Nice, where he remained for the duration of the war. In January of 1941, at age 72, Matisse underwent intestinal surgery. As a result, he was a virtual invalid for the rest of his life, unable to stand for more than a few minutes at a time. Unable to paint, he embarked on a series of 158 line drawings seeking to capture an image with a minimum of movement.[370]

In the latter years of the war, Matisse began to experiment with cut-outs and collage. This was a kind of breakthrough for Matisse, and his art began to be increasingly abstract as he proceeded. Matisse utilized the paper cut-out method exclusively until his death in 1954, at age 84.

ART FOR A NEW GENERATION

After the war, the works of the early modernists, Picasso and Matisse among them, were bought and sold for record prices as millionaire collectors and prestigious museums competed against each other for ownership. But as the financial value of the works of the modernist masters soared, for a new generation of younger European artists, basic survival was the primary concern.

For these artists, the bright cut-outs of Matisse and the tepid political art of Picasso seemed irrelevant and did not resonate at all with their own lives or experience. Instead, this new generation of European artists, attempting to process the aftermath of World War II and the harsh new realities of the emerging Cold War, produced images that expressed their bitterness, fear, and despair.

---

[370] Lydia Delectorskaya was asked how Matisse's drawings seem to have been done in a single flourish...she said she was "a pretty good eraser". (Jonathan Jones, *Lydia Delectorskaya, Henri Matisse (1947)*, *The Guardian*, December 1, 2001)

Alberto Giacometti was born in Switzerland in 1901 but spent most of his professional career in Paris. He spent the war in neutral Switzerland, returning to France at the conclusion of the conflict. He is best known for his tall, thin portrayals of the human figure which seem to suggest human frailty and weakness. Giacometti was interested in Existentialism and for many viewers, his art seemed to capture the tone of melancholy, alienation, and loneliness implied by that philosophy.[371] Giacometti, though, always denied that he was attempting to embody Existentialism directly in his art. On the other hand, Jean-Paul Sartre, the great Existentialist philosopher, definitely saw a connection, saying of Giacometti's work that "emptiness filters through everywhere, each creature secretes his own void."[372]

Francis Bacon was born in Ireland in 1909 but lived in both England and Ireland throughout his life. During World War II, Bacon volunteered for service, but was deemed physically unfit for active duty and was assigned to work in air-raid shelters instead. As it turned out, the fine dust in the shelters worsened his asthma and he was forced to give this up as well. Bacon did not take up painting until his late 30s and was entirely self-taught.

---

[371] Giacometti's figures not only suggested alienation, but aliens as well. At one point in the design process for *2001: A Space Odyssey*, Stanley Kubrick wanted tall, spindly aliens modeled on Giacometti's figures. (Michael Benson, Space Odyssey, pg. 64).

[372] H.H. Arnason, *Postwar European Art*, pg. 449

His images are grim, grotesquely distorted, and violent. This has been interpreted by analysts as his reaction to the plight of the world, or simply as a nihilistic existential attitude towards the meaninglessness of life.[373] Bacon's subject matter is almost exclusively the human form, especially the face. In many of his paintings from the immediate postwar period, the mouth of his subject is opened as if in the act of a horrendous scream. Bacon said that he borrowed this open-mouthed scream from a scene from the 1925 film, *Battleship Potemkin*, in which a panic-stricken nanny is shot in the eye.[374]

Jean Fautrier was part of the French resistance during World War II and was consequently arrested by the Nazis in 1943. After being released, he fled from Paris and took refuge in a psychiatric hospital where a friend arranged for him to have studio space. It was there that he created a series of small paintings he referred to later as the *Otages* (Hostage) series, made in response to scenes of Nazi atrocities he witnessed. Fautrier could hear the sounds of the torture and execution of French citizens carried out by the Nazis each night in the forest surrounding the hospital in which he had taken refuge. In his *Otages* series, Fautrier uses abstraction to mask the brutality and horror of the images.[375] These paintings, nevertheless, vividly convey the physical violence and inhuman cruelty inflicted by the Nazis on their prisoners.

Alberto Burri was not trained as an artist but as a doctor. After Italy's entrance into World War II in October of 1940, he was sent to Libya with the Italian army as a combat medic.

---

[373] Ibid, pg. 471

[374] ibid

[375] Karl Ruhrber, *Art of the 20th Century, Part 1*, pg. 254

In May of 1943 he was captured by the British who turned him over to the Americans for internment in a prisoner of war camp in Hereford, Texas. There, at age thirty, prevented from practicing medicine, Burri began to experiment with art to pass the time. At first, he tried drawing and painting, but later evolved an emphasis on texture and materiality, experimenting with unorthodox materials such as tar, sand, and glue. Following the war, Burri returned to Italy, taking up residence in Rome.

He is best known for his works entitled *Sacchi* (sacks), beginning in 1950. The material came from the sacks used to deliver food from the United States during the Marshall Plan. Burri began to sew the old sacks together on the canvas, the end result resembling the blood-stained bandages he had seen in his time in the field hospital. These torn and scarred images are generally regarded as a commentary on the brutality of war.[376]

Lucio Fontana was born in Argentina in 1899 but trained in Italy as a sculptor in the 1930s. In 1949 Fontana began to perforate a brightly painted canvas in a random, abstract way, revealing another painted canvas beneath. In the 1950s, Fontana slashed a spoiled canvas and realized that he could achieve a unique surface texture by so doing. He produced a series of monochrome, lacerated canvases which he called *tagli* (slashes). With these "slashed" paintings, Fontana would often line the back of the canvas with black gauze, so that a darkness behind the slash would shimmer, creating a mysterious illusion of depth.[377]

---

[376] H.H. Arnason, *Postwar European Art*, pg. 466

[377] Ibid, pg. 465

MUSIC IN POSTWAR EUROPE

On April 30, 1945, American jeeps pulled into the driveway of the Garmisch villa of Richard Strauss. The composer's seventeen-year-old son, Richard Jr., ran into Strauss's study shouting, "Grandpa, we are being evacuated within 20 minutes."

"Easy, easy," the composer said as he pulled a number of papers from a drawer. He walked out of the house to meet the soldiers. "My name is Richard Strauss. I am the composer," he said, holding out to them pages from his best-known compositions. "Here, you may look at them if you want." The Americans were dumbstruck. Strauss was not arrested and his villa was not commandeered by the military – instead, American officers arrived later to dine with him and his family. [378]

No composer better illustrates the moral dilemmas faced by artists under the Third Reich than Richard Strauss. During the Nazi years, he had accepted the offer of Joseph Goebbels, the Reich propaganda minister, to make him president of the Reich Music Chamber and served in that capacity from 1933 to 1935.[379] Strauss believed that by working within the Third Reich he would be able to enact reforms – new royalty schemes favoring classical composers and extension of composer's copyrights.

---

[378] Michael H. Kater, *Richard Strauss and Hitler's Reich: Jupiter in Hell*, The New York Times, January 6, 2002

[379] ibid

The price for this position of influence was intimate interaction with the Nazi leaders. He appeared at Nazi functions and socialized with the Nazi bosses when he was in Berlin. For Christmas 1933 he even gave Hitler a copy of *World History of the Theater*.[380] Years later Strauss expressed his regret, ruminating in his journal about "the price I had to pay for not keeping away, from the very beginning, from the National Socialist movement."[381]

On the other hand, Strauss refused to participate in anti-Semitic activities and used his position of authority to shield Jewish musicians within his sphere of influence.[382] As a result, the Nazis began keeping secret files on Strauss's poor attitude. In February 1934, he was denounced for failing to give the Nazi salute. It was reported later that Hitler himself began to see Strauss as an opponent of the regime and in league with "Jewish riff-raff".[383]

Things finally came to a head in 1935 when Goebbels ordered Strauss to resign the chamber presidency "on account of ill health." Strauss complied.[384] He complained in his private notes, "I consider the Streicher- Goebbels Jew-baiting as a disgrace to German honor, as evidence of incompetence, the basest weapon of the untalented, lazy mediocrity against a higher intelligence and greater talent."[385]

---

[380] Alex Ross, *The Rest is Noise*, pg. 324

[381] Richard Strauss, *A Confidential Matter: The Letters of Richard Strauss and Stefan Zweig*, pg. 119

[382] Michael H. Kater, *Richard Strauss and Hitler's Reich: Jupiter in Hell, The New York Times*, January 6, 2002

[383] Alex Ross, *The Rest is Noise*, pg. 324

[384] Michael H. Kater, *Richard Strauss and Hitler's Reich: Jupiter in Hell, The New York Times*, January 6, 2002

[385] Richard Strauss, *A Confidential Matter: The Letters of Richard Strauss and Stefan Zweig*, pg. 119

Strauss never considered leaving Germany. Now in his seventies, he was too old to begin a new life elsewhere. Furthermore, by remaining, he was able to use his dwindling influence on behalf of his Jewish daughter-in-law, Alice, and his grandchildren. However, as he discovered, there were limits to what he could accomplish. When he heard that Alice's Jewish grandmother, Paula Neumann, was being interned at the Theresienstadt concentration camp in Prague, Strauss attempted to intervene on her behalf. The regime pretended not to notice his appeals.

In desperation, the 71-year-old composer got into his limousine, and was chauffeured to the very gates of the concentration camp, where he stepped out and announced to the soldiers, "I am Richard Strauss, the composer." The soldiers ignored him and he returned empty-handed. [386]

He was still at his Garmisch home, protected by the American military, when his long, extraordinary career came to an end on September 8, 1949. His final composition, completed in the year preceding his death, was entitled *Four Last Songs*, an orchestral setting of three texts on the subject of death by Hermann Hesse, and one by Joseph Eichendorff. The music seems to glow with a gentle, ethereal light that corresponds to the words of the text which express a weary desire for rest. Strauss never heard the *Four Last Songs* performed – they were first performed in the Royal Albert Hall in 1950.[387]

Though Strauss was to some degree insulated from the horrors of the war, the young men who would become the next generation of European composers were not so lucky.

---

[386] Michael H. Kater, *Richard Strauss and Hitler's Reich: Jupiter in Hell*, The New York Times, January 6, 2002

[387] Wendy Thompson, *Richard Strauss, Four Last Songs*, Program Notes from the Philharmonia Orchestra, London

THE BATTLE FOR THE GERMAN MIND

Almost immediately after the death of Hitler, Stalin took his place as a threat in the minds of American leaders. U.S. policy called for Germany to be reinvented as a democratic, American-style society and a stronghold against the Soviet Union.

Part of this plan included a cultural policy of denazification and re-education, and it would have an important effect on postwar music.

The music policies of the Office of Military Government, United States (OMGUS) were summed up in a Psychological Warfare document titled, "Music Control Instruction No. 1":

> German musical life must be influenced by positive rather than by negative means, i.e., by encouraging music which we think beneficial and crowding out that which we think dangerous.[388]

O One of the composers placed in the "dangerous" category was Richard Strauss. "We must not allow such composers to be built up by special concerts devoted entirely to their works or conducted by them."[389] If composers like Strauss, deemed likely to reawaken feelings of Germanic supremacy were out, which composers would replace them? The obvious answer was, first, those composers, like Felix Mendelssohn, who had been banned by the Nazis. Secondly, it was decided that the music of well-known American composers, like Aaron Copland, should be actively promoted.

---

[388] Toby Thacker, *Music after Hitler, 1945-1955*, pg. 24

[389] Alex Ross, *The Rest is Noise*, pg. 348

Heavy-handed attempts to promote American concert music met with only limited success. At one such event, only thirty people turned up. The Office of Military Government decided to purchase the remaining 350 tickets and to distribute them to young musicians in the military. By so doing, the American occupation was not only funding the concerts but filling the seats as well.

DARMSTADT

The American attempt to redirect postwar German music would meet with much greater success in Darmstadt, a city that had been virtually destroyed by Allied bombing during the war. "Darmstadt is a city of the dead – literally and figuratively," wrote British scientist, D.A. Spencer in his diary in 1945, after passing through the city.

"Not a soul in its alleyways between red rubble that were once streets. Long, gaunt ruins…an overpowering silence everywhere."[390]

On the night between September 11th and 12th, 1944, the German city of Darmstadt was subjected to a devastating bombing raid by the British Royal Airforce. Ironically, in the memory of one survivor, the air raid will always bring to mind the charming music of Richard Strauss. On the night prior to the bombing, he vividly recalls listening to songs on the radio from the "sensuous world…portrayed in Strauss's magical music."[391]

After the war, in 1949, Darmstadt experienced a wholly different world of music as it hosted yet another American-sponsored experiment in the "reorientation" of German culture.

Wolfgang Steinecke, a man with a background in film and radio, proposed to set up a summer institute so that young composers might familiarize themselves with music which the Nazis had banned. The American authorities warmly backed the plan which was called, "The International Summer Courses in New Music".

---

[390] Martin Iddon, *New Music at Darmstadt*, pg. 2

[391] ibid

Arnold Schoenberg seemed to be the perfect match for Darmstadt. He had been denounced by the Nazis, and he was Jewish, but nevertheless completely German. His music was contemporary, so there was no possibility of it stirring pro-Nazi sentiments. Schoenberg quickly became the shining example for young German composers.

The Summer Courses in New Music 1949 season coincided with Schoenberg's 75th birthday, so it was decided to invite the composer to attend.

But government red tape and Schoenberg's poor health prevented him from coming.[392] Nevertheless, his presence was felt at the 1949 summer course: his *Five Pieces for Orchestra*, the *Variations for Orchestra*, the *Violin Concerto*, the *String Trio*, and the *Fourth String Quartet*, were all played. In fact, there was so much music by Arnold Schoenberg that American officials began to worry that the summer courses were becoming "one-sided" by promoting the twelve-tone method too much.

A memo by Colonel Ralph A. Burns, the chief of the Cultural Affairs Branch of the Education and Cultural Relations Division complained that "the over-emphasis on twelve-tone music was regretted."

Burns was especially disturbed by the snobbish behavior of a group of French students who arrived with their teacher, Rene Leibowitz, a dogmatic proponent of the twelve-tone method: "Leibowitz represents and admits as valid only the most radical kind of music and is openly disdainful of any other. His attitude is aped by the students."[393]

---

[392] Alex Ross, *The Rest is Noise*, pg. 350

[393] Martin Iddon, *New Music at Darmstadt*, pg. 22

Without intending to do so, the American government had become, in effect, the promoter of the most radical kind of modern classical music. The Darmstadt summer courses and their concerts were wholly subsidized by the city, and ultimately, the American occupation forces. The Darmstadt composers, therefore, had no obligation whatsoever to a paying public audience.

Meanwhile, concerts of traditional classical music carried on just as they had during the Nazi period and before. The result was a division between a classical establishment, somewhat tainted by association with Nazism, now struggling to survive economically, and on the other hand, a new avant-garde establishment - so violently opposed to Nazism that it disavowed all music of the past - subsidized by the American government, and therefore, completely insulated from the likes and dislikes of the paying audience.

MUSIC FOR THE COLD WAR

At the end of the Second World War, the former allies, America and the Soviet Union, did not completely demobilize their great armies. Instead, the two fully armed superpowers eyed each other warily across what Churchill called the "iron curtain" that had divided Eastern and Western Europe. The introduction of atomic weapons raised the stakes as tensions increased and the general mood darkened. As the Cold War standoff hardened, a similar kind of doctrinaire attitude began to take root in the world of music.

The modernist impulse had given birth to a variety of experimental musical languages and techniques in the early twentieth century: the atmospheric, impressionistic music of Debussy in France and in Germany, its dark counterpart, the dissonant, expressionistic music of Schoenberg, Webern, and Berg; the violent, primitivist rhythms of Stravinsky's *Rite of Spring*, and the neoclassical retreat to the safety of tonality during the years of World War II.

While all of this music was inventive and indeed revolutionary in its time, it would come to seem positively conservative in comparison with the radical music that appeared in the years following the war.

This remarkable new music was accompanied by an explosion of new theories, counter-theories, polemics, alliances, and splits, mirroring in a cultural form the polarized world of Cold War politics. But the dominant aesthetic that would define it all was one of dissonance, density, difficulty, and complexity.[394]

For the generation of European composers coming to maturity in the aftermath of the Second World War, twelve-tone music was particularly appealing, if for no other reason than that it was suppressed by Hitler and Stalin. For some, like Ernst Krenek, the use of the twelve-tone musical language even seemed like a moral imperative: "My adoption of the musical technique that tyrants hated most of all may be interpreted as an expression of protest and thus a result of their influence."[395]

Pierre Boulez was twenty years old when he first encountered twelve-tone music in the form of Schoenberg's *Woodwind Quintet* conducted and explained by Rene Leibowitz. (This is the same Rene Leibowitz who would later arrive at Darmstadt and become an object of consternation for Colonel Ralph Burns). This event would prove to be a turning point for Boulez.

---

[394] Alex Ross, *The Rest is Noise*, pg. 356

[395] Joan and Jean Strommer, *Transcendence in Music, Poetry, and Film, from Life the Human Quest for an Ideal: 25th Anniversary Publication, Book 2*, edited by M. Kronegger and Anna-Teresa Tymieniecka pg. 108

> It was a revelation. Here was music of our time, a language with unlimited possibilities. No other musical language was now possible. It was a radical revolution, for all former patterns were abolished. Music had now moved out of the world of Newton and into the world of Einstein. The old tonal idea was like a world defined by gravity and attraction. The 12-tone idea is based on a universe in perpetual expansion.[396]

Despite his initial enthusiasm, by 1948, Boulez had become disenchanted with Schoenberg for not realizing the full implications of the twelve-tone system, and for failing to bring about a revolution radical enough to encompass the realities of the new age. Specifically, he criticized Schoenberg for using the twelve-tone row as a musical theme rather than as a series of purely abstract interval relationships.[397]

Boulez believed that Schoenberg's system was now an antiquated paradigm, in need of modification, and he discovered the new model he was searching for in the music of French composer, Olivier Messiaen. Boulez had studied with Messiaen in 1944 and had remained within his circle of acquaintance, and was therefore aware of the radical new idea Messiaen hit upon in 1949.

In his piano composition, *Mode de valeurs et d'intensities* (Scale of Durations and Dynamics) Messiaen created scales, not only of pitches, but also of durations, dynamic levels, and articulations.[398]

---

[396] Joan Peyser, *To Boulez and Beyond*, pg. 154

[397] Richard Taruskin, ed., *Music of the Western World: A History in Documents*, pg. 507

[398] Paul Griffiths, *Modern Music, A Concise History from Debussy to Boulez*, pg. 142

Boulez began to apply this principle in his own compositions, using a similar technique to dictate each parameter of musical sound: pitch, duration, dynamics, and articulation, creating a radical new form of twelve-tone music which came to be called "total serialism", or simply, "serialism".[399] In a serial composition, a series of twelve is established for each parameter. In principle, no pitch should sound until the other eleven have sounded. Likewise, no duration should appear until all twelve have been used. No dynamic marking or articulation should be employed until all twelve have appeared.

Boulez strictly applied this technique to his *Second Piano Sonata* (1948), the *Livre pour quatuor* (1949), and his *Structures for Two Pianos* (1951). Since all elements of the musical sound are in continual circulation, the music is in a constant state of flux. Serial music seems cold, detached, and unemotional. Because there are no repeated themes or musical ideas, there is no musical narrative for the mind to follow. For the listener, there is no past to remember, no future to anticipate. The present moment is all there is.

The music created by serial techniques seemed strangely appropriate to the Cold War Existentialist world of the 1950s. The complex intellectual manipulation of charts and tables necessary for the composition of serial music seemed to mirror the scientific formulas and equations that had produced the atomic bomb which now overshadowed the world.

It could be argued that art is simply a mirror, reflecting the culture that produced it. If that is the case, the serial music of the 1950s offers a unique glimpse into the aesthetic disposition of this decade.

---

[399] ibid

Karlheinz Stockhausen was the German counterpart to Pierre Boulez. He was born on August 22, 1928, the oldest of three children born to poor parents of a rural background. After the birth of her third child, Stockhausen's mother began to suffer severe depression and was committed to a mental hospital in 1933, where she was killed eight years later as part of the Nazi euthanasia program. His father was conscripted into the military and disappeared on the Hungarian front.

As a young man, Stockhausen supported himself by playing piano wherever and whenever the opportunity presented itself. At one point he accepted employment from a traveling magician, "The Conjuror Adrion", for whom he provided suitable atmospheric music by improvising at the piano. Stockhausen and Adrion traveled the length of Germany, performing at colleges, cultural clubs, theatrical societies, and any other available venue. Looking back years later, Adrion recalled that when they would arrive in a new city, they would go straight to the hall to check the stage, the acoustics, and, of course, the grand piano.

> Karlheinz Stockhausen would seat himself at the piano, utterly composed, his eyes narrowing to a tiny slit, his head imperceptibly straining upwards. He played one note, then another, then a third, struck a few chords, and on his face you could see more and more clearly his displeasure at the instrument's unsatisfactory condition – and then there would be a look of unspeakable suffering, of reproach mixed with despair, from my distressed partner, and the exclamation (sometimes more of a scream), 'How am I supposed to make your magic music for you on this heap of [excrement]!?' And with equal regularity he would slam the lid shut.[400]

---

[400] Michael Kurtz, *Stockhausen, A Biography*, pg. 44

In 1951, Stockhausen attended the summer classes at Darmstadt, and there he heard a tape-recording of Messiaen's *Mode de valeurs et d'intensities*. Like Boulez, Stockhausen was immediately inspired by the idea of totally organized serial music and set to work creating his own composition. His first serial work, written in 1951, was entitled *Kreuzspiel* (Cross Play), for oboe, bass clarinet, piano, and percussion. Stockhausen explained the meaning of the title in terms of the distribution of the twelve pitches within the piano part:

> The piano begins in the extreme outer registers and progressively – through crossing of registers – brings into play six notes 'from above' and six notes 'from below'…the whole process then runs backwards in mirror form, so that at the end of the first stage all the notes are again in the extreme registers of the piano, as a result of the crossing process, however, the six notes from 'up top' are now 'down below', and vice versa.[401]

Stockhausen showed the score for *Kreuzspiel* to his friend Herbert Eimert, the director of the electronic music studio, NWDR, who presciently warned him, "If you make music like this, you will have to be patient for twenty years until you get a performance."[402]

The audience at the premiere was evidently unable to appreciate the subtle architecture of *Kreuzspiel* – the performance did not go well. In his book on the works of Stockhausen, Robin Maconie[403] offers several possible reasons for the failure of *Kreuzspiel* at its first performance:

---

[401] Ibid, pg. 41

[402] Ibid, pg. 43

[403] Robin Maconie was a student of Stockhausen, and this fulsome defense of *Kreuzspiel* can be assumed to reflect the opinions and attitudes of the composer.

"Classically-trained performers were not then used to listening to one another, nor to playing conversationally...they did not know what to do...", "the 1952 German audience, living in a time of political uncertainty looked to new music to revive a spirit of national identity...", "listeners were offended by the cool, personal self-sufficiency of *Kreuzspiel,* and also by its seeming to defer, by its salon-jazz character, to the vulgar influence of the occupying American culture."[404] Whatever the reason for its failure, Stockhausen withdrew the score, and did not revive it again until 1959.

By the middle of the 1950s, Boulez and Stockhausen had emerged as the two most important composers of what was being called "new music", and their language was the rigorous language of twelve-tone serialism.

SCHOENBERG VS STRAVINSKY: THE MUSICAL COLD WAR

After emigrating from Europe to the United States in the 1930s, Arnold Schoenberg eventually settled in Los Angeles, where he taught at UCLA and took private students. Schoenberg was delighted with the resurgence of his ideas in postwar Germany but was alarmed by the fanaticism of some of his adherents. Schoenberg had made a remarkable prophecy in 1909:

"The second half of this century will spoil by overestimation all the good in me that the first half, by underestimation, has left intact."[405]

He was especially disturbed by the attacks made by some of his admirers on Igor Stravinsky, who was then seen as the standard-bearer of Neoclassicism.

---

[404] Robin Maconie, *The Works of Stockhausen*, pg. 22

[405] Marshall Marcus, *Daniel Barenboim's Herculean challenge*, from *The Guardian*, January 25, 2010

For instance, when Theodor Adorno wrote an essay attacking Stravinsky, Schoenberg came to his rival's defense. Schoenberg wrote to the critic H. H. Stuckenschmidt: "It is disgusting…how [Adorno] treats Stravinsky. I am certainly no admirer of Stravinsky, although I like a piece of his here and there very much – but one should not write like that."[406]

By an ironic twist of fate, in the early 1950s, Igor Stravinsky, the champion of Neoclassicism and presumably the great rival of Schoenberg, was also living in Los Angeles, only a few minutes away from Schoenberg, though, as far as is known, the two never met. From his Los Angeles home, he watched as Schoenberg's twelve-tone method was adopted and adapted for use by the younger generation of composers in Europe and America. He received reports of his own music being booed in Paris by an upstart young composer named Pierre Boulez and his friends.[407] He was surely dismayed by the prevailing impression that his music was a relic of a bygone age while younger composers carefully studied the scores of Anton Webern.

For his part, Stravinsky had always been publically generous towards Schoenberg. In 1913, he criticized Vienna for ignoring Schoenberg, calling him, "one of the greatest creative spirits of our era."[408] As late as 1939, while Neoclassicism was at the peak of its popularity, Stravinsky said,

---

[406] Nicholas Lezard, *Quasi Una Fantasia: Essays on Modern Music by Theodor Adorno – review*, from *The Guardian*, February 21, 2012

[407] Alex Ross, *The Rest is Noise*, pg. 383 – As Alex Ross points out, Stravinsky did not at the time know Boulez had instigated this.

[408] Joan Peyser, *To Boulez and Beyond*, pg.108

> Whatever opinion one may hold about the music of Arnold Schoenberg (to take as an example a composer evolving along lines essentially different from mine, both aesthetically and technically)…it is impossible for a self-respecting mind equipped with genuine musical culture not to feel that the composer of *Pierrot Lunaire* is fully aware of what he is doing and that he is not trying to deceive anyone. He adopted the musical system that suited his needs and within this system, he is perfectly consistent with himself, perfectly coherent. One cannot dismiss music that one dislikes by labeling it as cacophony.[409]

Nevertheless, in the polarized, Cold War atmosphere of the 1950s, Schoenberg and Stravinsky represented two opposing musical camps, between which, like the United States and the Soviet Union, there seemed to be no possibility of compromise.

Everything changed on Friday, June 13, 1951, when Arnold Schoenberg died. At the time of Schoenberg's death, Stravinsky had been spending time with a young Julliard-trained conductor named Robert Craft. Craft had become Stravinsky's assistant and the two men had developed a close, almost father-and-son relationship. As a conductor, Craft was well-versed, not only in the works of Stravinsky but in the twelve-tone music of Schoenberg and Webern as well.

Almost immediately upon hearing of Schoenberg's death, Stravinsky began to question Craft about the twelve-tone technique. (Among his other merits, Craft was also a conscientious diarist, and carefully preserved the details of this period.) Over the next several years, Stravinsky set about learning a new musical language.

---

[409] Ibid, pg. 109

First, he absorbed Schoenberg's method. Following Craft's lead, he then moved on to the works of Webern. Stravinsky was drawn to Webern for the hard, clean edges of his music; for the nonexpressionistic purity of his art.[410]

Stravinsky cultivated a friendship with Boulez, even traveling to Paris in 1957 to visit Boulez in his Paris apartment. Stravinsky was "captivated by Boulez", Craft reports, "[and] with his new musical ideas, and his extraordinary intelligence, quickness, and sense of humor."[411]

By the end of the 1950s, all traces of tonality had disappeared from Stravinsky's work. Though many neoclassical composers, like Leonard Bernstein, felt betrayed by Stravinsky's adoption of Schoenberg's twelve-tone method[412], many others, like Aaron Copland, followed his lead.[413]

What Stravinsky did not know was that many of his twelve-tone compositions were being covertly commissioned by the CIA as part of a program, the aim of which was to demonstrate that America was on the cutting edge of cultural development and to counter the Soviet characterization of America as a culturally barren "nation of gum-chewing, Chevy-driving philistines."[414]

---

[410] Ibid, pg. 206

[411] Ibid

[412] "like a general defecting to the enemy camp," said Leonard Bernstein. Michael Steinberg, *The New York Times*, December 16, 1973

[413] In 1952, Copland said, "The twelve-tone composer...is no longer writing music to satisfy himself; whether he likes it or not, he is writing it against a vocal and militant [communist] opposition." (From *Aaron Copland: The Life & Work of an Uncommon Man*, by Howard Pollack, pg. 446). Whatever his reasons for adopting the twelve-tone method, it must be admitted Copland's twelve-tone compositions are not his best works.

[414] Frances Stonor Saunders, *The Cultural Cold War*, The New York Times, archive

In a 2001 book entitled *The Cultural Cold War*, author Frances Saunders reveals that, beginning in 1947, the CIA began covertly funding concerts by avant-garde composers, including Boulez and Stockhausen, with the original goal of "eject[ing] the Nazis from German musical life and licens[ing] those German musicians (giving them the right to exercise their profession) whom we believed to be 'clean' Germans," and to "control the programs of German concerts and see to it that they would not turn into nationalist manifestations."

However, as the Cold War got underway, the strategic focus of the cultural contest shifted from the German arena to the Soviet Union. The CIA saw the Cold War as primarily a psychological contest, one in which the Soviets had an early advantage.

> Experts in the use of culture as a tool of political persuasion, the Soviets did much in these early years of the Cold War to establish its central paradigm as a cultural one. Lacking the economic power of the United States and, above all, still without a nuclear capability, Stalin's regime concentrated on winning `the battle for men's minds'.[415]

In the Cold War "battle for men's minds", the CIA engaged the Soviets across a broad cultural front, funding concerts and secretly commissioning works by major modernist composers, including the newly converted twelve-tone Stravinsky.[416] As the Cold War progressed throughout the 1950s, another secretly funded project of the CIA, this time in the world of modern art, would prove to be wildly successful, beyond any reasonable expectation.

---

[415] ibid

[416] Ian Wellens, *Music on the Frontline: Nicolas Nabokov Struggle Against Communism*, pg. 121

Whether or not the New York school of Abstract Expressionism would have prospered to the extent that it did in the 1950s without the assistance of the CIA is a question that can never be answered.

CHAPTER TEN: ART AND MUSIC IN POSTWAR AMERICA

America emerged from the Second World War as the strongest nation on earth, both militarily and economically. With a monopoly on the atomic bomb and a booming economy, a general mood of optimism prevailed in the United States. During the war, there was plenty of work, but little to buy, thanks to rationing. After the war, with rationing lifted, Americans went on a consumer spending spree, with new homes, new cars, and new household appliances at the top of the list. This consumerism, in turn further fueled the economy, resulting in a GNP growth rate of 250% between 1945 and 1960.[417]

Just as World War II marked the end of European leadership militarily and economically, it also spelled the end of European dominance of the art world. The suppression of cultural life in Europe, as German military control spread across the continent during the war years, coupled with the clampdown on modern art in totalitarian countries, resulted in a mass exodus of artists from Europe to America. The presence in America, not only of European artists but also huge collections of modern art, added weight to the impression that the balance of cultural power and influence had shifted from Paris to New York.

In the late 1940s and 1950s, a dynamic new art movement called Abstract Expressionism emerged in New York City. Abstract Expressionism was the first purely American avant-garde art movement and its advent is arguably the most significant event in the history of modern art since Picasso and Braque created Cubism.[418]

---

[417] Tim McNeese, *The Cold War and Postwar America 1946-1963*, pg. 88-97

[418] Edward Lucie-Smith, *Lives of the Great 20th Century Artists*, pg. 240

The artists who created Abstract Expressionism were not young men – most were in their 40s and 50s [419] and most had worked together previously in a federally funded program called the Federal Art Project (FAP) that came into being during the Great Depression as a branch of the WPA. Nearly 10,000 artists were employed by the FAP during the years of its operation (1935-1943), and it created 200,000 separate works of art, including sculpture, murals, posters, photography, and easel art.

For the group that later became known as the "New York School" of Abstract Expressionists, the most important aspect of the FAP was the sense of community and comradery created among them. As they picked up their paychecks every week ($24.00 was the standard stipend), the artists got to know one another and became acquainted with each other's work. [420] One of these artists, Willem de Kooning said,

> The Project was terribly important. It gave us enough to live on and we could paint what we wanted…I had to resign after a year because I was an alien, but even in that short time, I changed my attitude toward being an artist. Instead of doing odd jobs and painting on the side, I painted and did odd jobs on the side. My life was the same, but I had a different view of it. I gave up the idea of first making a fortune and then painting in my old age.[421]

Artists living in New York in the 1930s and 1940s benefitted from an increasingly sophisticated network of museums and galleries. The Museum of Modern Art staged exhibitions such as, "Cubism and Abstract Art", "Fantastic Art, Dada, and Surrealism" and a major retrospective of Pablo Picasso.

---

[419] Norbert Lynton, *The Story of Modern Art*, pg. 227

[420] Newsweek, Volume 58, pg. 52

[421] Irving Sandler, *From Avant-garde to Pluralism: An On-the-spot History*, pg. 35

In 1939, the Solomon R. Guggenheim Museum opened, featuring modernist art, including a large collection of works by Wassily Kandinsky. All of this activity meant that artists in New York City were extraordinarily knowledgeable about trends in modern European art. In addition, many European modernists who had fled the upheaval caused by the war in Europe were living in New York. Personal contacts with artists like Marcel Duchamp and Piet Mondrian, made a huge impact on the American artists who encountered them and saw their works first hand. But it was Surrealism, with its close connection to Sigmund Freud, which was the single greatest influence on the Abstract Expressionists.

SURREALISM

In the years between 1922 and 1924, as the Dada movement was beginning to lose momentum, a new idea began to emerge in France. The self-declared leader of the movement, André Breton had trained in medicine and psychiatry and had served in a neurological hospital during the First World War, where he discovered Sigmund Freud's methods of psychoanalysis while treating soldiers suffering from shell shock. Ultimately, Breton became less interested in curing psychic disturbances than in exploiting them. He wanted to open a window on the disorderly inner world and make creative use of its contents. In a famous credo, Breton wrote, "I believe in the future resolution of the two states, apparently so contradictory, of dream and reality, in a sort of absolute reality, or *surreality*."[422]

In 1924 André Breton published his Surrealist Manifesto. He wrote that Surrealism is based "on the belief in the superior reality of certain previously neglected associations, in the omnipotence of dreams, and in the disinterested play of thought."[423]

---

[422] Steven Naifah, *Jackson Pollock, an American Saga*, pg. 412

Breton's ideas proved easier to express than to put into practice. The Freudian encouragement to draw on the creative reservoir of the unconscious was clear. But the methodology was somewhat ambiguous. Was it describing inspiration or technique? As it turned out, this question divided the Surrealists into two opposing practices: dream painting and automatism.

In his book, *The Interpretation of Dreams*, Freud developed the idea that the contents of the unconscious mind may be uncovered through dream analysis. Some surrealist painters, like Salvador Dali and Rene Magritte, attempted to illustrate their dreams; to realistically capture the illogical contents of the dream world, often by placing unrelated objects side by side. Breton had already suggested this idea, imagining "a juxtaposition of two...distant realities. The more the relationship between the two juxtaposed realities is distant...the stronger the image will be – the greater its emotional power and poetic reality." [424] In the works of Dali and Magritte, the unconscious mind became a source of inspiration, guiding the artist as he attempted to render faithfully, even realistically, a vivid image of the dream world, making use of all of his painterly technique and skill.

In another camp were painters who did not look to the unconscious mind merely as a source of inspiration, but sought to surrender conscious control altogether by employing a technique known as automatism.

---

[423] André Breton, *Surrealist Manifestos*, pg. 26

[424] Ibid, pg. 20

In Freudian psychology, free association is a technique in which the patient is encouraged to relate whatever thoughts come into the mind during the analytic session, without any censorship. The goal is that by so doing the contents of the unconscious mind can be revealed. Breton adapted Freud's technique of free association to artistic expression, developing techniques of "automatic writing", whereby rapid flurries of writing are carried out in the absence of any preconceived idea.[425]

Some surrealist painters adapted the idea of automatic writing to drawing, creating images without any deliberate conscious control. Many of Joan Miró's paintings were created by this kind of automatism: "Rather than setting out to paint something, I [simply] begin painting, and as I paint, the picture begins to assert itself, or suggest itself under my brush...the first stage is free, unconscious."[426]

JACKSON POLLOCK

During the heyday of Abstract Expressionism in the late 1940s and early 1950s, Jackson Pollock was, without a doubt the most famous member of the New York group. He was the focus of a feature story in Life magazine under the title, *Jackson Pollock – Is He the Greatest Living Painter in the United States?* Even today his paintings sell for hundreds of millions of dollars. In 2006, for instance, one of his paintings brought $140 million – the highest price ever paid for a painting at that time.[427]

In the beginning, however, he showed the least promise of any of the New York group.

---

[425] David Hopkins, *Dada and Surrealism*, pg. 17

[426] Robin Adèle Greeley, *Surrealism and the Spanish Civil War*, pg. 28

[427] Ed Pilkington, *Mexican splashes out record $140m for Jackson Pollock's drops of genius*, The Guardian, November 3, 2006

He was, in the words of art critic Hilton Kramer, "abysmally ill-prepared, by training or temperament or intellect..."[428]

During the Great Depression in the 1930s, Pollock worked for the Federal Art Project, collecting the usual $24 per week, creating nondescript examples of Americana, painted in a straightforward, representational way. In 1939, as World War II was getting underway in Europe, Pollock was a twenty-seven-year-old painter "whose accomplishments were negligible, and whose personality was already showing signs of fracture and disarray."[429] However, it was in 1939 that Pollock first came in contact with the work of Picasso, viewing Guernica at the Valentine Gallery in New York, and later that year, the huge retrospective, "Picasso, Forty Years of His Art" at the Museum of Modern Art.[430]

Pollock immediately dropped his attempts at representational art and plunged into the world of Picasso-influenced abstract painting. Pollock was undergoing Jungian psychoanalysis at this time and the awkward titles of his paintings reflect the influence of Jung's archetypes: *The She-Wolf*, *Male and Female*, *Guardians of the Secret*, and so on.

The idea which eventually led to Pollock's most important artistic breakthrough was the Surrealist notion of automatism, introduced to him by a fellow member of the New York group. Pollock was especially attracted to the idea that automatism might directly tap the unconscious mind. He soon hit upon another novel idea which would further remove conscious control from the production of his art: dripping the paint onto the canvas rather than applying it with a brush.

---

[428] Hilton Kramer, *The Triumph of Modernism*, pg. 76

[429] ibid

[430] ibid

This technique became Pollock's trademark. The works which he produced between 1947 and 1950 were all created by pouring, flinging, or dripping the paint onto the canvas as it lay flat on the ground, prompting the nickname, "Jack the Dripper".

The revolutionary aspect of Pollock's drip technique lies in the fact that the images reveal no evidence of the direct touch of the artist[431] – there are no brush-strokes. Rather, the paintings preserve a record of a bodily activity in which the artist's intent is transformed by the interaction of gravity, accident, and the unpredictable fluid response of the paint. For this reason, some art critics of the time referred to these works as "action paintings".

With increasing fame and attention from the media, Pollock found it hard to find the time and solitude he needed in order to create his paintings. Consequently, his creative output began to dwindle and his inspiration seemed to abandon him. Compounding the problem, his frequent visits to the Cedar Bar in New York, a favorite hangout for artists, attracted attention from friends and others who made it a point of honor to get him drunk. "For them, Jackson was a freak, just part of the entertainment, a notorious figure in the art world who had somehow succeeded in spite of himself."[432]

In 1954 he held a final one-man show. The quality of his work had noticeably deteriorated and his rate of production had slowed - he would soon stop painting altogether. He began a reckless affair which led to a separation from his wife, which further exacerbated his already notorious moodiness.

---

[431] However, they do reveal the indirect presence of the artist. In his *Number 10*, which is on display at the Museum of Fine Arts in Boston, Pollock's cigarette butt can be clearly seen, preserved by the enamel paint in the spot where it evidently fell from his mouth as he created the painting.

[432] Edward Lucie-Smith, *Lives of the Great 20th Century Artists*, pg. 265

On August 11, 1956, Pollock was killed in a single-car accident. He was drunk, and reportedly angry at the time of the crash, driving at eighty miles an hour when he failed to negotiate a turn.[433]

ARSHILE GORKY

Arshile Gorky was born in Turkish Armenia in 1904 and immigrated to the United States in 1920. Upon arriving in America at age sixteen, Gorky decided that he would become an artist, initially imitating the style of Cezanne, then Picasso. During the Great Depression in the 1930s, Gorky worked for the Federal Art Project and became acquainted with the other artists who would later form the core group of New York Abstract Expressionists. In 1937 the Whitney Museum bought one of his paintings – his first museum purchase. In 1944 he met the exiled Surrealists, including their leader, André Breton, who became an important influence on Gorky's mature style.

Arshile Gorky, *Cornfield of Health II* (1944) (Photograph by author)

---

[433] Steven Naifah, *Jackson Pollock, an American Saga*, pg. 793 (There were two women in the car with him at the time of the crash, one of whom was also killed – the other survived and wrote a book about Pollock, detailing the night of the crash.)

In 1946 Gorky suffered the first of what would become a string of devastating misfortunes. In January a fire destroyed twenty-seven of his paintings along with many notebooks and drawings. In February he underwent a dangerous operation for cancer. In June of 1948 he was involved in a serious automobile accident in which his neck was broken and his painting arm temporarily paralyzed. When he was released from the hospital, tensions in his marriage stemming from Gorky's suspicions of his wife's unfaithfulness led to a separation. In July, Gorky committed suicide, leaving a final note chalked on the wall nearby, "Goodbye My Loveds".[434]

WILLEM DE KOONING

Willem de Kooning was born in Rotterdam in 1904. He studied art at the Rotterdam Academy of Fine Arts and was apprenticed to a local firm of commercial artists where he continued to study until 1924.[435] In 1926 he came to the United States as a stowaway. He worked as a house-painter in Hoboken, New Jersey, before finally moving to New York. There he was befriended by Arshile Gorky, and the two struck up a mutually beneficial friendship.

> I met a lot of artists – but then I met Gorky. I had had some training in Holland, quite a training, the Academy. Gorky didn't have that at all. He came from no place; he came here when he was sixteen, from Tiflis in Georgia, with an Armenian upbringing. And for some mysterious reason he knew more about painting and art – he just knew it by nature – though I was supposed to know and feel and understand, he really did it better. [436]

---

[434] Edward Lucie-Smith, *Lives of the Great 20th Century Artists*, pg.253

[435] Ibid, pg.247

[436] Willem De Kooning, John Elderfield, *De Kooning: A Retrospective*, pg. 53

During the Depression, de Kooning worked for a time for the Federal Art Program but was let go because it was discovered that he was an illegal immigrant. By the 1940s de Kooning's work was being shown in exhibitions with other artists in the Abstract Expressionist movement. In 1951, his painting, *Excavation*, won the Logan Medal and Purchase Prize at the Sixtieth Annual of American Painting and Sculpture in Chicago, and in 1953, six of his paintings were shown at the Sidney Janus gallery in New York, which caused a sensation at the time.

Willem de Kooning, *Boudoir* (1951) (Photograph by author)

In the 1960s and 1970s, de Kooning's physical and mental condition began to deteriorate. At first, this decline was blamed on his heavy drinking, but eventually he was diagnosed with Alzheimer's disease.

Consequently, his works from the 1980s until his death in 1997 were the subject of some controversy. Claims were made that paintings attributed to him were composite efforts of studio assistants and possibly his wife, Elaine de Kooning.[437]

FRANZ KLINE

Franz Kline was born in Pennsylvania in 1910 and studied art in Boston in the early 1930s. Attracted to the romance of upper-class British life, he traveled to England in 1935, enrolling in Heatherley's School of Fine Arts in London. Kline married in England and would have applied for British citizenship, but this proved impossible for him, prompting his return to the United States with his British wife. In New York, he showed his work wherever possible, painted cityscapes, and murals in bars.

The turning point in his career came in 1943 when he met Willem de Kooning, through whose influence Kline began to move from figurative painting to abstraction. In 1949 de Kooning showed Kline how to use a Bell-Opticon projector to enlarge drawings onto a large canvas. (The New York group tended to paint on enormous canvases, having discovered the power of large images through their experience painting murals for the FAP). Kline immediately became intrigued with the possibilities presented by the projection of his drawings to large scale. He enlarged a drawing of his favorite chair to such an extreme degree that the image overlapped the canvas. Kline noted that under these circumstances the design became virtually abstract.

Another possible factor in his move from realism to abstraction was more personal. His wife, Elizabeth, began to exhibit signs of mental illness, aggravated by their precarious financial situation and her husband's uncertain prospects.

---

[437] Ibid, pg. 251

More than once they were forced to move because of eviction for non-payment of rent. Between 1938 and 1957 the Klines moved no less than fourteen times.[438] In 1948 Elizabeth was admitted to Central Islip State Hospital where she remained for twelve years, finally discharged in 1960.

Meanwhile, Kline's reputation began to grow. His new abstract images, created with the aid of the Bell-Opticon projector created a sensation. His trademark style was a stark black and white image, with bold, rough, single brushstrokes crossing the canvas, tracing the outline of some now-unrecognizable form.

Franz Kline, *Turin* (1960) (Photograph by author)

---

[438] Edward Lucie-Smith, *Lives of the Great 20th Century Artists*, pg. 261

Kline's success and reputation increased throughout the 1950s as museums competed for his works and as prices steadily escalated. However, in 1961 at the height of his success, Kline was diagnosed with heart disease, exacerbated by his smoking and hard-drinking lifestyle. He was hospitalized and died in 1962.[439]

MARK ROTHKO

Mark Rothko was born in Russia in 1903, as Marcus Rothkovich, the youngest of four children. Rothko's father, Jakob, immigrated to the United States in 1910, followed by his two oldest sons, who were threatened with conscription. Eventually, the entire family came to the United States, settling in Oregon. Seven months after their arrival, Jakob died unexpectedly, and young Mark Rothko had to deliver newspapers to pay for his education.

Despite these disadvantages, Rothko did well in school, graduating at age 17, and received a scholarship to attend college at Yale. After only six months, however, the scholarship was withdrawn, Rothko assumed, because of concealed anti-Semitism which was prevalent in Ivy League colleges at the time. In 1923 he dropped out of college to, in his words, "bum around a little bit."[440]

Eventually, he ended up in New York where he did odd jobs and began to paint. During the Depression, he enrolled in the Federal Art Project, through which he met Jackson Pollock, Willem de Kooning, and Arshile Gorky. After experimenting with various modern art techniques, in 1949 he hit upon his signature style: large blocks of contrasting, yet complimentary color, floating over a neutral ground.

---

[439] Ibid, pg. 262

[440] Ibid, pg. 241

Rothko painted only on enormous canvases which are intended to overwhelm the viewer, to create the sensation of being enveloped within the painting. In personal terms, Rothko felt he was painting "the great vacuum at the center of his being."[441] Elaine de Kooning wrote that "the tension of Rothko's work lies in its ominous, pervasive light - that of a sky before a hurricane…in his imperceptible shifts from one pure color to another, there is a sense of atmospheric pressure…"[442]

Rothko was highly secretive about his painting methods, refusing even to allow his studio assistants to be present as he painted. "I am a secretive person," he told his first assistant, "and whatever you see, it's private."[443]

It is now known, however, that Rothko created his paintings by gradually building up multiple translucent layers of opaque oil paint, sometimes as many as 20 layers, thinned and modified by a combination of natural and artificial substances.[444]

He further admitted to fellow artist, Robert Motherwell, that he liked to work under high-intensity lighting, arranged like stage lights, but when the work was shown, he insisted that it be under very low lighting, so that the blocks of color would seem to float in indefinite space. [445]

---

[441] James E. B. Breslin, *Mark Rothko: A Biography*, pg. 280

[442] Richard Williams, *Sounds like Mark Rothko*, The Guardian, January 31, 2002

[443] Ibid, pg. 317

[444] Jane Qiu, *Rothko's Methods Revealed*, Nature, February 1, 2009

[445] Edward Lucie-Smith, *Lives of the Great 20th Century Artists*, pg. 268

In the 1960s Rothko's reputation reached its highest point: he was invited to attend John F. Kennedy's inauguration in 1961 and he was receiving between $10,000 and $15,000 for his paintings.[446] In 1964 Rothko was commissioned by Houston art collector, John de Menil to create a meditative space in which his paintings could be shown to maximum effect. Rothko was given complete creative license, not only to produce the art, but also to design the space that would surround it, and he clashed frequently with the architect. The finished building, which is now called the Rothko Chapel, is lit only by sky-light, and the images he created for it are all in dark colors.

The chapel opened in 1971, but Rothko did not live to see it completed. His bouts of depression had become ever more frequent throughout the 1960s and finally gave way to complete melancholia. His drinking was out of control and he was taking heavy doses of barbiturates and anti-depressants. On New Year's Day in 1969, Rothko separated from his wife and moved into his studio.

In February of 1970 Rothko was discovered by his assistant, dead on the floor of his studio, in a pool of his own blood. He had ended his life by slicing open his arms with a razor. He was surrounded by the paintings he had created in the last year of his life: a series of stark black on grey images, reflecting his darkening mood.[447]

MORTON FELDMAN AND *ROTHKO CHAPEL*

When the Rothko Chapel was dedicated in 1971, New York composer Morton Feldman traveled to Houston for the opening.

---

[446] James E. B. Breslin, *Mark Rothko: A Biography*, pg. 5

[447] ibid

Feldman had been close to Rothko, and was, in fact, acquainted with all of the Abstract Expressionists in New York. Feldman had been introduced to the world of the New York painters after a chance[448] meeting with John Cage. Feldman attended meetings of the Eighth Street Artists' Club, the headquarters of the Abstract Expressionists, and developed close relationships with many of the artists, dedicating several musical compositions to them. While Feldman was in Houston for the dedication of the Rothko Chapel, he was commissioned by John de Menil to create a commemorative musical work in honor of the painter. The composition Feldman produced was entitled simply *Rothko Chapel*. Scored for voices, percussion, and viola solo, it is a quiet, slow-moving work evoking the hushed tone of the Rothko Chapel and the paintings themselves.

CIA PROMOTION OF ABSTRACT EXPRESSIONISM

A growing body of evidence suggests that the Central Intelligence Agency covertly funded and promoted Abstract Expressionism in the 1940s and 1950s in an effort to win the cultural cold war with the Soviet Union. Why would the CIA promote Abstract Expressionism?

In the early 1950s, the culture became a key Cold War battleground. The objective was to win the sympathies of influential western European intellectuals, the majority of whom detested what they perceived as the shallow, anti-intellectual, commercialized consumer culture of the United States, and it's "Coca-colonization" of the rest of the world.[449]

---

[448] No pun intended

[449] Greg Bamhisel, *Cold War Modernists*,

Initially, these attempts to promote American modern art were made openly. In 1947 the State Department organized the purchase of paintings and paid for a touring international exhibition entitled "Advancing American Art", with the aim of rebutting Soviet suggestions that America was a cultural desert. But the show caused outrage at home, prompting one bitter congressman to say: "I am just a dumb American who pays taxes for this kind of trash."[450] President Truman also denounced the exhibition saying, "If that's art then I'm a Hottentot".[451] The tour had to be canceled.

Those elements of the US government attempting to promote American culture now faced a dilemma. This presidential rejection, combined with Joseph McCarthy's hysterical denunciations of everything thought to be avant-garde or unorthodox, was deeply embarrassing. It discredited the idea that America was a sophisticated, culturally refined democracy. It also prevented the U.S. government from consolidating the shift in cultural supremacy from Paris to New York since the 1930s. To resolve this dilemma, the CIA was brought in.

A former CIA case officer, Donald Jameson, has publically confirmed the agency's involvement in Abstract Expressionism. "Regarding Abstract Expressionism," he said, "I'd love to be able to say that the CIA invented it, just to see what happens in New York tomorrow! But I think that what we did really was [simply] to recognize the difference [between the US and the Soviet Union].

---

[450] Frances Stonor Saunders, *Modern art was CIA 'weapon'*, The Independent, October 21, 1995

[451] "Hottentot", technically speaking, is a reference to a tribe in Southwest Africa. As a racist insult, however, it means primitive or uncultured.

It was recognized that Abstract Expressionism was the kind of art that made Socialist Realism look even more…rigid and confined than it was. And that…was exploited in some of the exhibitions."[452]

According to Jameson, the CIA established what it called a "long-leash" policy by which the Abstract Expressionists could be supported and promoted at "two or three removes". The centerpiece of the plan was an organization called the Congress for Cultural Freedom (the CCF) which, at its height, had offices in 35 countries and published more than two dozen magazines. The CCF would be the official sponsor of touring exhibitions; its magazines would provide useful platforms for critics favorable to the new American painting; and no one, the artists included, would be any the wiser.[453]

The question which cannot be answered is whether Abstract Expressionism would have arisen so quickly, or succeeded so thoroughly, without the support of the CIA.

---

[452] Frances Stonor Saunders, *Modern art was CIA 'weapon'*, *The Independent*, October 21, 1995

[453] ibid

CHAPTER ELEVEN: JOHN CAGE

John Cage is the most important and influential composer of our time. At least that's what author Kyle Gann attempted to write in his New York Times obituary for Cage until he was informed by his editors that he could not refer to Cage as a composer, but rather as a "music-philosopher".[454] Apparently the New York Times had no problem with Gann's assessment of Cage's importance or influence, but only with his vocation as a composer. Similarly, Arnold Schoenberg was once asked if he had any interesting American students. He replied that there were none. But then he smiled and said, "There was one – John Cage." Schoenberg quickly added, "Of course he is not a composer, but he's an inventor of genius."[455] This reluctance to acknowledge John Cage as a composer only serves to illustrate the point that his iconoclastic ideas have redefined the very notion of what it means to be a composer, thereby demonstrating his immense influence and importance.

John Cage was born in Los Angeles in 1912, the son of an inventor who built one of the first functioning submarines. Cage began playing the piano as a child but considered himself a poor student because he was uninterested in practicing scales. While in college, he became convinced that he would be a writer. He then persuaded his parents that going to Europe would be more useful to him than continuing in college. So in his third year in college, he dropped out and went to Paris.[456] In Paris, Cage came into contact with a wide variety of modern painting and music and became convinced that, if others were doing this, he could do it as well. Back in Los Angeles, he accordingly began to paint and write music.

---

[454] James Pritchett, *The Music of John Cage*, Introduction

[455] Richard Kostelanetz, *Conversing with Cage*, pg. 6

[456] Ibid, pg 2-3

According to Cage, those who heard his music had better things to say than those who saw his paintings, so he decided to devote himself to music.[457]

SCHOENBERG

In the 1930s, Arnold Schoenberg and Igor Stravinsky were both living in Los Angeles. For young musicians like Cage, these two world-renowned composers represented opposite musical philosophies, Schoenberg representing Modernism, and Stravinsky representing Neoclassicism. In 1933 Cage chose Schoenberg and Modernism. Cage relates the story:

> I went to see [Schoenberg] in Los Angeles. He said, 'You probably couldn't afford my price.' I said, 'You don't need to mention it because I don't have any money.' So he said, 'Will you devote your life to music?' and I said that I would.[458]

Cage studied with Schoenberg for two years. Finally, it became evident that he and Schoenberg had a fundamental difference on the subject of harmony:

> Several times I tried to explain to Schoenberg that I had no feeling for harmony. He told me that without a feeling for harmony I would always encounter an obstacle – a wall through which I would not be able to pass. My reply was that in that case I would devote my life to beating my head against that wall – maybe that's what I've been doing ever since.[459]

---

[457] Ibid, pg. 4

[458] Ibid, pg. 5

[459] ibid

THE PREPARED PIANO

Because Cage had an aversion to harmony, he initially considered himself to be exclusively a composer of music for percussion instruments. In 1938, he was asked to write music for a dancer named Syvilla Fort, for a performance at the Cornish School in Seattle.[460] The performance space was small, and there was no room for Cage's percussion instruments – the only available instrument was an upright piano which was built into the seating area. Cage hit upon the idea of inserting foreign objects between the strings of the piano, thereby changing its sound from a harmonic sound to a percussive sound.[461] In effect, this "prepared piano" became a one-man percussion ensemble. Bonnie Bird, a modern dance instructor at the Cornish School remembers the invention of the prepared piano vividly. Cage was at this time her accompanist.

> I had a couple of students who were just completing their fourth year. One of them was an absolutely beautiful black girl named Syvilla Fort...When Syvilla and I were discussing her graduation concert, I said she could have two or three pieces written for her by different composers available from the music department – and John was one of them...John came to me after the dance and said, "I have to have a gamelan orchestra." I laughed at him and said, "John, you're absolutely crazy – we can't even afford fifty cents!"...John played for the class on a beat-up grand piano – the dance studios tended to get the leftovers from the music students. It wasn't in the greatest condition; I had a little box behind the piano where I kept all the nuts and bolts and things that fell off...[462]

---

[460] Ibid, pg. 58

[461] ibid

[462] Peter Dickinson, *CageTalk: Dialogues with and about John Cage*, pg. 70 (As an incidental side note, Merce Cunningham was a student in Bonnie Bird's class at this time.)

One of the dances which Bird's students were practicing had a script which called for "telegrams to flutter to the stage". Bonnie Bird had the idea that, instead of telegrams, the dancers would flutter to the stage, sliding on a fireman's pole. She visited the local fire department to see about getting a pole but was informed that the actual pole which was solid brass, was quite expensive. Nevertheless, she visited the brass foundry to investigate, and was given a little piece of a pole for her trouble.

> I handed this piece of brass to John just at the beginning of a technique class. And I said, "Well, you can't have a gamelan; I can't have a brass pole." The upshot of this was that John took the piece of metal and put it onto the tray [of the piano]. The tray was a bit wobbly, and when John started to play the first chords for the warm-up exercise it fell off and rolled up the strings as he was playing. Of course, it made an extraordinary sound, and John, from that moment on, was gone as far as the class was concerned. He began ignoring us, playing different things and experimenting with this metal rolling on the strings...then he got tired of that and began inserting things from the box full of nuts and bolts into the strings and getting different qualities. By the end of class, he said, "I have a solution to the problem of the gamelan."[463]

ZEN BUDDHISM

In 1935 Cage married an artist named Xenia Kashevaroff, but their marriage began to unravel in the 1940s, and eventually ended in divorce in 1945. In the aftermath of the breakup, Cage's personal sense of identity and emotional life were thrown into turmoil. At the same time, he began to experience a professional identity crisis as well.

---

[463] Ibid, pg. 71

Like most musicians, Cage had been taught and had assumed, that the purpose of music was communication: to express feelings and ideas. However, he observed that in the 20th century all the composers were speaking a different musical language, and therefore, no communication was taking place. [464]

Cage himself had experienced the frustration of miscommunication. "I noticed," he said, "that when I consciously wrote something sad, people and critics were often apt to laugh."[465] In 1944, Cage had written a piece for prepared piano entitled *The Perilous Night* which, for him, was filled with feelings of grief and fear, but was dismissed by a critic as sounding like "a woodpecker in a church belfry".[466] "I had poured a great deal of emotion into the piece," Cage wrote, "and obviously was not communicating this at all. I determined to give up composition unless I could find a better reason for doing it than communication."[467]

In 1946, Cage enrolled in a class in Zen Buddhism taught by D. T. Suzuki, a noted author, and expert on the subject, and began a life-long embrace of Eastern philosophy which informed and inspired his work from that time forward.[468]

"I was in such serious necessity that I was on the edge of being unable to function," Cage said. "Though I do not want to blame Zen Buddhism for what I have done, I would not have done what I have done except for it."[469]

---

[464] Cage is perhaps the first 20th century composer to either recognize this, or to be honest enough to admit it.

[465] Gerald Larner, *John Cage interview: 'I gave up the notion of communication as impractical in my case'*, The Guardian, November 16, 1989

[466] Richard Taruskin, *The Danger of Music and Other Anti-Utopian Essays*, pg. 266

[467] ibid

[468] Joan Peyser, *To Boulez and Beyond*, pg. 174

[469] Richard Kostelanetz, *Conversing with Cage*, pg. 59

About this time, Cage met a musician from India named Gita Sarabhai. "Before she returned to India," Cage said, "I learned from her the traditional reason for making a piece of music in India: to quiet the mind thus making it susceptible to divine influence."[470] Since Cage had already found that, for him, communication was an inadequate reason for creating music, he adopted this rationale as a substitute. The question then became, what is a quiet mind? And, what are divine influences? Cage decided that "a sober and quiet mind is one in which the ego does not obstruct the fluency of things that come into our senses…Our business in living is to become fluent with the life we are living, and art can help with this."[471] In his book, *Silence*, Cage later refined and restated his philosophy:

> Our intention is to affirm this life, not to bring order out of chaos, nor to suggest improvements in creation, but simply to wake up to the very life we're living, which is so excellent once one gets one's mind and desires out of its way and lets it act of its own accord.[472]

Cage now came to believe that the purpose of music was not communication between the artist and the audience.

Rather, the purpose of music was to allow sounds to be themselves, and "in their being themselves to open the minds of the people who made them or listened to them to other possibilities than they had previously considered - to widen their experience, particularly to the making of value judgments."[473] A value judgment does not exist, except within the mind, Cage asserts.

---

[470] ibid

[471] ibid

[472] John Cage, *Silence*, pg. 95

[473] Richard Kostelanetz, *Conversing with Cage*, pg. 42

> When [the mind] says this is good and that is not good, it's a decision to eliminate from experience certain things. Suzuki said Zen wants us to diminish that kind of activity of the ego and to increase the activity that accepts the rest of creation.[474]

Cage's understanding of Zen Buddhism led him to a radical, new definition of music as simply a collection of sounds. He conceived of the whole range of sounds, including traditional "musical" sounds, noise-type sounds, and even the absence of sound, as equally usable in music. To accommodate this new world of sounds Cage developed a conception of musical form as an empty container into which any sound might be placed.

CHANCE OPERATIONS

In early 1951, one of Cage's students, Christian Wolff, presented him with a copy of the *I Ching*, an ancient Chinese text used for divination. Through a table of 64 hexagrams, questions may be posed to the *I Ching*, to which answers are obtained by means of chance operations such as tossing coins.

Cage immediately saw that the chance procedures of the *I Ching*'s divination table could be used for making complex musical decisions, thereby removing the will and taste of the composer entirely from the compositional decision-making process. [475]

Cage believed that he had discovered a way to realize his ideal of "a sober and quiet mind in which the ego does not obstruct the fluency of things that come into the senses". For Cage as composer, his job would no longer be the making of musical decisions, but instead, the asking of musical questions, for which the *I Ching* would furnish the answers.

---

[474] ibid

[475] Even though the motives and the media are different, this is essentially the same conclusion reached by Jackson Pollock when he embraced automatism in his drip paintings.

> I try to ask radical questions – questions that get at the root of things. If I succeed, then the answers – even though they come through chance operations – will be, I believe, revelatory in the sense of revealing to me more of creation than staying with my mind the way it was.[476]

The *I Ching* is also known as the *Book of Changes*. For this reason, Cage chose the title, *Music of Changes*, for his first composition written through consultation with the *I Ching*.

Cage drew several large charts, each concerned with some parameter of music: pitch, duration, dynamic level, tempo, and density (number of simultaneous sounds).[477]

The charts were made up of cells, each of which contained some musical element. To plot a single note, he tossed three coins six times (to correspond to the hexagrams in the *I Ching*).

The result would direct him to a number in the *I Ching*, which, in turn, would correspond to a numbered position on his chart. The entire procedure would be repeated over and over again to determine the note's duration, dynamic level, and all other parameters.[478] Silences are obtained through a separate "sounds" chart. Another chart was used to determine density (how many sound events would occur simultaneously). Another chart was used to determine structural changes such as the moving of cells within the charts.

---

[476] Peter Dickenson, *CageTalk: Dialogues With and About John Cage*, chapter 18, interview with Michael Oliver

[477] Cage's methodology was essentially the same as that of Boulez: the parameters of sound were identified, labeled, and controlled independently - the only difference being whether these parameters were manipulated by the will of the composer (Boulez) or by chance (Cage). The reader may judge whether or not there is any significant difference in the sound or musical effect between Cage's *Music of Changes* with Boulez's *Second Piano Sonata*. It is also interesting to observe that by removing the subjective ego of the composer from the compositional process, Cage has succeeded in creating the ultimate "objective" music – music which expresses nothing, aligning him philosophically with the stated desire of the Neoclassical Igor Stravinsky who claimed that "music is powerless to express anything at all."

The results were carefully transcribed and notated on a traditional musical staff. By this painstaking method *Music of Changes* was created.

CAGE AND DUCHAMP

Cage first met Marcel Duchamp in the early 1940s at a party given by art collector Peggy Guggenheim.[479]

The two men became good friends and Duchamp asked Cage to write music for his part in an abstract film called *Dreams that Money can Buy*. Cage treated Duchamp with deference, not wanting to burden him with a friendship until he learned in the 1960s that Duchamp's health was failing. He then began to actively seek his company. Knowing of Duchamp's love of chess, Cage, as a pretext, asked Duchamp to teach him the game. For two weeks in 1966 Cage and Duchamp were together every day. "We're great buddies," Duchamp told an interviewer, "we have a spiritual empathy and a similar way of looking at things."[480]

There were obvious similarities between the two of them: Cage once considered becoming an artist, and still experimented in art. Duchamp wrote a musical composition in 1913 called *Erratum Musical*, a work for three voices, composed by chance – Duchamp wrote musical pitches on 25 cards and drew them randomly from a hat.[481]

But there were differences as well. Cage explained that Duchamp, "often chose the simplest method. In *Musical Erratum* he simply put the notes in a hat and then pulled them out.

---

[478] Joan Peyser, *To Boulez and Beyond*, pg. 183

[479] Peter Vergo, *The Music of Painting*, pg. 334

[480] Kenneth Silverman, *Begin Again, a Biography of John Cage*, pg. 228

[481] ibid

I wouldn't be satisfied with that kind of chance operation in my work…it simply doesn't appeal to me…I enjoy details and like things to be more complicated."[482]

When Duchamp died in 1968, Cage was asked to do something to memorialize his friend.

He subjected the dictionary to chance operations based on the *I Ching*, arranging for the results to be printed on interchangeable pieces of Plexiglas, entitling the finished work *Not Wanting to Say Anything About Marcel*.

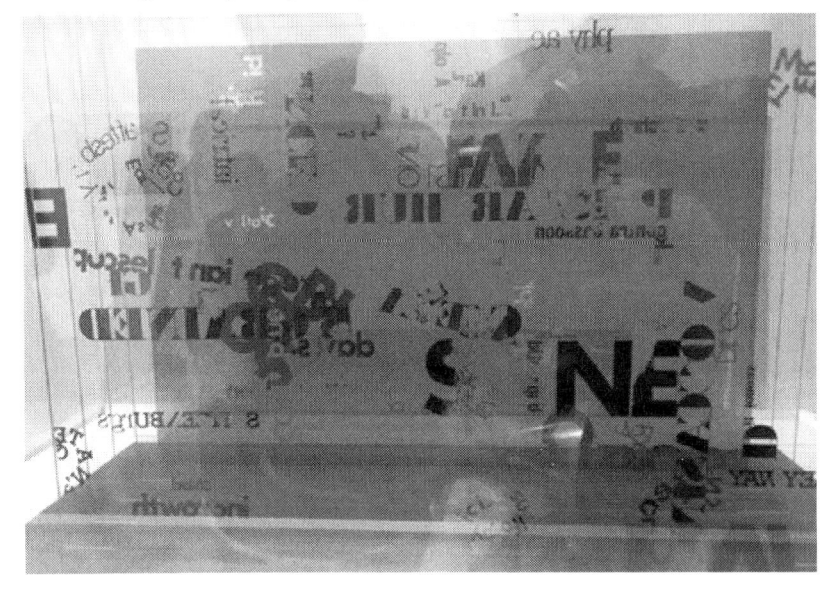

John Cage, *Not Wanting to Say Anything About Marcel* (1969)

(Photograph by author)

While living in New York, Cage became close to the Abstract Expressionists, even joining their artist's club which congregated on Eighth Street in lower Manhattan. Cage gave several lectures to the group and they proved to be a receptive audience for his ideas and his music.[483]

---

[482] Peter Vergo, *The Music of Painting*, pg. 334

[483] Steven Johnson, *A Junction at Eighth Street*, from *The New York Schools of*

Two younger artists, Jasper Johns and Robert Rauschenberg, not part of the Abstract Expressionist circle, came directly into Cage's orbit.

During the summer of 1951 Rauschenberg had been working on a series of monochrome paintings known as the *White Paintings*, several panels consisting of nothing but ordinary house paint uniformly applied to the canvas with a roller. These paintings by Rauschenberg had a tremendous impact on Cage. He wrote later that the *White Paintings* by Rauschenberg gave him the courage to create what has since become Cage's most famous (or infamous) work.

4'33": NO SUCH THING AS SILENCE

According to Cage, he had been considering a project like 4'33" for several years but had abandoned it for fear of being dismissed as a cynical prankster.

"I was afraid," he said, "that making a piece that had no sounds would appear as if I were making a joke."[484]

The title, 4'33", refers to the duration of the work: four minutes, thirty-three seconds, during which the performer does nothing. It was first performed at the Maverick Concert Hall in Woodstock, New York, on August 29, 1952, by Cage's friend, the virtuoso pianist, David Tudor. In the audience that night were fellow composers Morton Feldman and Earle Browne whose works were also on the program. Also present were vacationing members of the New York Philharmonic, curious about the activities of the musical avant-garde. Apart from turning the pages of the music, Tudor merely sat at the piano, not touching the instrument at all. [485]

Music and Visual Arts, pg. 7

[484] Kyle Gann, *No Such Thing As Silence: John Cage's 4'33"*, pg. 16

[485] Will Hermes, *The Story of 4'33"*, NPR 100 Fact Sheet

Recalling this first performance, Cage said, "People began whispering to one another, and some people began to walk out. They didn't laugh – they were irritated when they realized nothing was going to happen, and they haven't forgotten it 30 years later: they're still angry."[486] Cage speculated on the reason for the hostility of the first audience:

> They missed the point. There's no such thing as silence. What they thought was silence, because they didn't know how to listen, was full of accidental sounds. You could hear the wind stirring outside during the first movement. During the second, raindrops began pattering on the roof, and during the third, the people themselves made all kinds of interesting sounds as they talked or walked out.[487]

In the conversation after the concert, it became evident that the anger of the audience had not dissipated. David Tudor recalls that a local artist stood up and said, "Good people of Woodstock, let's drive these people out of town!"[488] What no one in the audience that night could have known was that they had just witnessed a significant historical event, the premiere of the "pivotal composition of this century".[489]

MUSIC AFTER 1952

Cage's music after 1952 became increasingly radical and his scores began to resemble navigational charts in which a performer is confronted with a baffling variety of choices.

---

[486] Richard Kostelanetz, *Conversing with Cage*, pg. 65-66

[487] ibid

[488] American Masters*: I Have Nothing To Say And I Am Saying It*

[489] David Revill, *The Roaring Silence*, pg. 166

Chance, indeterminacy, and a multiplicity of choices were factors that dominated Cage's works in the following decades. For example, in one of his works from 1958, Cage specifies that the piece can be performed by "any number of players using any number and kind of instruments." Another piece calls for "any number of players and sound-producing means."[490]

In 1959 Cage and long-time collaborator, David Tudor, recorded an album for Smithsonian-Folkways entitled *Indeterminacy*. The plan was simple but audacious: Cage read 90 original stories, his speed determined by the story's length. In another room, beyond earshot of Cage, David Tudor performed miscellaneous selections from Cage's piano works and played pre-recorded tape from Cage's electronic experiments. Cage's speaking and Tudor's sounds proceed independent of one another, sometimes complimenting each other, sometimes colliding with one another. The result offers a unique glimpse into Cage's philosophy.

In his later years, Cage devoted himself exclusively to a series of compositions usually referred to as the "Number Pieces". These works were created on commission, and the titles refer to the number of players for which he is writing. For instance, the first of these, written in 1987, is entitled *Two*, written for flute and piano. In the event of a subsequent piece being commissioned for the same number of players as a previous composition, the new work would be designated by a superscript, as in Two^2 (1989).

---

[490] Peter Vergo, *The Music of Painting*, pg. 346

Eventually, there were 43 of these "number pieces" completed by Cage before his death in 1992. All of the number pieces make use of a similar compositional device: time brackets. Each player is given a part consisting of a sequence of time brackets – a short set of notes (chosen, of course, by chance procedures), bracketed with a time duration attached to it. The idea is that the pitches within the time bracket must be played within the time specified, but their exact placement is left to the discretion of the performer. The players make no effort to coordinate their parts.[491]

John Cage's long career as a composer had begun after Arnold Schoenberg, whom he idolized, urged Cage to give up composition because of Cage's aversion to harmony. Schoenberg had said, you will come to a wall and will not be able to get through, to which Cage responded, then I will devote my life to beating my head against that wall.

Ironically, during the last summer before his death, Cage began re-reading Schoenberg's *Harmonielehre* (Theory of Harmony), having at long last evidently overcome his aversion to harmony.

Los Angeles Times Classical Music critic Mark Swed spoke to Cage on the telephone just hours before his death on August 12, 1992. After being told that a rainstorm was expected in New York City that night, Swed suggested to Cage that it would be a good, spooky night to read Schoenberg's *Harmonielehre*. "Oh, I finished that," replied Cage, "Isn't that marvelous?"[492]

---

[491] James Pritchett, *The Music of John Cage*, pg. 200

[492] Mark Swed, *John Cage's genius an L.A. story, The Los Angeles Times*, August 31, 2012

CHAPTER TWELVE: POSTMODERNISM

Postmodernism is notoriously difficult to define. As the name implies, it positions itself as being after Modernism, and therefore different than and superior to Modernism, since it has evidently supplanted it. In the view of some writers, Postmodernism itself is now passé, even before it could be adequately defined: "It was sad to see postmodernism disappear before we could explain it...and now we are faced with a dilemma, what shall we call this new thing towards which we are going?"[493]

Postmodernism is simply a convenient label for a series of art movements that arose beginning in the 1960s and onwards. Like Neoclassicism, it is a reaction against certain aspects of Modernism. However, unlike Neoclassicism, which was a conservative reaction, Postmodernism is anarchic and nihilistic, and seeks to be even more radical than Modernism.

Postmodernism can also be understood as an outgrowth or extension of Dada.

But just as Dada marketed itself as "anti-art", though it *was* art nevertheless, Postmodernism markets itself as anti-Modernism, but is, nevertheless, simply another of the many faces of Modernism. Postmodernism does, however, have some distinguishing characteristics:

---

[493] Raymond Federman, quoted in *The Cambridge Introduction to Postmodernism*, by Brian McHale

1. *Postmodernism is cynical.* Whereas most modernist art (with the exception of Dada) took itself very seriously, postmodernist art tends to be mocking and cynical. As an example, Google the sculpture by Maurizio Cattelan which stands outside the Milan Stock Exchange and you will see a photo of an enormous marble hand with its middle finger extended.

2. *Postmodernism delights in mixing high and low culture.* Modernist art was generally associated with the elite class and was consequently seen as a mark of cultural sophistication. By contrast, postmodernist art delights in low culture and kitsch – it is a kind of cultural garage sale. The social philosopher Jean-François Lyotard uses the word "eclecticism" to explain this tendency and suggests that it is a defining mark of contemporary culture: "You listen to reggae; you watch a western; you eat at McDonald's at midday and local cuisine at night; you wear Paris perfume in Tokyo and dress retro in Hong Kong; knowledge is the stuff of TV game shows."[494]

3. *Postmodernism is unabashedly political.* For the most part, Modernism was more concerned with psychology than politics. By contrast, postmodern art tends to be highly politicized, making frequent use of the images of popular or notorious politicians and political slogans.

NEO-DADAISM

One of the first manifestations of Postmodernism was called Neo-Dadaism, and primarily refers to the work of two New York artists, Robert Rauschenberg and Jasper Johns who, in the late 1950s were closely associated with John Cage.

---

[494] Jean-François Lyotard, *The Postmodern Explained: Correspondence*, 1982-1985, pg. 8

Robert Rauschenberg was born in 1925 in Port Arthur, Texas. He had a difficult childhood, and in school was a poor student and uninterested in sports. He briefly attended college, but was expelled, and was subsequently drafted into the Navy where he worked as a neuro-psychiatric assistant. There he learned, as he related later, "how little difference there is between sanity and insanity, and [I] realized that a combination was essential."[495]

When he was discharged in 1945, he returned to Texas to find that his family had moved without informing him, and that his house was now occupied by strangers. He used the GI Bill to study art, first at the Kansas City Art Institute, then in Paris, and finally at the experimental Black Mountain College in North Carolina, where he came in contact with John Cage, who was teaching there at the time. Quickly coming under Cage's influence, Rauschenberg began to radically simplify his style, reaching an extreme in 1951 when he created a series of all-black and all-white canvases, painted using ordinary enamel house paint applied with a roller, straight from the can.[496]

In 1954, Rauschenberg, now living in New York, met Jasper Johns, and the two artists formed a close working relationship. "He and I were each other's first serious critics… [We] literally traded ideas. He would say, 'I've got a terrific idea for you', and then I'd have to find one for him."[497]

---

[495] Edward Lucie-Smith, *Lives of the Great 20th Century Artists*, pg. 296

[496] ibid

[497] Ibid, pg. 297

One of Rauschenberg's best-known works is entitled *Bed* (1955). He called this kind of assemblage a "combine", because he combined various real-world objects to form the work of art. It consists of a pillowcase, a sheet, and a quilt, all splattered with paint and attached to a traditional canvas. For some observers, the work seemed to imply extreme degradation – both of the person associated with the object, and of art itself.[498]

Monogram (1955-1959) is an iconic work by Rauschenberg. This is another of his "combines" which came into being after Rauschenberg saw an Angora goat in a second-hand store and paid fifteen dollars for it. The official catalog description of *Monogram* gives a comprehensive inventory of materials used in its production: "oil, paper, fabric, printed paper, printed reproductions, metal, wood, rubber shoe heel, and a tennis ball on canvas with oil and rubber tire on Angora goat on wood platform mounted on four casters."[499]

Jasper Johns was born in Augusta, Georgia, in 1930, and was raised in extreme poverty in various towns in the South, being passed between grandparents, uncles, and aunts after his parents divorced. To please his parents he enrolled at the University of South Carolina but dropped out after only one year. He went to New York in 1949 and entered a commercial art college where he applied for a scholarship. He was told that he would receive one on the basis of need, since he did not deserve it on the basis of merit. He refused and left to work as a messenger, and then a shipping clerk, before being drafted into the army.[500]

---

[498] Norbert Lynton, *The Story of Modern Art*, pg. 283

[499] Robert Rauschenberg Foundation, New York, New York

[500] Edward Lucie-Smith, *Lives of the Great 20th Century Artists*, pg.299

After being discharged, he returned to New York and entered City College on the GI Bill, but lasted only one day. In 1954 Johns was introduced to Robert Rauschenberg. Gradually the two men became friends, then lovers in a triangular relationship with a girl named Rachel Rosenthal, who lived on the floor above Johns in their apartment building. At about this same time, Johns experienced a kind of artistic epiphany and destroyed all the art he had created up until that point. He explained,

> Before, when anybody asked me what I did, I said I was going to become an artist. Finally, I decided I could be going to become an artist all my life. I decided to stop becoming and be an artist.[501]

Soon after this experience, Johns created the work which marked the turning point in the development of his individual style. It came about as the result of a dream in which he saw himself painting an American flag. He then acted out his dream, painting the flag, filling the whole field of the canvas.

He used an old medium, pigment mixed with wax, and the result had an old-world richness that stood in stark contrast to the flat, straight-from-the-can enamel house paint being used by the Abstract Expressionists at this time.

But the work which first won recognition for Johns was his *Green Target* (1955). As the name implies, *Green Target* is a set of concentric circles (i.e., a target) painted various shades of green, using the same encaustic method used to produce his *Flag* (1954). The *Green Target* was shown in an exhibition entitled "Artists of the New York School: Second Generation".

---

[501] Ibid, pg. 300

The show was seen by an art dealer named Leo Castelli, who had just opened his own gallery. Two days later, Castelli and his wife came to visit Robert Rauschenberg, to propose giving him a show. Rauschenberg had by now moved in with Rachel Rosenthal in the apartment above Johns. When Johns was mentioned, Castelli, remembering the *Green Target*, asked to see Johns work as well, and was taken downstairs to his studio. Castelli was thunderstruck: "I saw evidence of the most incredible genius," he said later, "entirely fresh and not related to anything else." Castelli's wife bought a painting on the spot and Johns was given a show of his own. The exhibition opened in January of 1958 and was a great success. The Museum of Modern Art bought four works for its own collection, and several of its trustees made private purchases. Only two works remained unsold. From this point forward, Jasper Johns was a celebrity in the New York art world.[502]

BRITISH POP ART

Richard Hamilton was born in London in 1922 and began his art education in 1934. In 1952 he was one of the founding members of an artist's organization called the Independent Group which met at the Institute of Contemporary Arts in London, one of its main objects being the study of popular imagery.[503]

Hamilton helped organize a number of exhibitions which illustrated the philosophy of the group, the most important of these being "This is Tomorrow", opening in 1956. The exhibition outraged conservative British opinion at the time. Especially provocative was Hamilton's collage, *Just what is it that makes today's homes so different, so appealing?*, an image which shows

---

[502] ibid

[503] Ibid, pg. 303

> ...a room containing a blown-up cover of Young Romance and an immense tin of ham on the coffee-table, a muscle-bound Mr. Universe flaunts his physique and clasps a shamelessly phallic tennis racket. It thrusts out of his groin like a giant lollipop, and the words "Tootsie POP" are splashed across its orange wrapping paper.[504]

This image is considered one of the first examples of "Pop Art". In the following year (1957) Hamilton offered the first formal description of "Pop Art".

He wrote that Pop Art was "Popular (designed for a mass audience), Transient (short-term solution), Expendable (easily forgotten), Low cost, Mass produced, Young (aimed at youth), Witty, Sexy, Gimmicky, Glamorous, and Big business".[505]

Hamilton associated with many of the 1960s rock stars and was invited by Paul McCartney to design an album cover for the Beatles – the result was the *White Album*.[506] He would also prove to be a strong influence on the 1960s American pop artists Andy Warhol and Roy Lichtenstein.

David Hockney was born in 1937 in Bradford, England. By the age of eleven, he knew he wanted to be an artist. When he arrived in the Royal College of Art in London in 1959, he realized that there were two very different attitudes towards the practice of art:

---

[504] Richard Cork, *Richard Hamilton: The prophet of Pop Art*, The Independent, February 9, 2014

[505] Fiona MacCarthy, *Richard Hamilton: they called him Daddy pop*, The Guardian, February 7, 2014

[506] Rebecca Steel, *Richard Hamilton: The Chameleon Of British Pop Art*, Culture Trip, April 20, 2017

> I realized that there were two groups of students there: a traditional group...doing still life, life painting, and figure compositions; and then what I thought of as the more adventurous, lively students, the brightest ones, who were involved in the art of their time. They were doing big, Abstract Expressionist paintings.[507]

Hockney first tried to paint in the style of the Abstract Expressionists but found that, for him, abstract expressionism was non-expressive. At the time it was considered "anti-modern" to include lifelike figures in art, so he began including words in his paintings in an attempt to humanize them, as in *We two Boys Together Clinging* (1961).

An exhibition in 1961 called the "Young Contemporaries" marked Hockney's emergence as one of the leaders of the new Pop Art movement. In 1963 he traveled to California, and the Los Angeles lifestyle soon became a major feature in works such as *Portrait of an Artist (Pool with Two Figures)* (1972).

Hockney is one of the wealthiest and most influential British artists of the 20th century. He has always maintained that he is not a "pop artist" since he rarely deals with mass media or culture in his art, but because he was a pupil of Richard Hamilton he is usually included under the pop art label.[508]

Hockney was tangentially touched by a scandal in 2013 when his 23-year-old assistant, a former rugby player named Dominic Elliott, died under unusual circumstances stemming from a binge of drinking, cocaine, and ecstasy at Hockney's home in Yorkshire, England.

---

[507] Edward Lucie-Smith, *Lives of the Great 20th Century Artists*, pg. 305

[508] Rebecca Steel, *Richard Hamilton: The Chameleon Of British Pop Art, Culture Trip*, April 20, 2017

Witnesses said that Elliott, after being told that Hockney had left the house, reportedly threw himself headfirst over a 10-foot balcony, but was unhurt by the fall. He then went into the bathroom and drank from a bottle of drain cleaner. Soon after, he asked to be taken to a hospital but died before arriving.

Hockney was not personally charged or implicated in the death. Nevertheless, he sold the Yorkshire home. He now maintains a residence in Malibu, California, and an office in West Hollywood.[509]

AMERICAN POP ART

The Pop Art movement developed concurrently in the 1960s in America and Britain, but it was in America that the prime source of much of the imagery of popular culture originated, and American artists, steeped in this imagery, gravitated naturally towards it.

The publicity surrounding the abstract expressionist artists in the 1950s, the grandiose seriousness of their pronouncements about the deep meaning of their works, the carefully cultivated legends of their tormented yet heroic creative lives and the air of high-priced commerce associated with their art, all but invited a mocking, frivolous reaction from the next generation of artists.

The word "pop" was used to refer to a wide range of artistic activities. What they all shared in common was a reliance on mass-media images, and as a result, the media celebrated this movement in an unprecedented way.

---

[509] Paul Peachey, *David Hockney's assistant died after drinking acid at artist's Bridlington home*, August 29, 2013

The name also implied a connection to the world of popular music, whose iconic stars were emerging at the same time. The artists drew on intentionally mixed sources, mingling images from commercial advertising, from pinball machines and comic books, and any other aspect of popular culture that caught their attention.

Roy Lichtenstein was born in 1923 in New York City and his childhood was quiet and uneventful. His study of art at Ohio State University was interrupted by the war when he was drafted in 1943. After the war he returned to Ohio State and finished his education, earning a bachelor's and a master's degree in art. In the late 1950s and early 1960s, he experimented with abstract styles and accepted a teaching position at Rutgers University in New Jersey, bringing him into close proximity to New York City.

Lichtenstein found his unique style as the result of a joking challenge from one of his children. "I'll bet you can't paint as good as that," his son said, pointing to a Mickey Mouse comic book. Responding to his son's dare, he reproduced six frames from the comic book, making minimal changes from the source material.

> The idea of doing [a cartoon painting] without apparent alteration just occurred to me ... and I did one really almost half seriously to get an idea of what it might look like. And as I was painting this painting, I kind of got interested in organizing it as a painting and brought it to some kind of conclusion as an aesthetic statement, which I hadn't really intended to do to begin with. And then I really went back to my other kind of painting, which was pretty abstract. Or tried to. But I had this cartoon painting in my studio, and it was a little too formidable.

I couldn't keep my eyes off it, and it sort of prevented me from painting in any other way, and then I decided this stuff was really serious ... I would say I had it on my easel for a week. I would just want to see what it looked like. I tried to make it a work of art. I wasn't trying just to copy. I realized that this was just so much more compelling.[510]

It was at this same time that he began to incorporate other elements that would become part of his signature style: Ben-Day dots[511], and speech bubbles. Lichtenstein took some of his comic book paintings unannounced into the Leo Castelli Gallery and was immediately accepted for exhibition there. His career was uniformly successful from that time forward. In his later life, Lichtenstein applied the Ben-Day dot technique to other non-comic book subjects such as Chinese landscapes and nude figures.[512] Lichtenstein died of pneumonia in 1997, at age 73. His last words, like a comic book character in one of his paintings, were, "Well, here I go!"[513]

When Andy Warhol saw Roy Lichtenstein's comic-book paintings in the Leo Castelli Gallery in 1961, he became angry at what he considered to be a fellow artist trespassing on his territory. For his part, Lichtenstein made light of the situation, dressing up as Warhol at a Halloween party.[514]

---

[510] Eric Shanes, *Pop Art*, pg. 84

[511] Colored dots used as an inexpensive method of coloring and shading comic books, named for Benjamin Day who invented the technique in 1879.

[512] Marcus Field, *Roy Lichtenstein: The Man Who Turned Mickey Mouse Into a Masterpiece*, The Daily Mail, January 26, 2013

[513] Sarah Churchwell, *Roy Lichtenstein: from heresy to visionary*, The Guardian, February 23, 2013

[514] ibid

Andy Warhol, born Andrew Warhola in Pittsburgh in 1928, was the best known of all the American pop artists. His celebrity was based as much on his flamboyant lifestyle and carefully cultivated persona as on his art.

Warhol studied art at the Carnegie Institute, graduating in 1949. He left immediately for New York where he found employment as a commercial artist and illustrator - his specialty was drawing shoes. He eventually worked his way up to the most prestigious glossy magazines and the most exclusive department stores in New York. In the course of his work, he gained a thorough knowledge of the processes of mechanical reproduction and even invented some new techniques of his own.

He also designed sets for an avant-garde theater group on the Lower East Side. It was through this group that he became acquainted by Bertolt Brecht's theory of alienation – the idea that a work of art must deliberately distance the spectator and invite judgment, rather than identification.[515]

In 1960 Warhol made a series of paintings based on newspapers and fragments of comic strips. The images were projected onto the canvas and filled in by hand. No established gallery would accept them, and Warhol felt himself to be at an impasse. A friend jokingly suggested that he should paint dollar bills or Campbell's soup cans – objects that were so familiar that people had ceased to notice what they looked like. He initially tried painting the images by hand, but since literalism was the goal, he decided to silk-screen them onto the canvas.

---

[515] Edward Lucie-Smith, *Lives of the Great 20th Century Artists*, pg. 316

The Campbell's Soup cans were exhibited in the summer of 1962 in Los Angeles and created a sensation. That same year Warhol created 200 One Dollar Bills using the same silk-screen method. (This painting sold at Sotheby's in 2009 for a remarkable 43.7 million dollars.)[516]

The soup cans and dollar bills were quickly followed by a series of images of Marilyn Monroe, Jackie Kennedy, and other celebrities.

Andy Warhol, *Mao Tse-Tung* (1972) (Photograph by author)

With his sudden success, Warhol could now afford his own studio on East 42nd Street, which he renamed "The Factory", where he mass-produced his silk-screened prints and made experimental films with the help of a group of friends and hangers-on.

---

[516] Carol Vogel, *Warhol Fetches $43.7 Million at Auction, New York Times,* November 11, 2009

The Factory by then had become a hangout for a bizarre gang of characters: runaway girls, aspiring socialites, transvestites, hustlers, and addicts. In June 1968 Warhol became the victim of his self-created mythology. He was shot and critically injured by a mentally unbalanced feminist extremist named Valerie Solanas, who was angry with Warhol for not returning a script she had submitted to him. Solanas shot Warhol three times before her gun jammed. Doctors were able to save him only by opening his chest and manually massaging his heart.[517]

Characteristically, Warhol later had himself photographed by fashion photographer Richard Avedon, showing off his scars from the incident. Though he survived the attack, he never fully recovered.

He was forced to wear a corset for the rest of his life in order to protect the incisions.[518] Solanas was diagnosed as a schizophrenic and sentenced to three years in prison.

Warhol always claimed that his work had no significance, social, artistic, or otherwise. In 1968 he said,

> The reason I'm painting this way is because I want to be a machine. Whatever I do, and do machine-like, is because it is what I want to do. I think it would be terrific if everybody was alike…In the future, everybody will be world famous for fifteen minutes…If you want to know all about Andy Warhol, just look at the surface of my paintings and films and me, and there I am. There's nothing behind it.[519]

---

[517] Annys Shin, *The Day Andy Warhol Was Shot*, The Washington Post, May 25, 2017

[518] Farah Nayeri, *Warhol and Avedon Form an Unlikely Tandem in London*, The New York Times, March 8, 2016

[519] Norbert Lynton, *The Story of Modern Art*, pg. 294

Andy Warhol died in 1987 as the result of what should have been a routine gallbladder operation. Because of his terror of hospitalization, Warhol had delayed serious treatment of his gallbladder until he was forced to submit to an operation. The surgeon found Warhol's gallbladder full of gangrene – the organ fell apart as it was being removed. Nevertheless, Warhol survived the surgery and seemed to be recovering – he was cheerful and taking calls in his hospital room. However, the next day he was found dead by a nurse. The autopsy revealed heart failure as the cause of death. Medical historian, Dr. John Ryan, in an in-depth analysis of Warhol's death, points out that Warhol was in very poor physical condition at the time of his surgery, due to dehydration and the effects of his longtime addiction to amphetamines.[520]

NOUVEAU RÉALISME

Nouveau Réalisme (translated "the new realism") could be seen as the French counterpart to American and British Pop Art. Artists associated with Nouveau Réalisme made extensive use of collage and assemblage, sometimes incorporating real objects directly into their work.

Yves Klein, probably the best known of the Nouveau Réalisme artists, was born in France, in the city of Nice in 1928 and spent a disturbed childhood shuttling back and forth between bohemian parents, a possessive childless aunt, and his grandparents. He was a poor student and habitual truant.

His poor academic performance made it impossible for him to join the Merchant Marine Academy as he had planned, and he ended up opening a small bookshop in one room of his aunt's electrical appliance store.[521]

---

[520] Mary Kekatos, Revealed – *The Secrets of Andy Warhol's Death*, from *The Daily Mail*, February 21, 2017

[521] Edward Lucie-Smith, *Lives of the Great 20th Century Artists*, pg. 337

In 1947 he discovered an interest in judo, taking classes at the local police school. In 1953, with financial help from his aunt, he traveled to Japan to enter the Kodokan Judo Institute in Tokyo – the most prestigious judo school in the world. In Japan, Klein started taking chemical stimulants to help him prepare for judo contests, and began a lifelong dependence on amphetamines, which probably contributed to his early death. He eventually attained the level of Black Belt – Fourth Dan, a higher level than any Judo expert in Europe. He returned to France, determined to make a mark in the world of French judo. However, the French Judo Federation rejected him, and even refused to recognize his Japanese qualifications. [522]

Klein moved to Spain and attempted to reinvent himself as an artist, even going so far as to create a book of reproductions of his non-existent past paintings, back-dated to give himself a track record. Returning to Paris, his attempts to make a place for himself in the French art world met with failure until he met an adventurous art dealer named Iris Clert who was attempting to make a name for herself in the Parisian avant-garde. It was a perfect match, mutually beneficial for both parties, and Clert became Klein's co-conspirator for many of his subsequent projects. This began a period of frenzied activity for Klein.

According to an official catalog, he produced some 1077 artworks between the years 1956 and 1962, and he found himself at the center of the newly created Nouveau Realisme group.

But he was also becoming increasingly idiosyncratic and unstable: a book he published in Belgium, for instance, predicted mankind's immediate evolution into an age of levitation, telepathy, and immateriality.[523]

---

[522] Peter Schjeldahl, *True Blue, An Yves Klein retrospective*, The New Yorker, June 28, 2010

[523] Thomas McEvilley, *Yves the Provocateur: Yves Klein and Twentieth-century Art*,

He created a long series of monochrome blue paintings, the color being so intense that it was later patented as "Klein International Blue". Having created his own trademarked color, he then began applying it to various objects. In 1958 he created a scandal with his exhibition at Clert's gallery entitled Le Vide (The Void), in which the windows of the gallery were painted blue, the rest of the interior painted white, but otherwise left empty.[524]

Klein not only created a large number of paintings during this period, but he constantly invented new techniques. One such procedure, called by him "anthropometries", involved painting a woman's body with blue paint and pressing her against the canvas. Another technique involved burning composition board with a flame-thrower. [525]

Klein suffered a major heart attack in 1962, at the Cannes Film Festival, after viewing a film in which he had participated by recreating his anthropometries. Unknown to Klein, the film had been edited in a mocking way, presenting his work as part of a sneering compilation of bizarre cultural practices from around the world designed to shock Western audiences.

Klein died after a second heart attack three days later, at the age of thirty-four.[526]

Arman, along with Yves Klein, was one of the founding members of the Nouveau Réalisme group. He was born Armand Pierre Fernandez, in 1928, in the city of Nice, France, where he later met and befriended Yves Klein at the local police judo school.

---

pg. 138

[524] Norbert Lynton, *The Story of Modern Art*, pg. 331

[525] Edward Lucie-Smith, *Lives of the Great 20th Century Artists*, pg. 338

[526] Peter Schjeldahl, *True Blue, An Yves Klein retrospective, The New Yorker*, June 28, 2010

In 1957, emulating Vincent Van Gogh who signed his paintings with his first name, "Vincent", Armand began signing his paintings with "Arman". When he immigrated to the United States in 1973, he formally changed his name to "Arman Pierre Arman", but used "Arman" as his public persona.

Although he originally considered himself to be an abstract painter, between 1959 and 1962 Arman began developing other techniques for which he is better known. One of these is the "Poubelle", which is French for "trash bin". Arman's "poubelles" are assemblages of garbage, often displayed in a Plexiglas box. Arman acknowledges that he was inspired by the German Dada artist, Kurt Schwitters, who made collages out of old bus tickets, newspapers, and other bits of garbage salvaged from postwar Germany. Arman is probably best known for his so-called "Accumulations", collections of common and identical objects. For instance, his *Big Parade* (1976) features multiple trombones, joined together in pairs, bell-to-bell, in a surrealistic large mass. In his 1977 work, *Hammers*, a number of hammers are joined together in a bunch, all seeming to be pounding the same invisible nail.

Some of Arman's accumulations are enormous public monuments – *The Clocks*, for instance, stands outside the Gare St. Lazare railway station, Paris, France.[527]

---

[527] In 1953 Arman married French electronic music composer, Éliane Radigue, who specializes in creating long, slow-moving electronic compositions reflecting her interest in the philosophy of Tibetan Buddhism.

Another artist closely associated with Nouveau Réalisme goes by the name of "Christo", though he was born Christo Vladimirov Javacheff in 1935 in Bulgaria. In 1957, during the Cold War, he escaped to the West by bribing a railway officer and stowing away onboard a train transporting medical supplies.[528] He met Jeanne-Claude de Guillebon in Paris in 1958 and since that time, Christo and Jeanne-Claude have collaborated together on art projects. Since 1994, all works attributed to Christo were retroactively credited to Christo and Jeanne-Claude.

Christo's work is based on objects wrapped in fabric. In the late 1950s and early 1960s, he wrapped small objects, like bottles and cans. By the middle of the 1960s, he was wrapping larger objects, like motorcycles and chairs. Beginning in the 1970s, Christo and Jeanne-Claude became more ambitious – in a project begun in the 1970s, but only concluded in the 1990s, they wrapped the German Reichstag with fabric. In the 1980s Christo and Jeanne-Claude surrounded islands off the coast of Florida with pink fabric. Christo, who is still living (Jeanne-Claude died in 2009), has plans for new and even more ambitious projects, such as wrapping one or more skyscrapers in New York City.

Christo insists that his art has no message or deeper meaning beyond the immediate aesthetic impact. He reflects sadly on the temporary nature of his art

> Do you know that I don't have any artworks that exist? They all go away when they're finished. Only the preparatory drawings and collages are left, giving my works an almost legendary character. I think it takes much greater courage to create things to be gone than to create things that will remain.[529]

---

[528] Jacob Baal-Teshuva, *Christo and Jeanne-Claude*, pg. 11

[529] Byan Solomon, *Christo's Back With The Unimaginable*, i-Italy, June 8, 2016

MINIMALISM

Minimalism as an art movement emerged in the late 1950s as an alternative to Abstract Expressionism and continued to grow in influence throughout the 1960s. In one sense, Minimalism is an extension of the concept of abstraction, the idea that art should have its own reality without imitating something else. In traditional painting, the work of art represents some aspect of the real world: a landscape, or a portrait of a person, or some experience of the artist – a feeling or emotion.

Minimalism, like abstract art, makes no attempt at all either to represent the outer world. It does, however, have some identifying characteristics which distinguish it from other forms of abstract art:

1. Minimalism often makes use of single or repeated geometric forms.

2. Minimalist art exhibits no trace of emotion or intuitive decision making, and little about the artist is revealed in the work.

3. Minimalist artists reject the notion of the artwork as a unique creation reflecting the personal expression of a gifted individual, seeing this as a distraction from the art object itself. Instead, they created objects that were as impersonal and neutral as possible.[530]

4. Minimalist art is self-referential – it does not refer to anything beyond its literal presence. The materials used are not worked to suggest something else.

---

[530] This idea parallels the philosophy of Marcel Duchamp in his various justifications of his "readymades".

Frank Stella, now considered to be the "Father of Minimalism" was born in 1936 in a suburb of Boston. He had just finished his college degree at Princeton when he created his so-called "black paintings" which consisted of nothing but black strips, laid out in rows, fanning out in different directions, all with evocative titles like *The Marriage of Reason and Squalor* and *Die Fahne Hoch!* (The Banner High), named after a Nazi marching song. His black paintings caused a sensation when they were first seen in an exhibition at the Museum of Modern Art in New York in 1960, alongside works by Jasper Johns and Robert Rauschenberg.[531]

Stella denied that his paintings had any deep meaning: "What you see is what you see". He also tried to minimize the importance of artistic technique, "I tried to keep the paint as good as it was in the can." [532]

Nevertheless, compared to later Minimalist artists who appeared in the 1960s, Stella exhibits a high degree of painterly craft.

After his initial success with his black paintings, Stella began increasingly to incorporate color into his images. In the 1960s, he created a series of ever-more-complex canvas shapes called Irregular Polygons, in which the shape of the canvas determined the content of the image. This was followed by a group of paintings called the Protractor Series, paintings made on circular or semi-circular canvases. Stella's work has continued to evolve and in 2015 the Whitney Museum of American Art celebrated his long career with a major retrospective exhibition highlighting 60 years of work.[533]

---

[531] Jonathan Jones, *The Prince of Whales*, The Guardian, April 4, 2001

[532] ibid

[533] Blake Gopnik, *'Frank Stella: A Retrospective'*, The New York Times, December 4, 2015

Carl Andre was born in Massachusetts in 1935 and is regarded as one of the leading members of the 1960s Minimalist movement. After studying art in the early 1950s, he went to work in the Boston Gear Works, where he earned enough money to travel to England and France in 1954. The following year he joined the United States Army Intelligence agency in North Carolina. In 1957 he moved to New York where he worked as an editorial assistant in a publishing house. Shortly thereafter he began making sculptures out of wood, influenced by his friend, Frank Stella.

Typical of Andre's art is *Equivalent VIII* from 1966, which consists of 120 bricks arranged in a rectangular shape. *Equivalent VIII* was purchased by the Tate Museum in London in 1972, and it was featured in several exhibitions in the following years. However, in 1976 a controversy over the work erupted in the press. The Sunday Times ran a story about recent acquisitions by the Tate Gallery, illustrated by a photograph of *Equivalent VIII*.

The story sparked a firestorm of controversy. The Tate was ridiculed for, as many people saw it, being conned into buying a pile of bricks. As a result of the hullabaloo, *Equivalent VIII* is probably the best-known work of contemporary art in the Tate's collection. The controversy surrounding *Equivalent VIII*, however, pales into insignificance in comparison to the imbroglio that would engulf Andre's life in 1985.

Carl Andre first met artist Ana Mendieta through a mutual friend in 1979, and the couple eventually married in 1985. Andre was older – 50 to her 36, and to many friends, they seemed temperamentally incompatible. In addition, the couple had a reputation for drinking and fighting.

At 5:30 AM on the morning of September 8, 1985, the doorman at 11 Waverly Place heard a sound from far above him which sounded like a woman pleading, "No, no, no, no, no." He then heard a sound which sounded to him like an explosion, as a body landed on the roof of the next-door deli. Ana Mendieta had fallen from the window of the 34th-floor apartment she shared with Carl Andre.

When police arrived, responding to Andre's hysterical 911 call in which he claimed that his wife had committed suicide, they noted fingernail scratches on his face and arms.

Andre was charged with second-degree murder. At his trial, he waived his right to a jury, and his case was instead decided by the judge, who acquitted Andre on all charges.[534] As a result, showings of Andre's work are regularly protested by women's groups.

MINIMALISM IN MUSIC

In the 1960s, just as Minimalism was taking hold in the field of visual arts, a group of young American composers began to apply to music the same principles they observed in Minimalist art, creating music that was self-referential, non-expressive, and above all, repetitive.

It was strictly an American phenomenon, free from European Modernist angst, and inflected with the optimism of the American Pop culture. As composer Steve Reich, explained,

> Schoenberg gives a very honest musical portrayal of his times. I salute him – but I don't want to write like him. Stockhausen...and Boulez were portraying in very honest terms what it was like to pick up the pieces of a bombed-out continent after World War II.

---

[534] Ronald Sullivan, *Greenwich Village Sculptor Acquitted of Pushing Wife to Her Death*, The New York Times Archives, February 12, 1988

> But for [an] American in 1948 or 1958 or 1968 – in the real context of tail fins, Chuck Berry, and millions of burgers sold – to pretend that instead we're really going to have the dark-brown angst of Vienna is a lie, a musical lie…[535]

Minimalism in music began on the West Coast, primarily attributable to the creative activity of one man. La Monte Young was born in 1935 in a log cabin in Bern, Idaho.

The first sound he recalls hearing was the sound of the wind blowing under the eaves of their log cabin. He described the sound as "very awesome, and beautiful, and mysterious."[536]

In 1940 he moved to Los Angeles with his family. He later said that he loved California because of its "sense of space, sense of time, sense that things could take a long time, that there was always time."[537]

He was initially attracted to the 12-tone music of Arnold Schoenberg, and then became fascinated with Anton Webern.

He began to notice that in a Webern 12-tone composition, particular pitches tended to recur in the same register, whether high, middle, or low, and that these recurring tones created a hidden through-line in the music. He applied this observation to his own compositions, by creating 12-tone works in which each tone was sustained for a very, very long time. He called these compositions "long tone" pieces.

---

[535] Robert Fink, Repeating Ourselves: *American Minimal Music as Cultural Practice*, pg. 118

[536] Keith Potter, *Four Musical Minimalists: La Monte Young, Terry Riley, Steve Reich, Philip Glass*, pg. 23

[537] ibid

He traveled to Darmstadt to attend the summer courses in 1959, and there he came in contact with Karlheinz Stockhausen and John Cage. In the early 1960s, he relocated to New York where he was warmly received by the downtown artist community, including Yoko Ono and Andy Warhol.

By this time Young had become a heavy user of psychedelic drugs, and become interested in the classical music of India, in which the tambura plays a constant drone throughout the composition. About this time Young gave up traditional music notation in favor of evening-length ritual improvisations which he called *Theater of Eternal Music*.

Terry Riley was born in 1935 and grew up in the foothills of the Sierra Nevada. He met La Monte Young in 1958 while studying at Berkeley and experimented with Young's "long tone" composition style. Riley learned an important lesson from Young, that music need not "press ahead to create interest."[538]

Experimenting with tape recorders, Riley discovered the effects that were possible by threading a long loop of tape through two different machines, one set to play and the other set to record. What Riley learned from experimenting with tape loops was that a sense of static drone could be produced, not just from long tones, but also by active musical figures which repeated continually.[539]

Riley applied this idea in a composition called *In C*, which takes the form of 53 modules, each containing a brief melodic figure.

---

[538] Alex Ross, *The Rest is Noise*, pg. 495

[539] One person who took special note of Riley's innovations was Pete Townshend of The Who, who dedicated their song *Baba O'Riley* to Terry Riley after hearing Riley's 1969 composition, *A Rainbow in Curved Air*. (Tom Service, *A Guide to Terry Riley's Music, The Guardian*, January 28, 2013)

Each musician in the ensemble is instructed to proceed from one module to the next at his or her own pace, tailoring the music to the needs of each instrument, and the musical desires of the moment.

The first four modules from *In C* by Terry Riley

The musical motives of each module are derived from the seven notes of the C-major scale, giving the piece its title, *In C*. The whole composition is rhythmically organized by the piano, which plays two high Cs, which pulse without variation throughout.

The premiere took place on November 4, 1964. Alfred Frankenstein, the classical music critic for the San Francisco Chronicle attended the second performance, and wrote his review under the title "Music Like None Other On Earth".

Frankenstein identified the primary characteristics of this new music which would later be called Minimalism: first, the melodic material is simple; second, the harmony is likewise simple, but develops greater complexity as the work proceeds; third, there is a restricted rhythmic vocabulary; fourth, the tempo is quick and unchanging; fifth, the volume level is constant. Apart from these clinical observations, Frankenstein describes his personal reaction to the music in transcendental, almost religious language:

> Climaxes of great sonority and high complexity appear and are dissolved in the endlessness. At times you feel you have never done anything all your life long but listen to this music and as if that is all there is or ever will be, but it is altogether absorbing, exciting, and moving too.[540]

---
[540] Robert Carl, *Terry Riley's In C*, pg. 53

At the premiere of *In C*, the piano was played by a twenty-eight-year-old named Steve Reich who had only recently met Terry Riley. It was Reich who suggested adding the repeating high Cs on the piano, an addition which organized the piece around a tight, unwavering pulse.[541]

Steve Reich was born in New York in 1936, just one year later than La Monte Young and Terry Riley. Like most American teenagers in the 1950s, Reich grew up listening to music on recordings: Bach, Stravinsky, Charlie Parker and Miles Davis. After initially studying philosophy at Cornell, Reich switched to Julliard where he began to study music seriously.

Reich moved to San Francisco in 1961 where he immersed himself in the lively music scene. At night he frequented jazz clubs, seeing John Coltrane perform at least 50 times.

During the day he studied African drumming, fascinated by the interlocking rhythm of traditional African music.[542]

In 1964, Reich met Terry Riley and played the piano part at the premiere of Riley's composition *In C*. By 1965, the psychedelic movement was in full swing. La Monte Young and Terry Riley embraced the hippie culture, attracting tie-dyed fans to all night improvisations. Reich, however, began to grow uneasy with certain aspects of the San Francisco scene, especially the rampant drug use. He moved back to New York, shedding his psychedelic associations.

While in San Francisco, Reich, like La Monte Young and Terry Riley, had experimented with tape loops. In one notable experiment which resulted in a tape composition called *It's Gonna Rain* (1965), Reich recorded a San Francisco street preacher named Brother Walter.

---

[541] Alex Ross, *The Rest is Noise*, pg. 497

[542] Ibid, pg. 498

Reich was drawn to the sound of the street preacher in the first place because of the sheer musicality of the sound. "Sometimes when people speak, they almost sing," Reich explained.[543]

Brother Walter was preaching about Noah's Flood, and Reich isolated the phrase "it's gonna rain" from the sermon, turning it into a tape loop. "Tape loops are little bits of tape that are spliced together so that they just go around and around and around and repeat themselves," Reich said. "And when you take a bit of speech like 'It's gonna rain,' the way he says it, you really begin to hear the music of what he's saying and what he says increasingly blended together so it's hard to separate them.."[544]

While working with the tapes, Reich made a surprising discovery. Having placed two tape loops, both with recordings of Brother Walter saying, "it's gonna rain", on two separate tape machines, Reich found that as the tape machines, running at slightly different speeds, grew increasingly out of sync, unexpected rhythmic combinations took place. Reich describes the process:

> There are two loops of his voice, starting in unison. And then one slowly creeps ahead of the other… And so they go out of phase. It's like a canon or a round, like 'Row, Row, Row Your Boat.' And you get first a kind of shaking, a reverberation, and then you get a sort of imitation and gradually you begin to hear it as a round. And that's exactly what happens in this piece.[545]

---

[543] Tom Huizenga, *Fifty Years Of Steve Reich's 'It's Gonna Rain'*, NPR, January 27, 2015

[544] ibid

[545] ibid

When he returned to New York, Reich became intrigued with the idea of two live performers becoming gradually out of phase, producing the same effect he had achieved with two tape recorders. Initially, he doubted whether human performers could play with sufficient precision to mimic the phasing effect of the machines, so he decided to put it to the test, using himself as the subject.

> ...late in 1966, I recorded a short repeating melodic pattern played on the piano, made a tape loop of it, and then tried to play against that loop myself, exactly as if I were a second tape recorder. To my surprise, I found that while I lacked the perfection of the machine, I could give a good approximation of it while enjoying a new and extremely satisfying way of playing that was both completely worked out beforehand and yet free of reading notation, allowing me to become completely absorbed in listening while I played.[546]

Having satisfied himself with the concept, Reich notated the composition, which he called *Piano Phase*. Two pianos begin playing in unison, playing the same pattern over and over again.

One piano stays within a fixed tempo while the other gradually speeds up, becoming increasingly out of phase until the two pianos are a full beat apart. Then the process is reversed until they are synchronized again. At this point, the pattern is changed and the phasing begins again.[547]

---

[546] Steve Reich, performance notes for *Piano Phase*, published by Boosey & Hawkes

[547] ibid

Opening of *Piano Phase* by Steve Reich

Reich spelled out his philosophy in a 1968 essay entitled *Music as a Gradual Process*: He wrote, "I am interested in perceptible processes. I want to be able to hear the process happening throughout the sounding music."[548] Reich offers three analogies to illustrate what he means by "musical process":

> pulling back a swing, releasing it, and observing it gradually come to rest; turning over an hourglass and watching the sand slowly run through the bottom; placing your feet in the sand by the ocean's edge and watching, feeling, and listening as the waves gradually bury them.[549]

The philosophy of Steve Reich represents a radical departure from the practice of both Pierre Boulez and John Cage, whose procedures – whether serial or chance operations – informed and guided the composer, but were absolutely hidden from and imperceptible to the listener. Reich summed up what he believed to be the major achievement of Minimalism:

> What my generation did wasn't a revolution, it was a restoration of harmony and rhythm in a whole new way, but it did bring back those essentials that people wanted, that people craved, but in a way they hadn't heard.

---

[548] Steve Reich, *Music as Gradual Process* (1968)

[549] ibid

> Now, we're living back in a normal situation where the window is open between the street and the concert hall.[550]

Philip Glass was born in Baltimore, Maryland in 1937. He studied music at Julliard, where he was taught the methods of Neoclassicism, and he became friends with his classmate, Steve Reich. Glass survived in New York by working odd jobs. At one point he even formed a moving company with fellow-composer Reich, carrying furniture up and down the narrow staircases of New York apartments.[551]

Glass was repelled by the European avant-garde. He called it a "wasteland dominated by these maniacs, these creeps, who were trying to make everyone write this crazy, creepy music."[552] Instead, he was attracted to nonwestern music, especially the music of India. Unlike Reich, who developed his musical ideas based on instruments becoming out of phase, Glass chose to work on the purely rhythmic level, adding and subtracting notes from a set, much as is done in Indian musical improvisation.

The early phase of Glass's career culminated in the monumental work, *Music in Twelve Parts*, written over a four-year period between 1971 and 1974 and taking four hours to perform.

Glass acknowledged his musical debt to Steve Reich in a 1968 composition entitled, *Two Pages for Steve Reich*. However, in 1969 the title of this composition was shortened to *Two Pages*.

Whether this change reflected or precipitated a cooling in the formerly friendly relationship between Reich and Glass is unclear, but in the 1970s a true rivalry began to develop.

---

[550] Alexis Petridis, *Steve Reich on Schoenberg, Coltrane and Radiohead*, The Guardian, March 1, 2013

[551] ibid

[552] Timothy D. Taylor, *Music in the World: Selected Essays*, pg. 107

Over the following decades aesthetic differences between the two minimalist composers became more pronounced – Reich and his ensemble tended to circulate in classical and academic circles while Glass embraced the world of rock music with ever-increasing enthusiasm, performing high-decibel sets with his own ensemble in rock clubs, and collaborating with rock stars like Paul Simon and David Byrne of the Talking Heads.[553]

Today, Philip Glass is probably best known for his musical contribution to numerous films, documentaries, and television programs. IMBD lists 135 film credits for him, including music for *The Truman Show* and *Battlestar Galactica*.

---

[553] Richard Taruskin, *Music in the Late Twentieth Century: The Oxford History of Western Music*, pg. 391. Taruskin suggests that Reich had a snobbish prejudice against rock music, which does not seem to be the case. He points out that Stockhausen shared a similar prejudice against rock music until he appeared on the cover of *Sgt. Pepper's*.

POSTSCRIPT: WHAT COMES NEXT?

As we look back from our vantage point in the twenty-first century to the art and music of the twentieth century – the explosion of creative activity, the progression of "isms", the manifestos and polemics – the sheer energy expended in the creation and promotion of art – it is difficult to imagine anything remotely like it ever happening again.

In 1992 Francis Fukuyama published a book entitled *The End of History* in which he argued that, with the end of the Cold War and the seeming triumph of liberal democracy, history as a linear story of social and ideological evolution may have reached an endpoint – a point of stasis.

Fukuyama's thesis is focused on politics and government, but a similar case could be made for cultural evolution as well. It may very well be that, like a fast-moving river that finally empties into the sea, art and music, in terms of evolution and development, have reached a similar endpoint, an "end of history", a point of stasis. If this is indeed the case, the primary reasons are globalization and technology.

We live in a world of instant access to culture. Cell phones, the Internet, Wi-Fi, laptops and PCs – all of the familiar and ubiquitous technological apparatus of the modern world – have created a situation in which the majority of the world's population has access, through either cell phones or the Internet, to the entire scope of artistic and cultural activity, from every part of the world, from the beginning of time until the very moment in which you are reading this.[554]

---

[554] The United Nations estimates that 47% of the world's population has access to the Internet and 75% are using mobile phones.

Musicians and artists have access to an audience made up, potentially, of every individual on the planet. Anyone who is interested in art or music has access to any particular style or genre, from any period of history, and it is as easy to access as a click of a mouse or a few taps on an iPhone touchscreen. This means that all periods of art and music history now exist simultaneously. It could, therefore, be argued that, in effect, the linear flow of time, at least where music and art are concerned, has ceased to exist, or at least, to be relevant.

This does not mean that artists no longer create. On the contrary, art is being created today on an unprecedented scale. Andy Warhol's prediction that everyone would have fifteen minutes of fame has not been literally fulfilled, but something very much like it has taken place. With instant and simultaneous access, both for the creator and consumer of art, there is no longer a linear progression from one style to the next; there is no clear narrative of one "ism" leading to another. Everything that has ever been created exists side by side with everything being created today and everything that will be created tomorrow.

From our vantage point here in the twenty-first century, living after "the end of history" has taken place, we can look back at the composers and artists of the twentieth century, their colorful and tortured lives, their idiosyncratic enthusiasms, their bold pronouncements and manifestos, and view them with a new fondness and appreciation. They not only gave us great art – they gave us a great story as well.

Printed in Poland
by Amazon Fulfillment
Poland Sp. z o.o., Wrocław